T0370046

TO DIE WITH SUCH MEN

SHANNON MONAGHAN

To Die With Such Men

Frontline Stories from
Ukraine's International Legion

HURST & COMPANY, LONDON

First published in the United Kingdom in 2025 by
C. Hurst & Co. (Publishers) Ltd.,
New Wing, Somerset House, Strand, London, WC2R 1LA
© Shannon Monaghan, 2025
All rights reserved.

Distributed in the United States, Canada and Latin America by
Oxford University Press, 198 Madison Avenue, New York, NY 10016,
United States of America.

The right of Shannon Monaghan to be identified as the author
of this publication is asserted by her in accordance with the
Copyright, Designs and Patents Act, 1988.

A Cataloguing-in-Publication data record for this book
is available from the British Library.

ISBN: 9781911723899

This book is printed using paper from registered sustainable
and managed sources.

www.hurstpublishers.com

Printed and bound in Great Britain by Bell & Bain Ltd, Glasgow

I, with two more to help me,
Will hold the foe in play.
In yon straight path a thousand
May well be stopped by three.
Now who will stand on either hand,
And keep the bridge with me?

Thomas Babington Macaulay, "Horatius at the Bridge"

Then I thought of my sins, and sat waiting the charge that we
could not withstand,
And I thought of my beautiful Paris, and gave a last look
at the land,
At France, ma belle France, *in her glory of blue sky and*
green field and wood.
Death with honor, but never surrender.
And to die with such men—it was good.

Herbert Kaufman, "The Hell-Gate of Soissons"

The conversations relayed in this book occurred mostly in English, and I have transcribed them as accurately as video recording and combined memories can allow. Unless they were relayed after the fact in English, all translations from French are my own. Almost all conversations between the members of Charlie Team were in French; I have noted this explicitly in the text only in certain cases, in order to help highlight the challenges of operating with multiple languages in the midst of combat. Conversations in Ukrainian or Russian are reproduced in the original, or were relayed to me after the fact in English, or else have been translated by one of the native speakers on the team.

CONTENTS

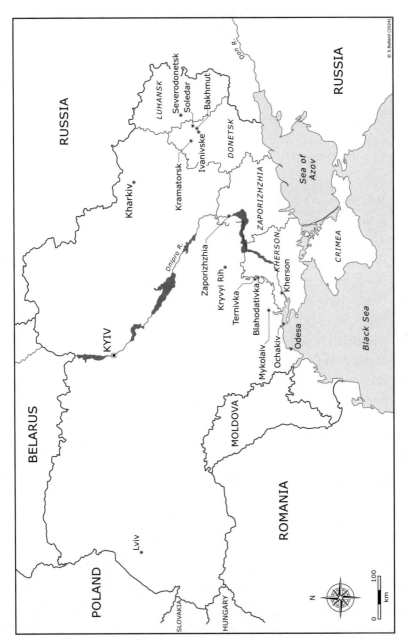

Ukraine

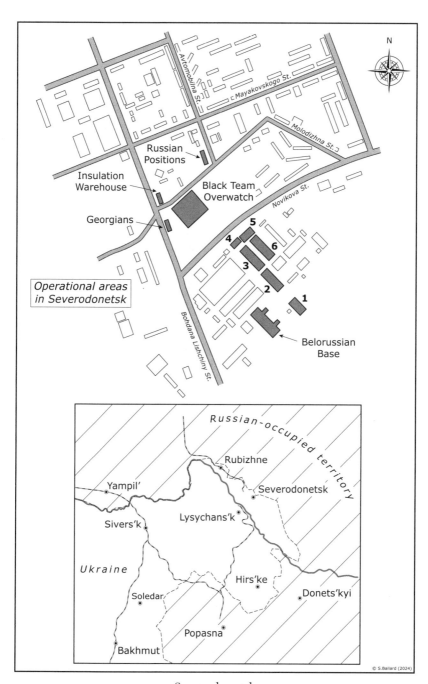

Operational areas in Severodonetsk

Severodonetsk

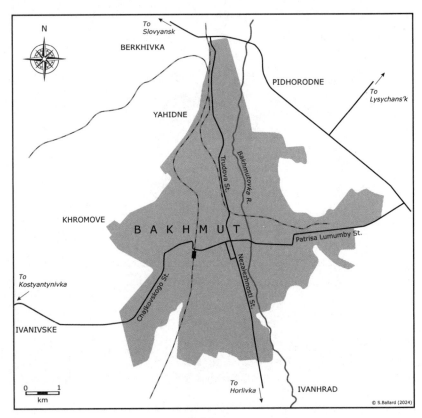

Bakhmut

THE BATTLE FOR KYIV

The driver went as far as he could into Irpin without getting the truck blown up. Artillery was everywhere, crashing into the streets, the high-rises, everything, destroying what had once been a nice suburb of a major European capital. Sixty men were crammed into the back of his military lorry. The driver stopped. The order came to pile out.

Ginger[1] stepped into the street. The American was wearing sneakers. He had a shitty, makeshift plate carrier, no helmet, and an RPK machine gun ("a big-boy AK") with four drum mags, a broken front sight, and no rations except the water bottle in his cargo pocket and the candy bar in his back pocket. He expected to be out for four days. He had trained for years to fight the Russians. But he had trained with a NATO force, with the best and shiniest tools that money could buy. There he was required to carry a fifty-pound pack full of all the contingencies. *Fuckin' nothin' like this.*

"The Russians are that way," said a Ukrainian officer with a heavy accent, gesturing as the artillery exploded all around them, turning the place to rubble. He pointed in the opposite direction. "The friendlies are that way."

He pointed back towards the Russian positions. "Go kill them."

* * *

Ginger was just shy of his twenty-fifth birthday. Energetic, with eyes that formed crinkling laugh lines hidden behind combat-proof glasses, and a dark red beard that bestowed his nickname, he was gloriously foul-mouthed, absolutely hysterical, and icily brave, a former infantry sergeant in the U.S. Army. He had served in Afghanistan and in Europe, the latter as part of Atlantic Resolve, an operation designed specifically for Russian deterrence. He had always joked that it was just an excuse for the army to take people away from their families. Now the Russians had finally invaded, but NATO wasn't taking the bait. He had gotten out of the military less than a year before, and had been working as a welder at a fab shop outside Fort Riley, Kansas.

Oh man, Ginger had thought, watching the Russian mobilizations on the border that November, *this thing's about to go down*. He started talking to an old army buddy about re-enlisting. *Now this, this could be World War III.*

Soon after the invasion began, it became clear to Ginger that the U.S. was never going to put boots on the ground. He started asking around. He was specifically trained to use the heat-seeking, fire-and-forget anti-tank missile called the Javelin, so he contacted the Instagram page "Saint Javelin." The founder put him in touch with the defense attaché at the Ukrainian Embassy in Washington, D.C.

On March 3, he told his boss and co-workers, "Hey, dude, I'm going to Ukraine."

"Are you serious?" everyone replied.

"Yeah."

"We freakin' knew you would," they said.

"Yeah, that's what my momma said," Ginger responded.

He put his job on hold, sold his apartment and his car, and got on a plane to the capital. He went to the Ukrainian Embassy and found the defense attaché.

"Do you realize what you're going to do?" the officer asked.

"Yeah."

"Do you realize that this isn't like anything you've probably seen before?"

"Yeah."

"Are you ready to kill?"

"Absolutely."

The officer handed over a phone number. "He'll get you over there."

What he received next was a ten-digit grid. *Holy shit, what is this?* thought Ginger. He plugged it in. It was the coordinates for a border crossing between Poland and Ukraine, about an hour's drive from the Polish city of Rzeszów.

Shit, he thought. He bought a plane ticket and flew directly to Rzeszów from New York.

Ginger landed in Rzeszów on March 5 and met what he called a "sketch-bag dude" from the Ukrainian Army (UA). This man was in charge of getting the Westerners through the Rzeszów checkpoint and into the main UA training base, Yavoriv, an hour west of the city of Lviv.

At midnight the Ukrainian put him on a bus with what Ginger identified as "a bunch of other randos" and sent him across the border and to the Yavoriv base.

The Ukrainians were sorting their volunteers into two basic groups that formed the International Legion. Those with combat experience and high-level military training went to the "special teams," run by the Ukrainian Defense Intelligence (GUR), roughly the military intelligence wing of the army. Those without experience went to be trained and put into equivalents of the territorial defense forces.

Ginger, a trained, deployed veteran with Javelin experience, was picked for a team at Yavoriv almost immediately. He was astonished by the diversity of the volunteers around him. Europeans and Americans seemed to make sense in terms of geography, but there were people from everywhere, even a few Korean SEALs. There were also what he called "an absolute ridiculous amount" of British people, many of whom melted away quickly: they'd made a hasty decision to buy what from Britain was a very inexpensive plane ticket on the budget airlines.

There were even British civilians, including one kid who got dubbed the "combat sandwich maker." He was eighteen years old, six months out of school, and had spent his entire brief career working at Subway. He had no military training whatsoever.

"Dude, what are you going to do out there?" Ginger would ask. "Are you going to start whippin' up some cold cuts in the trenches? What experience do you have? There is no amount of training that you can conduct in the next month that will ever prepare you for what you're going to see out there." The combat sandwich maker was sent to the standard training units.

The Russians were pushing towards the capital, trying to encircle it. Ginger's team was sent straight to Kyiv to help in the attempt to stave off the decapitation strike. He arrived just as the vicious battle for a suburb called Moschun closed. Now they would go to another suburb: Irpin.

The Ukrainian military attaché had told him not to bring his own kit, that he would be supplied. He didn't want to get arrested flying over because someone thought he might be some sort of right-wing paramilitary freak, so he packed only civilian gear. By then the place was in a panic, and there wasn't enough of anything for anybody— hence the sneakers, janky plate carrier, and broken front sight.

"If we go to war with Russia, the infantry will probably never get into a fight," the American officers had always teased when Ginger was deployed in Europe previously.

"Bullshit!" came the traditional response of the 11-Bravos, the infantrymen.

But the head-shaking from the other side was real. "You wouldn't make it through the fields that are getting smashed by artillery."

In Irpin, they fought street to street through the city, with artillery exploding everywhere. They did call for fire missions, building clearance, and reconnaissance. *Like nothing I'd ever even imagined*, Ginger thought. *Like a movie. Surreal.* The whole time the air was filled with an unreal amount of artillery. Everything was exploding. The entire ground shook.

As Ginger stepped off the truck, a former U.S. Navy SEAL was walking into the arrivals hall of the Warsaw airport. He looked around. A Slavic-looking man was holding a sign that said one word: "Legion." The SEAL headed for the sign. The man holding it said there was a bus leaving at midnight.

The American had been following the conflict since the war started in the Donbas in 2014. He'd had a flight scheduled from Thailand, where he had been teaching English after leaving the SEALs, but then Covid hit and Ukraine closed its borders, so he lost all of his money on the ticket. He'd wanted to help by working as a trainer for the Ukrainian Army as it Westernized.

As the Russian buildup started, he began to follow the situation more closely. Once the war got under way, he was afraid that he'd missed his chance; he assumed that the borders would be closed and that the Russians had air superiority. But they didn't. He bought a plane ticket, flying through Helsinki to Warsaw.

His name was Dan. Thirty-five years old, of medium height with a swimmer's lithe and toned physique, he had brown hair, a strong, square jaw that gave him a ruggedly handsome but also intimidating appearance, and a bull neck. He had served in the SEALs for twelve years. Quiet and professional, as one special operator of World War II once said of a teammate, "In the most dangerous situations he appeared phlegmatic to the point of indifference, not because he lacked the intelligence to feel fear, but because he possessed the priceless self-discipline that can conceal and suppress it."[2]

Now other men approached Dan: foreign fighters going in the opposite direction. They had been at the terrible fight in Moschun, not far from Bucha, and had been scared off by Russian artillery and the highly trained, non-conscript Russian Airborne Forces (VDV) units that were operating there.

"Hey, you going over there to fight?" one of the other foreigners asked the SEAL. "Man, I don't know." He and his buddies were full of horror stories.

Now I understand why generals in the old days would shoot people fleeing and stuff, Dan thought. *You can have guys who are pretty ready to do it, and built for this sort of thing, but if you run into a dude on your way there who got scared to death, it can be kinda disheartening.*

"Yeah, I'm going anyways," the SEAL said. *Some poor eighteen-year-old sap nutted up and charged the beaches at Normandy*, he thought. *Fuck, I've gotta be able to do this.* He was given a phone number for a guy organizing foreigners. It was all ad hoc, very unofficial. Then he climbed onto the midnight bus.

The bus arrived at Yaroviv in the middle of the night. The men were put into tents. Dan still had the contact information for a guy he hoped to find. "Hop in the tent with me," said the other man. "We'll get you all set up, get you a gun." The SEAL went to sleep, and was woken by a massive explosion.

Everyone scattered out of the tents. Dan ran for the woodline and huddled up against a tree. In his mind flashed all the images he'd seen of American Predator drones mopping up "squirters" in wood-lines with thermal sights. He heard fast movers—fighter jets—and assumed that they were being targeted by enemy planes which were about to circle back around for everyone they'd missed. It turned out to have been a Russian cruise missile. The jets were Ukrainian, scrambling to try and intercept.

Dan had been a close air support controller, known as a JTAC, in the SEALs, responsible for coordinating between ground forces and air assets. He had plenty of experience calling in close air support, but it had always been directed at someone else. Now he was on the receiving end. He hunkered down for a few minutes and waited.

Panic ripped through the base. People were yelling and scream-ing. *I've never understood that*, Dan thought, looking around quietly. *Why do you think that yelling is going to fix anything?* He got up and saw that the sun was starting to rise. He found his contact again, a calm, level-headed American Ranger.

The base was in chaos. Then the foreigners were given word: go out to the helipad in the woods to defend it from a possible air assault. This translated in the moment to an assumption that an air assault was imminent. "Prepare for an airborne invasion," they were told.

People were scared to death already. Rumors started ripping through: the Russians had landed, they were in the woodline, they were encircling, they'd taken over the base.

Finally the Ukrainian officers said, "Look, this is what you're here for. Anyone who doesn't want to do it, muster here, we'll put you on a bus and send you back across the border."

The strike generated a mass exodus. Even people who were already in Kyiv left because of the Yavoriv cruise missile: they assumed that the Russians were targeting foreigners, that they would hunt down and find them. It was useful, Dan decided in retrospect, in filtering out people who were not the right fit. Ginger's combat sandwich maker was among those leaving. He went home.

Dan spent the night in the woods guarding the helipad. He later realized that there had been little likelihood of an airborne assault; the Ukrainians had simply needed something to do with the panick-ing foreigners, so they gave them a job in a safe place, well away from the hardened structures that would attract any further strikes.

As the sun came up, Dan discovered that they were actually on a massive base: there would be no Russians coming out of the treeline anytime soon, at least not without making a lot of noise first.

"Hey, you guys can come and sleep back in the tents!" they were told. *Nah*, thought Dan. He slept in the woods that night, by himself, keeping away from the structures. He jumped into a team, and a few nights later they were loaded into a bus and sent to Kyiv. The first night they were called back because of Russian air assaults. The next night they set out again.

The bus was full of a bunch of Georgians, a few Americans, plus some Poles and Brits packed in. The windows were blacked out; they slept on the luggage. It was a fourteen-hour drive. *A miserable road trip*, Dan thought. *One of the worst road trips ever.*

Kyiv was in the process of being surrounded. The level of fear in the air was intense. The van broke down as they neared the city, so they got out and unloaded their gear on the side of the road. "A truck will come pick you up," they were told.

A military truck came by. There were four guys in the back, coughing their lungs out. They started ribbing the new guys immediately, joking. Dan watched in amusement, but some others had never experienced it before and got, as he put it, "all butt-hurt about it." "This is just how it is," he explained. "These guys have all been in the shit and we just showed up, bright-eyed and bushy-tailed."

One of the new guys had goggles on his helmet, nice tactical goggles. "Oh yeah," one of the veterans said, eyeing him. "The last dude who showed up with goggles died."

They arrived in Kyiv and rolled up to the barracks. *We look like a shit show*, Dan thought, looking around. *A total gypsy camp.* No one else was packed right: guys had multiple bags, with stuff hanging off them, looking more like tourists than soldiers. Dan had nothing but a rucksack, ready to move anywhere at any moment.

He walked in the door and saw a guy with hair awry and flip-flops, sitting and eating. Cool, nonchalant, comfortable in a war zone, plus the hair: Dan identified him immediately as a fellow American special operator. "Dude," he said, introducing himself, "I want to be in your unit. Get me out of this shit show." They did a quick background review. The other guy turned out to be a Ranger. "Alright," said the Ranger, happy to have an experienced SEAL on board, "you can roll out with us in the morning."

They gave Dan a quick brief for the next morning's mission. That night, he went down hard with what he strongly suspected was Covid. His was the version with the very bad intestinal ailments. He spent the night throwing up, with a splitting headache. The team left him in the barracks, and he went back to bed. He was told they would be back in three days.

Three days later, Dan was just barely recovering, but the team wasn't back. He went wandering downstairs, emaciated and haggard but mobile. On the first floor he found some Ukrainian officers. "Hey," he said, "where are my guys?"

"They'll be back tomorrow," he was told. "Nothing's wrong."

Relieved, he turned and started to crawl up the stairs and into bed. Then he heard a voice behind him. "Um, who are you?"

No one had updated his status with the staff office. They'd had him down as a deserter; the military intelligence men had been out looking for him. They cleared it up while Dan went back to sleep.

"We're gonna clear through this area of buildings," Dan was told on his first op a few days later. They loaded into a truck and drove along a little side-route they had been taking into Irpin, trying to avoid the artillery. He was still sick and prone to motion sickness anyway, and nearly threw up all over the guys in the back of the truck. He barely knew who was on his team. He stuck close to the easily identifiable Ranger with the long hair.

The artillery was everywhere as they got out of the truck. Dan had no idea what was going on. They ended up clearing into a tall apartment building. It was twelve stories, with a modern, slightly undulating exterior and rounded corners: a nice place. For them it was a convenient position. They were trying to aim a rocket at a Russian BTR personnel carrier that was down in a park below them. They could see its nose sticking out from a partially covered position.

That should have been a quick in-and-out, Dan realized when they got back to their base. *We took all day to do that*. There seemed to be a local habit of sticking around. *After you've killed the enemy, and it's not your job to stay, then leave.*

He'd been in plenty of urban combat in Iraq. *But that was more fun*, he thought. *It's much scarier against Russians*. They fought very differently. In Iraq and in Afghanistan, where he had also fought, the overhead was cleared by a Predator, so you didn't have to worry.

Now he was looking all over the place, checking windows for snipers; wondering why they were stopping in the street. But he found that the Russians fought very differently from his previous enemies. Unlike the Iraqis, they didn't try to leave one guy here and another guy there; they were no small men in suicide vests tucked into false walls, ready to clack themselves off when you entered to clear the room. The Russians were a stronghold force. They took a building, and they held it. There were no stragglers taking potshots.

Likewise, his job was no longer to clear a building, fingerprint everyone, and own it. Now they were clearing something in order to move through. It was much faster and much more targeted.

Back in the girls' dorms that had been turned into the International Legion's barracks, Dan ran into a tall, handsome Black American who pointed out where they could do their laundry. He was a twenty-eight-year-old Texan, with a beautiful smile, kind eyes, calm voice, and a rich, thick dark beard. They called him Tex. He had beaten both Dan and Ginger to Kyiv.

Despite the calm and kind demeanor—Tex could make friends with anyone and genuinely enjoyed helping people—he was a hard-bitten fighter, what everyone would call a true natural, an honest-to-God one-in-a-million. He was the guy that all of those fancy selection programs for SEALs, Rangers, and Green Berets were trying to find, but they had missed him: a minor youthful indiscretion meant that his paperwork wouldn't be looked at. Tex had absolutely no military background.

An attempt to join the French Foreign Legion years before had failed due to a minor injury; a failed marriage had intervened in the meantime. But he had been carefully tracking the situation in Ukraine. When he saw it looking like it might come to a flashpoint, he put his affairs in order: if it happened, all he would need was a plane ticket. Two days after Russia invaded, he got on a one-way flight to Romania.

Tex had negotiated with a taxi driver in Bucharest to get him to a small town called Tulcea, where a water crossing over one of the Danube's final branches would take him into Ukraine.

While he was waiting for the ferry, he bumped into two Ukrainians who spoke English. They had been working abroad but were going home to defend their country. They promised to help Tex get into one of the units. It would be two more days before President Zelensky declared the creation of the International Legion.

He crossed the Danube branch, the final reaches of Romania, and the end of the Danube itself. He and his new Ukrainian friends stepped onto Ukrainian soil at Izmail, in the Odesa Oblast, where the first checkpoint guards were alarmed to find a tall, imposing Black man carrying Ukrainian hryvnia and a bunch of Russian rubles. The guards held the occupants of the car—donated to them by Ukrainian civilians fleeing in the other direction—at gunpoint.

Tex's phone was dead and he couldn't communicate in the local language. His new friends talked him through. Two days later, they got him on a bus that connected to a train that took him to Odesa. He had a contact who was trying to help him join the Ukrainian Marines, but they were processing volunteers in Lviv, on the opposite side of the country. Tex got on another train and headed west.

The train was incredibly crowded; there were refugees everywhere. His contact for the Marines couldn't come, but other men helped him find his way to a different unit headquarters nearby. Finally, he heard about the brand-new International Legion and found the building known as "the school." There, an officer sitting at a child's desk interviewed him. Volunteers were closely questioned: why are you here? What is your experience?

He was accepted, and told to join the units for those who needed training. He was put on a bus and sent to Yavoriv. There he saw a small group of Westerners who were clearly operators. The body language, the confidence: they were not like the rest. *Why are they different, though?* he wondered. *Why aren't they in uniform or participating in the stuff we're all doing?* He had been issued the standard kit of the Territorial Defense-style section of the Legion, including boots and winter gear.

Soon he joined them. They confused Tex with another guy, a former American Marine who had served with one of the guys in the group. "Look, if you guys are gonna go fight," Tex said, "I'd love to come. I'll carry all of your stuff, I'll load your magazines. Whatever you need me to do, I'll do all of that."

Several of the guys were against it; they only wanted former special operators. But two men disagreed. "Just let him come. We have room for two more people. Just let him come."

Tex's initial contract was cancelled. He gave back his standard kit, grabbed a plate carrier, skipped out of training, signed a new contract, and joined the GUR special team. They loaded onto a bus and were driven to a hotel in Kyiv.

After a few hours in the hotel, someone called a meeting. "Pack your stuff for forty-eight hours. We're going out." Tex packed what limited stuff he had.

Downstairs was a Ukrainian officer in his mid-thirties named Vadym, a tall, slender, but muscled bald man with a goatee-like beard, piercing eyes, and a countenance that left one in no doubt that he was a fierce and experienced fighter.

"If you want to fight," said Vadym, "get on the truck." They loaded up and drove out to a small suburb called Moschun.

When they stopped, mortars and artillery were falling everywhere. Houses were burning. Tex saw several elderly people step out onto the road. They had just climbed out of some rubble. They were bleeding, and their heads were all messed up. *What the hell is going on?* Tex thought. One of the vehicles ahead of his was hit by a mortar. They kept going.

They stopped at a school building. Everyone got out.

Vadym gave the order: "Everyone with combat experience, get on the left side of the road." Everyone moved over except Tex and two other people, one of whom was known as Skinny Jeans, on account of his preferred legwear.

One of Tex's buddies said, "Just lie." Tex tried to be sneaky, but Vadym looked back just as he crossed. The Ukrainian smirked. *Well, that's my pass*, Tex thought.

They advanced into the town. Packs were left in the rear. They moved up into the trench line, where they left three quarters of their men. A handful of guys were taken into a house fifty meters in front of the trench line. There were no comms. All hell was still breaking loose: artillery, small arms fire, and tanks, all in a fairly small town.

These Russian troops were not conscripts. They were VDV, the Russian airborne troops, all contract soldiers.

The artillery was hard and close; hot frag fell in Tex's lap. Military-grade drones, the big Russian Orlan-10s, floated above them all day, flying the trench line from one end to the other. In his trench, Tex was carrying only an FAL FNC rifle which he could tell was subpar.

The artillery was so heavy that they had to move over towards their right flank in order to dig in additional fighting positions. Tex and a Brit with him stopped to chat with a Ukrainian machine-gun position on their way. "Is your camera on?" one of the Ukrainians asked, clearly hoping the answer was yes. *Strange vibe*, thought Tex. But they were friendly and gave the Westerners the lay of the land. Tex didn't even know what town they were in.

That night, the artillery intensified. Tex and the Brit went out to get water and passed the machine-gun position again. It had taken a direct hit in the night, and both Ukrainians were dead. *That's crazy!* Tex thought. *We were just talking to them.*

A small group of volunteers moved past Tex's position. A few minutes later, they were back: two of their guys had been shot. Tex couldn't find his group's medic, so he put the tourniquet on one man and walked him to the casualty collection point. The second man required chest seals: he'd been shot through and through on his right side. The only things either complained about were the tight tourniquets and bandaging.

Soon someone asked for two volunteers for a small operation on the other side of the village. Everyone else started complaining about their guns jamming or a lack of mags. Tex and his British friend looked at each other and stood up.

The American began to get worried when the Ukrainian officer started briefing them. He spoke English but not very well: "You will take knife, and you will go to building."

Oh man, thought Tex, *I don't have a knife. I don't know why I would need a knife to go to a building ...*

"Knife" turned out to be a person. He took Tex and the Brit to the new location. Knife's role was as bait: he was going to try to get armor and armed personnel to engage him, so that Tex and the Brit, tucked into an elevated position, could shoot anti-tank rockets back at the Russians. Tex could see the exhaust from the diesel engine. But before they could take out the armor, the Russians shifted their artillery and started to get very close to them. They were forced to pull back.

A few days later they were withdrawn from Moschun. They had no idea if they were winning or losing. But throughout the artillery was relentless: 24/7, nonstop, the Russians kept shelling the suburb. They were pulled back to Kyiv, where they got a few days to rest and recover.

People started to leave in droves. Winston Churchill had cracked that during war the truth must be protected by a bodyguard of lies, but when he arrived, what Ginger found in Kyiv was closer to the Churchill line about the Soviet Union: a riddle wrapped in a mystery inside an enigma. Rumor was constant, overheated, everywhere; you could practically cut its presence in the air with a knife. He'd come back from an op to find a bunch of new faces and people generally, as he put it, "freakin' out." They talked about Kyiv getting surrounded, that they were all going to die.

It's like mass hysteria everywhere, Ginger thought. "What did you come here to do, then?" he demanded. "You all showed up here to fight, and now that the fight's at your doorstep, you wanna leave?" It was chaotic. The city was getting missiled all day, every day, and was surrounded on three flanks. It was a dark time. Originally it was said that the International Legion had twenty thousand volunteers, from dozens of countries. (One, India, was initially added by mistake. Tex, sporting a beard that could make a Sikh jealous, was asked where he was from. Not wanting to identify himself, he had done a dead-on impression of a Punjab accent, and thus the legend was born.) By the end of the first few months, there would only be a thousand volunteers remaining. Some were killed or wounded, but most were casualties not of the war but of their own fear: they left.

"I've seen some dudes who were supposed to be the best of the best that the United States, Britain, France had to offer, and they turned around and fuckin' ran. All that experience, all that training was for nothing because they couldn't actually handle the fight itself," Ginger said later. Tex stayed.

Their Legion unit was chaotic; people were coming, going, all over the place. Logistics were messy. Everything was under pressure. People didn't know one another very well. Ginger thought everyone around him was bleak and professional, just waiting to die.

One day Dan saw Ginger in line in their dorms, waiting for food to be delivered. He looked so young. The infantryman was wearing his favorite and only comfortable civilian t-shirt. It said "Never strong enough" and "Live large," with a giant American flag on it. "Definitely an American," another of the foreigners declared to Dan.

For his part Ginger thought that Dan looked straight out of central casting. *Like a knock-off Elvis Presley*, Ginger thought, *but skinnier.* Dan was stuck in too-large, desert-camo battle-dress. *Swallowed,* thought the infantryman, *by this GI Jane-era Navy SEAL-type shit. He looks straight out of a fuckin' movie. Like a corny, act-of-valor Navy SEAL movie. The lead role for sure.*

The SEAL was dead straight. His face showed no emotion. Ginger thought he never smiled, nothing. "Hi. Nice to meet you. I'm Dan," said the older man when they were introduced. *Wow.*

With all the moving pieces, they tried to become more structured. The teams were broken down into two basic units, Alpha and Bravo. The gear and the food situation were still wonky. Everything had happened so fast. The logistics were stretched to breaking point.

There were no MRE ready-to-eat meals, and very little official food supply. The men fighting to take back the city would eat whatever was left in the cupboards of the houses as they cleared through; it was freezing cold, and they were out on mission for three or four days at a time. At one point the Ukrainian Army distributed gruel. *I thought that was just fake stuff for Oliver stories, which they feed poor orphans*, Dan thought. *But it actually exists! And they feed it to soldiers.*

They were constantly hungry. On one mission Dan and the Ranger he'd met on his first day in Kyiv walked into a Ukrainian position in Irpin while a Russian tank was tearing up the neighborhood around them. Someone complained that they were hungry. The Ranger looked around, saw a well-fed-looking Ukrainian, and said, "I bet this fat-ass knows where to find food!" The tension broke. Generally, though, they were on their own.

One day Dan talked about the food situation to Prym, a gregarious but very literal Ukrainian who had served in the French Foreign Legion and who operated as their second-in-command under Vadym. "Hey, man," the SEAL said, "the guys are getting thin, I had to punch an extra hole in my belt."

"Oh, you want food, man? Here you go!" said Prym enthusiastically, handing over boxes of cookies. There were lots of cookies to go around, but protein was harder to come by.

Kit was a similar story. In Yavoriv, Dan had gotten a set of plates. He taped them into his t-shirt, a slick little trick he'd taught himself while fighting with the SEALs in Iraq. He had a helmet, but he judged it more harm than good, so he left it behind. He carried a CZ Bren 2 and little else. *It's a good thing we train worst-case scenarios*, he thought of his time in the SEALs, *because this is close to a worst-case scenario.*

Badass, thought Ginger when he saw it. It looked like Dan wasn't wearing plates at all. Despite the absurdity, it looked very cool. Tex's plate carrier was ancient, but at least the plates were steel and would have done something. He exchanged his FAL for a NATO-chambered CZ Bren 2. The joke was that the war was like *Call of Duty:* you "level up." Guys leave, you find something: slowly, you build a full kit.

"Light is right," the common saying in the SEALs, became the mantra. Ginger, initially weirded out by the lack of the standard U.S. Army fifty-pound pack, found himself quite happily sleeping on straight-up, ice-cold concrete or huddling with a bunch of other guys in an unheated basement to keep warm. But after Irpin, he would never again carry extra weight. *I would rather be cold at night than not be able to move*, was his position. *I'd rather be a little uncomfortable for a few days.* He never took even a day backpack unless he had to carry team kit, like extra rounds for the Carl Gustaf rocket, or the radio. He put water bottles in his ammo dump pouches, food in his cargo pockets, ammo in his webbing, and just rolled. *There are a lot of times when you have to freakin' beat feet out here. You don't have time to go pick up your bag, and you sure as hell don't have time to run with a fifty-pound pack on*. Dan, still taping plates to his t-shirt, had run light for years. SEALs tended to run slicker than most people, and he ran slicker than most of his fellow SEALs. For years he'd had a rule that if he went on a few ops and didn't use a piece of kit, he'd stop carrying it. After twelve years in the SEALs, he had stripped his system down to the essentials only.

* * *

Tex was happy to see that Irpin was more built-up, with apartment buildings—better for absorbing artillery hits than the more rural town of Moschun and its exposed trench lines. It made the artillery seem much less threatening. The teams kept going out, for missions ranging from forty-eight to seventy-two hours, would push as far as they could, get backfilled, then rest and repeat. One day Tex's team pushed forward into Irpin, where they ran into another group of Americans. A sniper with them said that there was armor ahead in a park, but it was disabled. They planned to assault up the park using the defilade as cover. Three men ahead of Tex started running up the park to a hill. Just as they reached the top, Tex heard an incredible amount of fire open up from a BTR. Vadym, their unit's leader, was standing right next to him, screaming for them to come back. They had to abandon a bag but managed to exfil without casualties, jumping over fences to escape while the artillery came down all around them.

On one mission Dan found himself patrolling through a poorer, lower section of the city, very unlike the usual high-rises of Irpin. He was surprised. *This feels out of place.* The section looked older, like a village that had been converted to a suburb as the city encroached on it. The houses were small cottages, very close together. There were tall, bad fences all around them, allowing the men to sneak through holes. Trees formed a sort of a canopy, though many had become the casualties of artillery fire, and were snapped in half. Many of the buildings had huge black marks around windows and doors, the result of rocket and artillery fire. *This has been artyed to shit*, Dan thought, looking at the destroyed and damaged buildings. Things were on fire everywhere; there was smoke.

It was cold, with snow on the ground. The gloom was heavy. Crows and the occasional barking dog could be heard between the booms of artillery, like a weird combination of a World War II movie and a creepy story from the Brothers Grimm.

Dan was further back in the line, running his standard CZ Bren and carrying a big anti-tank NLAW on his back. Ahead of them was a Russian headquarters position. It was still very early. Neither the Russians nor the Ukrainians liked to operate at night; for the last twenty years, the Americans had loved little better than to operate in the dark. Now they finally had night vision. It was not the best, but it was functional enough.

The Russians were completely unaware: moving around, making coffee, not wearing body armor, rifles more than arm's length away. It wasn't the perfect L-shaped ambush of standard doctrine, but "it was perfect because they weren't ready for it," as Dan put it later. The enemy had no idea that they were there. The front of the patrol opened up, killing the first few guards at the front of the house. Return fire broke out; they started to break contact and melt away. A Ukrainian member of the unit couldn't resist the temptation to use the rocket he'd been carrying around for the whole mission. The range was bad and he didn't have a good shot, so he mortared the thing at the Russian position. Soon enemy artillery came in to try to smash the team on their egress.

Dan's team went back a few days later to clean the place out. The Russians had pulled back, leaving only a skeleton force. Now they destroyed what was left. When Dan moved up, the porch was littered with dead Russians. They had accidentally set the house on fire. It had collapsed on a Russian tank parked next to it.

Ginger knew that the Russians were well equipped, far better than the Americans' enemies in Iraq or Afghanistan. But in Irpin the Russian soldiers were often conscripts, and they could be very unpredictable. One day Ginger's team got into a five-hour firefight with a Russian position. They then exfiled. Hours later they returned to check on the position, only to find a bunch of conscripts standing around, smoking cigarettes, with zero situational awareness. They "waxed 'em all," as Ginger put it. There was a mission where they tried to take out a BMD-1, a Russian infantry fighting vehicle, only to have one of their guys end up with a bullet in his lung (he hauled himself out as the team literally ran and climbed over fences to exfil). On another occasion Ginger watched two BTRs start smashing his position while he stood eating a Milka cookies-and-cream chocolate bar (because there were no MREs), eyeballing the tracers that looked like something out of *Star Wars* as they laced into the building next to him. Once he was tucked into the windowless back of an armored personnel carrier and poked his head out on feeling a particularly bizarre movement, only to realize that they were on a pontoon bridge. And at another time, the all-balls Vadym stopped to take a smoke break while standing in the midst of an active artillery zone so that he didn't bother anyone in the vehicle. It was chaos, but they were winning.

They did a modified version of many of the special operations missions of the Global War on Terrorism: clearing buildings. Then, SEALs or Green Berets or Rangers would clear buildings, searching for high-value targets, doing counter-terrorism work. Now, the International Legion units were moving forward, performing the standard "Battle Drill Six": entering and clearing a room. They'd clear ground and go home, where Ginger would "take a shower with some cockroaches," and then less experienced Ukrainian units like the Territorial Defense or civilian militias would move in and hold the positions, often under ferocious artillery bombardment. Sometimes they would have to retreat, then everyone would perform the whole dance over and over again.

Told to clear a section of Irpin, Tex's team went through much more quickly than expected, so they started to push to the edge of the city. They rolled up on another Russian headquarters building. Vadym and a few Americans ran in to clear it. Someone threw a grenade, which set fire to something, and the whole building burned down next to an abandoned Russian tank. Another Russian position a few hundred meters away had already been cleared. Tex followed.

On his way, he saw a pink blob on the ground. He walked up to look closer: it was a brain. A whole, perfect, intact human brain, just sitting on the pavement. *Holy shit*, he thought. He walked a few more paces and found a helmet that had been shot through and completely destroyed. *Well okay, that's probably that guy's helmet.* In the building he came upon Russian kit, personal items, the works. Tex grabbed the cell phones, cameras, and tablets to turn them over to military intelligence. The other teams started to push to the edge of the city as well.

The civilians poured out of their buildings. Dan looked around in surprise. Old ladies came out, giving them kisses. *Well, that's different*, he thought, accustomed to Iraq and Afghanistan. It hit home: *We're the good guys.* He'd grown up watching old black-and-whites of Americans rolling into France during World War II as liberators. He'd grown up idolizing those men. *Only instead of some pretty French girl it's an old babushka. Holy shit*, he thought. *This is it. This is what that feels like.*

They settled down to wait. Dan felt badly for the civilians: wherever soldiers went, artillery fire followed. Prym, in charge of the op, insisted that they stay. "Let's move a few buildings back," the men argued. They were just going to get smashed.

"No, *suka*,"[3] Prym insisted. "We must stay here and watch for the Russians."

They settled in. They were hit by something; the debate raged over whether it was a shell or a mortar or a tank. In the morning they egressed, being backfilled by a Ukrainian unit.

Tex, in a different position, realized that even with the Russians gone it wasn't a safe spot. The Russians had the coordinates and could easily smash it; perhaps the retreat was a *maskirovka*, a deception, and they would come back to slaughter them in the night. The British former paras in the unit were on edge that night. Tex, watching them, was nervous. The paras wouldn't sleep and held security at all times, insisting that they wouldn't die in their sleep. Nothing happened. The next morning they were backfilled by some Georgians and Belorussians, and went back to Kyiv. The next day, all of Irpin was declared clear.

In the wake of the Russian retreat they found running BMP fighting vehicles, tanks, ammunition caches, weapons, the lot. But it was disturbing to see how prepared the Russians had been. Every twenty-five to fifty meters was an entrenched position. There were lots of fortified houses and fortified intersections. *Somebody up top, the big man in Irpin, knew what he was doing,* Ginger thought. *His sol-diers were just useless.*

They returned to their dorms in the girls' school, where there were posters of boy bands on the walls and the remnants of a feminine, civilian life everywhere. Told they would be moving out, they packed their bags for their next mission.

2

ZAPORIZHZHIA

The new mission set was simple: armor hunting. Zaporizhzhia is mostly open, agricultural land, former steppe and part of the area that makes Ukraine famous for its "black earth," from which the country produces a prodigious amount of grain and also derives its two-toned, wheat-gold and sky-blue flag. "Just farmland with small treelines that separated each plot," as Tex put it. Now it was a playground of the Russian aggressor, who was focusing much of his forces around besieged Mariupol in an attempt to create a land bridge to occupied Crimea. The wide open spaces were dotted with small villages of around a dozen houses each, where the Russians hid their tanks and BMPs. The idea was to hunt as much armor as possible, creating enough of a ruckus in the rear to draw pressure away from the siege of Mariupol, where Ukrainian units, and quite a few civilians, were holed up in the bombarded Azovstal steelworks. They had ten Javelin missiles and one command launch unit, or CLU, to fire them. "We want you to get ten damn kills" was how Ginger understood the order. *Okay, roger that.*

"Pack just combat equipment for three days out in the field," Dan was told. He left a bunch of his stuff in the dorm in Kyiv. He packed a rucksack and hopped in the van. They drove south, stopping in Zaporizhzhia city for the night to sleep, and headed out to their operational area in the morning.

Their new billet was a huge, former aircraft parts-making factory and warehouse, the equivalent of three or four stories high. It had a large, open room, with machining equipment along it in rows, with crates of scrap metal and wood lying around. The usual factory detritus marked the shop floor, with metal shavings and black soot everywhere.

Some Ukrainians were already there. They had claimed a space in the basement and used a fireplace down there, but the Legion teams had to hunt out their own accommodation. *Well, we aren't sleeping out in the field, which is what I thought we were going to be doing,* Dan mused.

At the ends of the building were offices and hallways, where they made up spaces to sleep. The office walls had photos of the aircraft they had made parts for until the war started. Dan crashed in the warehouse's little library room.

They eventually built their own fire in a metal crate, in the big warehouse room, and created a warm, cozy spot to hang out. MREs were delivered, this time Canadian, which Dan declared the best combination of taste and operational efficiency. They always had an easy-to-cook meal and a snack like jerky that was easy to put in your pocket.

Dan would watch as Ginger and Rob, a very posh British officer from a storied old regiment, did their daily odd-couple routine. "Dude," Ginger would say, "you're like all the bad parts of a girl-friend. And you're fat. I don't even know what to do."

"Fuck you, ya fuckin' wanker!" Rob would respond. "We should've kept the colonies."

Just being soldiers, man, thought Ginger. *Just being ignorant and belliger-ent.* He wasn't even sure if they were joking, but it was still hilarious.

It was not good infantry fighting terrain. The only cover was in a series of narrow treelines, or hedgerows, that were probably grown as windbreaks. They were not large, and the Russians were well aware that anyone trying to sneak up on them had to come through that cover, so they frequently hit the greenery with hours and hours of artillery or mortars, just in case. The Russians used full-on, old-school scorched earth tactics, like something out of previous centuries.

In order to hunt armor, they needed to get their missiles in good range of enemy equipment. This put a premium on Jav gunners like Ginger, who was soon in high demand from both Alpha and his own Bravo team. For his part the tall, well-built Tex joked that the guys liked to load him down with gear, probably because he made it look easy. He often carried extra missiles for the Javelin in support.

The Legion men would move in a single file line, sneaking up to a spot where intelligence suggested they might find Russian armor, and then tried to get their NLAW or Javelin gunner in a position to hit the thing. Mostly they spent a lot of time being very, very cold and very, very tired from their five- to twenty-kilometer movements through artillery barrages to potential and often absent targets. *We probably got shot at by a thousand rounds of artillery*, thought Ginger by the time they were done.

It was a difficult task. Near Marfopil', Ginger watched a series of BTRs and BMPs "driving around like they were using them from grocery getters," as he put it, but they were just a bit too far away in their treeline, about 2,300 to 2,400 meters out.

Finally, a target presented itself at about 1,800 meters. Ginger set up the Javelin and started to get a lock on the target. He engaged the seeker. The battery coolant unit (BCU) popped, and the command launch unit (CLU) failed, causing the BCU to burn out. They had two more missiles, so he shut down the CLU, thinking it was overheating. The BTR was still parked; the rest of the team watched in high tension, anxious to hit the target. "You guys need to shut the hell up," Ginger said. "This takes time. There was a CLU failure. I don't know what's wrong with it. There's no way to *know* what's wrong with it. The CLU failed."

He ran the testing parameters. It passed everything, so he hooked up the CLU to the second missile. He engaged the seeker trigger to get a lock. Another CLU failure. The BCU went up, he thought, *like a damn Christmas tree.*

Everyone was pissed. They pulled back, because they couldn't get close enough to hit it with an NLAW, which needed to be about six hundred meters away. At that distance, they'd be smashed, possibly on the way in but definitely on the way out.

They went back, fetched a new CLU from a nearby Ukrainian unit. The next morning, they returned. They sat for seven or eight hours but saw zero more pieces of armor.

One day Dan and the rest of Alpha team went out to the Ukrainian front, to a small village on the forward line. Their destination was further east, past the line of Ukrainian control and towards the Russians. There were BTRs in a woodline which they were hoping to hit with a rocket. They found a river with good cover that would let them approach the Russian line.

They crept up to the Russian line and came to a nearly deserted village of half-a-dozen or so low, old brick cottages with a small, narrow dirt road lined by waist-high fences. There were alder bushes tucked here and there, but they were still leafless, giving a scraggly, skeletal vibe. It was April, but it was functionally still winter: grey, cold, and lifeless. Dan took a look around. "This is the village where Hansel and Gretel got eaten!" he joked. "If you wanted to take your kids trick-or-treating and scare the shit out of 'em, this is the village to do it in." It was eerie. There was even a little old lady in one of the houses, though her look was classic babushka. *No witchy appearance*, Dan thought. *That would have been the cherry on top.*

Prym, in command of the mission, added to the atmosphere by disappearing. He had gone on a recce but forgot to tell anyone. There was no angle on the nearby BTRs. Prym came back and started breaking into one of the cottages. *What the hell is he doing?* wondered Dan.

"We must stay here tonight!" said Prym.

This village was closer to the Russian front line than the Ukrainian line. Any Russians would only have to check half-a-dozen or so houses. It was not a good spot to be in, especially in the looming darkness.

"There's no reason," said Dan. "We don't have an angle. We're not watching anything, we're not observing anything. We're not providing intel. We're just risking our butts out here for the night."

Prym was adamant. The Russians have thermal, he argued; we can't leave.

"They're just as uncoordinated as you are!" Dan tried to convince him. "They'd have to launch the drone, with a thermal, spot us, then coordinate artillery on us all while we're on the move." But Prym was firm. Everyone else wanted to get out.

Mortars started coming into the village. *They know we're here,* thought the SEAL. Any squared-away commander could easily have wiped them out with twenty or thirty infantrymen. It was freezing cold, and the mortars kept coming in. Some of the guys thought they heard radio mikes keying up outside, though Dan never heard them. *They could no problem kill us right now*, Dan thought. But they stayed. It was a small, two-and-a-half-room cottage on the first floor, with a staircase leading to another room upstairs. A fireplace in the middle heated the whole house.

Probably one of the scariest nights I've ever had, thought Dan afterwards. *Terrible decision-making*. But he realized that the Americans really had the monopoly on night fighting. No one else was quite as comfortable at night, especially under night vision. The village had one saving grace. Dan, who had followed the "combat gear only" orders to the letter, picked up a coffee mug there. It was glass, with a big handle. On it was painted an adorable, whimsical image of a little brunette girl wearing a red dress with white polka dots and a big Mickey Mouse ears headband, carrying a bunch of lollipops like a bouquet and a paper coffee cup under her arm. It had something written on it in Ukrainian, but he was never sure what it said.

Another mission took Dan to what he called "the Soviet officer's house" in the last row of cottages in the village that marked the Ukrainian forward line, abutting open fields and farmland. It had a separate cellar, a chicken coop and barn combination, plus a fruit tree. The main house was single-story, with no basement. It had a proper entryway. To the right was a room that Dan eventually slept in. The master bedroom was straight ahead, and to its left was a large living room. At the front of the house, opposite Dan's room, was a little bathroom and the kitchen and kids' room, which conveniently for the team contained bunk beds. *A really cool setup*, Dan thought, looking around. The fireplace in the kitchen touched the living-room wall, which had a tiled patch, allowing the fireplace to radiate heat throughout the house.

The local Ukrainians would bring them wood, so they could have some heat and boil water for coffee and MREs. They also had the usual visiting mortars. The guys were out in the backyard when one round landed right next to the room Dan had been sleeping in. He was horrified, because he'd left his SAW light machine gun in the bedroom. They sheltered, but once he heard the break in the usual four- or five-round salvo, he ran back in to grab his gun and drag it into the cellar.

25

He took photos of the place later: the outside of the pale blue house was pockmarked with mortar fragments. The window was broken and blown open, throwing glass onto the furniture he'd been sleeping on, where the SAW was lying. But it was in one piece.

The SAW was the legacy of one of their British paras, who had found it in an armory in Kyiv. Dan had been shocked to see it. It was a Mark 46, a version that had been developed by the SEAL teams in order to produce a more chopped-down, lighter SAW. The Brit brought it to Zaporizhzhia but then left the team for another project. Dan adopted the weapon: "Hey, it's a 46, Team guys are the ones who designed that, I want that gun."

It got him a gun he liked, a weapon whose role also put him number two in any patrol, behind the point man. It was much heavier than the Bren 2, but it had an added benefit: the SAW man didn't have to carry a Javelin. Dan was happy to make the trade.

The day after Dan's visit to the Hansel and Gretel village, Ginger's Bravo team went out, working with the Ukrainian Army (UA) on a joint offensive. Two UA tanks and an infantry company were meant to move west to northeast. The Legion teams would move west to east, then north, along a ravine. They were supposed to hit a particular town at a specific time.

The timing was off. The mission brief began at 4 p.m. for a mission that was meant to kick off at 5 p.m. The plan included a five-mile on-foot movement, so they were, by necessity, late. The UA went on with the offensive, got smashed, and pulled back.

But the Legion team kept going. It was nearly dark. It was low-tech: only their temporary commander Yuri, who had taken over Vadym's role as unit leader when the other man was promoted to head of the whole Legion, had the directions, and no one had night vision. *Terrifying*, thought Ginger, *walking through a war zone at night, no idea where you're at, no compass, no map, no nothing, and no NODs* [night optical devices, or night vision]. *And you're expected to follow this guy who hopefully knows where he's going.*

They got to a spot that looked like a reservoir dam for a series of fields, though it held no water. They set up on the dam's ridge, which had plenty of good cover and concealment. From their elevated position they could look right down on a little village, about a thousand meters away.

For ten or fifteen minutes, they couldn't see anything. It was the perfect engagement distance, but they had nothing. Ginger, along with his British officer pal Rob and two other men, grabbed the Javelin and moved two hundred meters down into the field below them, towards the town.

"You guys have thirty minutes to make something happen, or we're leaving, 'cause we're all alone out here," said Yuri. "We have no backup."

Alright, whatever, Ginger thought.

The rest of the fire team pulled security on the ridge. Ginger's group moved up to a nice thin treeline. Ginger moved a few steps out and to the left. From there he could see what he thought was an MLRS rocket-launcher truck.

"I've got eyes on, it's hot, somebody's in it, the exhaust is hot, the tires are hot," he confirmed, looking through the thermal on the Javelin CLU. Rob said that the taillights were on. *I've gotta hit this thing*, Ginger thought.

It was about seven hundred meters away. Ginger got the missile up on his shoulder, running the system. He tried to set up for the shot, but he kept being knocked and shifted by the wind, over and over again. It was getting dark, the sky the dim, ominous grey-blue of an oncoming storm. *So frustrating*, he thought.

"Guys, I can't get a lock," he said. He asked one of the other men with him, another trained Jav gunner, to help him. The other man knelt and put Ginger in a bear-hug, stabilizing him. Ginger slowly built the Jav's target box around the back end of the truck. It locked. He held the seeker trigger. The other man stood to his side, stabilizing Ginger's shoulder with his right hand.

"Prepare to fire," he said.

"Okay, roger that," came the response.

Ginger squeezed. As soon as he pulled the trigger, everything slowed down, as though the world had entered slow motion. The Javelin has a soft launch, so when it spits the missile out of the tube, it will seemingly hang in the air for a second, and then the missile will fire its own engines and take off.

It happened so slowly in Ginger's mind that he thought he could reach out and grab the rocket. *It's right there*, he thought. *I could grab it and walk away with it. So weird.*

The missile took off. Once he saw the soft launch go, he started to disassemble the CLU. His brain had shut down; he was simply moving. The CLU was in his left hand. They took off in the opposite direction. All he could hear were explosions.

As they ran, their team leader called back to the men on the ridge.

"Where are you?" came the response from the ridge.

"We're right in front of you, I'm looking at you!" said Ginger's team leader.

"We're gonna need a better description than that."

"Dude, we can see you."

"Yeah, no. We need to know where you are. Put your hand in the air and start waving right now."

What? thought Ginger. They each put a hand in the air and started waving as they ran.

"Okay, you need to fuckin' run. Hurry the fuck up."

They dead-sprinted the last 120 meters. They got up on the ridgeline. Ginger was completely gassed. They'd done a five-mile movement in and just sprinted back, with Ginger holding the heavy, awkward CLU.

"We need to get out of here. We need to leave." No one would tell the Jav team anything.

They marched back, climbed onto their waiting BTR, and drove out.

What Ginger had thought was an MLRS truck was actually a fuel truck attached to a BTR which was sitting next to a house, where there was also ammunition. The fuel truck blew up. The BTR burned down, cooking off all of its ammunition. The house they were parked next to burned down. Ginger had heard it while he was running away at a dead sprint.

He was in awe. *I had no idea.* It was incredibly loud. For an hour they could hear the pops of ammunition cooking off. *Insane.* It was right before darkness, so the men could look back as they pulled out, riding on top of their own BTR, and see the fire. Every time he looked back, Ginger felt a tingle go up his spine, and he'd smile. *I fuckin' did that.*

The Javelin is a fairly technical device. The training program is a week long, but at the end of it the trainees never fire the actual rocket: they're too expensive. Everything is done on very high-end simulators. *That was my first time ever actually firing a Javelin.*

Back at the warehouse, two of the men from the ridgeline pulled Ginger aside. "Hey, man," they said, "there were between five and six hostiles probably about a hundred meters away from you guys walking in the same direction."

"What?"

"Yeah. There was a team following you guys out of the woodline. That's why we were trying to get eyes on you."

"Why didn't you fucking shoot those guys!"

"Dude, we were watching you the whole time. We didn't think they could see you, but they knew that you were out there some-where," since they had just fired a Javelin from the position. "We didn't want to alert them and have them shoot at you while you were in the open."

Ginger's heart just sank. "Dude, you're telling me that there were six guys following us through an open field, and they didn't engage us and you didn't engage them?"

"Yeah, dude, I don't know what to tell you, but it happened."

For the next two or three days, Ginger tried to make sense of what they were telling him. He asked the other men from the ridge-line, and they said the same thing. Everyone said six men: hence their confusion, because they knew that the Javelin team had only four guys. *Fuck,* thought Ginger. *How did we not hear them? How did we not see them? How did we not pass them when we went out there?*

It kept him up for days, trying to make sense of it. Finally he gave up: he never could. Maybe there was dead ground, a trick of the terrain. But the hostiles were armed, and they were following the Jav team. *Why didn't they shoot? They see us with our dicks in our hands, we're all blown out, we're all tired, running in the opposite direction, that's easy kills.* He didn't believe it at first, but everyone said the same thing. *Super weird. I would've engaged that target! I would have one hundred percent engaged that target. Even if you were worried about us being engaged, you should be able to wipe them out before they even got a chance to fire at us.*

He could never rationalize it either way. He couldn't make sense of it, so he just didn't believe it.

The Javelin is a great weapon, but like all weapons it has its limitations. The Ukrainians in command of the foreigners were often confused by its capabilities, frequently thinking that it worked as a sort of giant sniper rifle that fired a rocket instead of a bullet. But a Javelin is a complex, dual-computer, soft-launch rocket. It is self-guided, but that means that it takes time to acquire and lock onto a target, something very different from just clacking off a round with even a .50-caliber sniper rifle.

After Ginger's initial success, Alpha borrowed him for a new attempt on Russian armor. They waited for hours. As soon as Prym would see something, he would start freaking out. "Ginger! Ginger! Ginger! Javelin, get it! Right there, right there!" No distance, no direction, no description, nothing.

Finally, one of the foreigners would give Ginger a distance and description, and he would be able to track with the digital thermal sight in order to find the target. Often these targets were out of range: the CLU can see further than the rocket can actually lock onto. You can see to 2,500–3,000 meters, but you can only lock up to 2,000 with the version Ginger was using. Prym, in his excitement, would often forget the range limitations.

Ginger would hurry over, power up the rocket, and realize the target was too far away, leaving Prym angry or upset. "Dude, you have to understand, there are limitations to this weapons system," the American would say. "It's not an end-all, be-all. I can't shoot everything under the sun with this thing. I have my ranges, I have my ability to hit targets at distance when they're moving. I can't hit a moving target at 2,000 meters, but I can hit a moving target at 1,000 meters."

But Prym was so energetic, he would find targets everywhere. Finally Ginger would say, "Prym, do you want to take over? Do you want to use this?"

"Mate, no, I don't know how!" Prym would always reply. "I don't understand!"

"Then don't tell me what to do with the weapons system if you don't know how to use it yourself!" Around and around they went, almost hourly.

Dan watched, the SEAL impressed both with the young infantryman's knowledge and with his unruffled ability to hold his ground. *This guy knows his shit. We need this guy.*

There are two sights on the Javelin: the CLU, which can be used as a separate thermal, and each missile's own on-board computer. On the CLU, on a narrow field of view, on a 2x zoom, is a 24-magnification thermal optic. When you switch over to take the shot, the screen goes black, and it takes two to three seconds to back off and connect to the warhead's sight. That's a 4x thermal with no zoom. What you can see at 2,000 meters on a 24 magnification on a thermal camera is completely different from the missile view—but only the missile is going downrange. You might not even be able to see the target at all between the first and second views. It can be easy to lose a target at distance. It is also a fairly slow process: it takes at least five minutes to get through the whole firing process with a good, clear, easy shot. "And five minutes feels like a really, really, really long time," said Ginger.

Alpha was skunked. They went out again, still borrowing Ginger. They had gotten a few knock-off NODs, so they started out in the middle of the night, arriving at their target location at 4 a.m. They sat all morning, shivering in the bitter cold. *This is the coldest I've ever been in Ukraine*, Dan realized, though it was already mid-April.

Dan and Ginger walked forward from the treeline, the SEAL serving as the assistant gunner. He helped Ginger set up the CLU and the rocket, then tucked back into the treeline, where it wasn't as cold, *a slightly not-as-miserable position*, he thought. Dan felt bad for Ginger, huddled in the wind in front of him. *Man, he is jackhammered.*

Ginger sat on the CLU's thermal. It was so cold that the Russians didn't want to move much either. Finally, the first thing he saw that day, around 6 a.m., was two Russians standing at a small four-way intersection in the road, about 2,300 or 2,400 meters away.

"Hey, I've got eyes on two guys," he called on the radio, "sittin' in the middle of a four-way intersection to the northeast. Are you tracking these guys?"

"How far are they?" came the answer from the treeline.

"About 2,400 meters."

"No man, we can't see 'em, we can't see 'em."

"I'm literally staring at these guys. They've got like a rocket or something."

"*What?*"

"Yeah. They're playing with something out there."

The guy standing on the left-hand side suddenly took off running. *What the hell?* thought Ginger. "Hey, guys, that one guy just beat feet." Then there was a *whoomp*: a huge cloud of smoke appeared in the thermal, obscuring everything else.

"Holy shit! He just got blown up!" Ginger exclaimed.

"*What?*"

"He just fucking exploded!"

As Ginger looked through the CLU, he saw a vapor trail heading towards them. *Oh my God.*

Dan looked up. "*Incoming!*" he shouted, along with Tex and the other men with him.

Everyone hit the deck. The Ukrainian kid with them took off running. *I have never seen somebody move so fast*, Ginger thought. He was flying through the treeline. *What the hell?* The Jav gunner tucked up around the CLU as if it could somehow protect him. *There's no way.*

Whatever it was flew right overhead and hit the farmhouse behind them.

"What the hell was that!" everyone exclaimed.

"I don't know, I thought he blew up!" Ginger responded. He could no longer see the Russian through the huge smoke cloud obscuring the thermal.

Everyone started laughing, then settled back down.

Five minutes later, Ginger was back on the CLU's thermal, scanning. He heard a noise overhead, vaguely familiar. "Is that a jet?"

"No, there's no way," said the men in the treeline. "They don't have air out here, we have AA [anti-aircraft units]."

"Dude, that sounds like a jet," Ginger said. He got back on the thermal, and saw it: a Russian fighter. "Guys! There's a fucking jet coming right towards us!" he exclaimed.

"No!"

"*Yes!*"

"Should we leave?"

"I don't know! I've never seen a jet before. Never in my life have I had to deal with this situation. I don't know," Ginger replied.

"We gotta do something!"

"Stand by," called Ginger, out in the open by himself, watching on the CLU.

"We're not going to leave," said Prym, in his accented English. "He's not going shoot us. We're too small target, it would be waste."

"Yeah, that's a great assumption to make. That this guy won't come drop a 500-pound bomb on us," Ginger snapped.

"No, no, no, mate, he's not coming for us, I promise!" said Prym.

Then Ginger heard it: the repeating burps of the jet's 30 mm cannons. He watched the rounds impact through the CLU. The jet wiped out the Ukrainian mortar position that had been covering them, killing seven or eight men, destroying the guns, and blowing up the ammunition. Soon afterwards a jet, probably the same one, hit the nearby town, killing twenty-five men, blowing up a Ukrainian BTR, and nearly wiping out the whole UA unit there, but not before the Ukrainians managed to shoot it down with a Stinger missile.

They started to realize that at about the same time every day, mortars flew up and down the forward line. It seemed to be a standard Russian procedure: putting a mortar on a vehicle and driving up and down smashing things. They planned a simple op to take it out: they would head out in the afternoon, ambush the vehicle with a Javelin, and return.

They moved up to the forward line and checked in with headquarters. But the UA had spotted a BTR that they wanted the Americans to take out, just as Bravo had done earlier. Their simple ambush was turning into a full-on operation.

Now it was daylight, and they were now required to walk up to the Russian line. A quadcopter drone appeared overhead. They were usually Ukrainian, though not always.

"Hey, man," the guys asked Prym, "is that ours or the Russians'?"

"It's not ours," said Prym, marching forward.

"Wait a second! It's broad daylight. This thing is staring right at us." They were also getting updates: the BTR they'd been told about was now accompanied by a few technicals, then a BMP. The force was growing, there was a drone overhead, and the Russians were on edge because they'd been hit by a Jav team the day before.

On the SEAL teams Dan had done lots of studies of missions that went wrong. They were always taught that it was not just one thing, but a sequence of red flags, that led to problems. *That's hap-*

pening right now, he realized. *Things are lining up.* Prym was still trudging along. They looped around a different treeline, trying to throw the Russians off.

Attack helicopters showed up and started strafing the front line. The team hunkered in the leafless treeline, hoping to God that the helicopters didn't turn around and light them up. The Russians were nervous of Stingers, though, so left quickly. So did the Americans: it was time to go.

They were there for nearly a month, but didn't have enough density on the ground to tempt the Russians away from Mariupol. The Legion decided to move them to a new operational area. Ginger got one more kill before they left, another Jav gunner on the team got one more in Zaporizhzhia, and another further south as a trainer for a Ukrainian unit.

The warehouse got bombed right after they left to refit in Kyiv. The running joke was that they were now actually in Purgatory, and that they'd died in the warehouse, like a strange, Ukrainian wartime version of the TV show *Lost*.

3

THE TALL MEDIC

After they arrived at the girls' dorm barracks in Kyiv and took showers, an older American soldier named Eric brought Ginger and a few other guys out front. Standing in front of them Ginger saw what seemed like a seven-foot-tall blond man, wearing a headband, t-shirt, cargo pants, sandals, and a completely disarming grin.

"What's up, guys?" chirped the cheerful blond giant. "I'm Greg!"

What the fuck? thought Ginger. *Who the fuck is this guy?*

Greg was actually 6′ 5″, twenty-eight years old, towering and lanky but well built. He had a handsome face like some sort of old-school eastern European film star, apart from being blond-haired and pale-green-eyed, with an infectious, goofy grin. What Ginger called a headband was actually a bandana, a habit that the Ukrainian-born Canadian had picked up while working in hospitals in Mexico. His favorite was the one he called his "good luck clowns bandana," checker-blocked in alarmingly bright shades of blue, red, green, and yellow, with the namesake clowns on it.

He had been born in Ukraine to a family with a long history of fighting proudly for their country, though given the complexity of twentieth-century politics this meant that he had family members who had been sent to the Gulag, fought with Ukrainian nationalist partisans, and avoided liquidation after World War II by an offer from the French to join their Foreign Legion; one of them had even won the ultimate USSR honor of Hero of the Soviet Union. He believed, not in a right-wing way, in an essential Ukrainian national-ism: that they were a people and an independent country and should stay that way. As a child he was one of the few students in his school who would habitually speak in Ukrainian rather than Russian. His name was actually Grygorii, and he told everyone to abbreviate his last name to "T-Rex," because it was so long.

His father, a successful businessman who had gone into politics, chose to move the family to Canada when Greg was still in grade school. When he graduated from high school and didn't know what to do with himself, he ended up back in Kyiv. Not long after, the Maidan Revolution kicked off in 2013, when the people rose up and threw out the president, Viktor Yanukovych, who had tried to throw over democratic desires for further integration with Europe for a program that would have kept them, like Belarus, as a vassal state of Russia.

After Greg recovered from what he called "injuries sustained" during the protests, he signed up for insurgent training with civilian militia groups; they thought there was going to be partisan warfare in the forests. They had expected a full Russian invasion any day. Crimea was gone, and the protests looked like they might turn into Budapest or Prague 2.0: the Russians had a long history of sending in the tanks when the people in what the Russians considered to be their satellites expressed independent desires. That the Cold War was over seemed to have changed less than people thought.

In training he met an older, gruff former German special forces medic. "He was a complete psychopath," Greg said, "but an amazing medic, and he made us do awful, unspeakable things to each other, but for whatever reason I really liked it." *Shooting is fun*, Greg decided, *but this medical thing is kind of interesting*.

The invasion scare settled down. Over the following years, he did odd jobs to support his medical training and earned a degree from a university in Canada as a paramedic. Along the way he worked in hospitals in various places, including Mexico and Africa. When the war broke out he was enrolled in a master's program in remote medicine and had been accepted for a training program run by the U.S. Special Forces, the Green Berets.

In late 2021, Greg had been working in a hospital in Africa, racking up hours for his medical training. He was keeping an eye on the Russian buildup on the Ukrainian border. But this didn't look like previous buildups. They weren't training; they were just lurking, staging near the border. *This one might be the real deal*, he thought.

By the end of January, he was back in Kyiv, at his family's apartment. A friend connected him with the Georgian Legion, which was helping train civilians who wanted to prepare for the invasion. Greg assisted with the training and began to reestablish his contacts from the Maidan Revolution, trying to figure out how best he could help if war broke out. He started collecting medical supplies.

When Putin gave his big speech, "an hour of him rambling that Ukraine was not a country, or a people ... he kind of rewrote history there, but whatever," Greg knew: the war was actually happening. He went into the kitchen and saw his father. "Dad, we're getting invaded," Greg said. "Yep," his father replied.

On the evening of February 23, Greg met up with a few friends. They went out for coffee, sitting and chatting. Greg checked his Instagram and saw that Russian conscripts were painting "Zs" and zeros on their tanks and armor. "Okay, guys," he said to his friends, "we're getting invaded this week."

"No, no! That's not gonna happen," everyone said, brushing it off.

"This is *Russian* military. You do not paint something on a vehicle with a permanent paint for no reason. You don't do that in training, you don't ever do that," Greg responded.

At 4:30 a.m. he woke from the sound of explosions. He checked the news. *Yep*, he thought. *They're firing rockets at us.* He was ready for it, but it was a surprise all the same. He ran around grabbing socks, medical supplies, food. He burst into his father's room. "Dad, we're under attack!"

"Who is attacking us?" replied his father, still half asleep.

"Who? Who? Turkey!" snapped Greg. "Who do you think?"

Everyone connected to the Georgian Legion received a Google pin drop: *muster here.* His father gave him a partial lift, and he ran the rest of the way. Greg arrived last, because he had to run through "half the town," as he put it. The address turned out to be the headquarters of the GUR, the Ukrainian military intelligence. They were handing out AK-47s. *Unfortunately, no AK for me*, thought Greg: the GUR had run out.

Everyone—a host of Georgians, Ukrainians, and about ten foreigners—was told that they would be taken to a military base and given better weapons and gear. *Hell yeah*, thought Greg. They were loaded onto vehicles. It was still rush hour in Kyiv. They fought through traffic, taking a roundabout route: north in order to hook west. The base was on high alert when they arrived. Everyone got out, standing around in the parking lot. Greg looked around. "What's this?" he asked, pointing towards something two hundred meters away from them.

"Oh," someone said. "That's the Hostomel airport."

They could hear jets near the airport. They were still standing around talking when they heard a *ka-BOOM*. *What the actual fuck!* thought Greg, diving into a drainage ditch for cover. There was a little chain-link fence in front of him. He looked up to see four Ka-52 attack helicopters, flying towards them just fifteen meters above the ground.

"Shit, guys!" he exclaimed. "These are the Black Sharks!"

"Oh, Ukrainian?" asked the guys around him.

"Well, we don't have these in our inventory, so I doubt it," Greg replied.

One of the Georgians got up, with no helmet, no vest, and nothing but an AK-47 under his shoulder. He was walking around, smoking a cigarette. "This is not okay, buddy!" said Greg.

"*Russians!*" said the Georgian, with a heavy accent but a voice that sounded almost bored, pointing. "*Russians!*"

"Yes, we know!" laughed everyone else. *Thank you, Captain Obvious*, thought Greg. "You see that helicopter? Your AK is going to do *nothing* to it!"

The men around Greg—he still didn't have a gun—shot at the helicopters, but Greg could see the bullets bouncing off. The helicopters started to take everything around them apart. They sheltered in a brick building. Greg looked out and saw a bigger helicopter flying with a BTR personnel carrier suspended below it on ropes. *Well, that's a come-to-Jesus moment*, he thought, *okay, shit. This isn't good*.

The men around him were yelling in Georgian; they piled out of the building. Greg caught up with an Australian running ahead of him. Everyone was scrambling into trucks. Greg and the Australian saw a truck driving towards them, the one that had driven them there. But the driver plowed right past them.

Everyone ran. Helicopters flew over, strafing them. At one point Greg took cover lying in a field, and looked up to see a jet banking around them. *Very scary.*

Along the way he managed to get a helmet. He picked up an AK-47 from a dead man. He also found a brand-new, U.S.-manufactured Airtronics RPG-7 rocket launcher, something he'd been trained on after the revolution. Terrified kids were dropping things in their desperation to escape. Greg was delighted and very proud. As he went he searched for RPG rounds; he found half a dozen.

He walked twenty kilometers out with his AK, helmet, his med bag, and the RPG and its rounds. Ahead of him was a collection point on a road. He saw a Ukrainian officer standing there.

"Oh!" said the officer, noticing him, "thank you for bringing the RPG." He reached out and took the hard-won prize from the very pissed-off medic.

They climbed into vehicles and were taken to a national guard base in Kyiv, near the airport. They were told to shelter from expected bombing. Greg was picked to defend the building, and was posted in the stairwells. In the skies above him were planes dogfighting. Bombs fell everywhere. *I'm going to die this time*, he thought. He took out his journal and started writing in it for the first time. *Pretty damn terrifying.*

Someone handed the Australian an RPG. He was an experienced soldier, and both he and Greg had been hanging out with the Ukrainian recon soldiers, men who had been fighting since the war started in the Donbas in 2014. Most of the men sheltering in the basements were inexperienced kids, who were mostly police- and not military-trained, if they were trained at all.

"Okay, Greg," they said. "You were an RPG loader?"

"Yes," he said. It had been part of his insurgent training.

"Okay. We're making these teams. There's Russian tanks coming down this road. You guys are going to go out and ambush them."

Bizarre, thought Greg. He had been having coffee with his friends in this beautiful city, which looked like an eastern European Paris, a day before. Now he was with an Australian, preparing to shoot rockets at invading Russian tanks.

They sat poised for an hour, waiting. Then someone came out to get them. "Russian tanks got blown up, they're not coming here." They went back inside.

Greg stayed at the base for several days as the city was bombed. At one point a Russian sympathizer took a potshot at them at night from another building nearby. They shot back and wounded the guy; the police cleared his building, arrested him, and took the documents that he'd left. Then two *agent provocateur* vehicles, perhaps forward elements of Russian recon, attempted to do a drive-by on the checkpoint in front of the building, killing one policeman and wounding two others.

They couldn't have been locals, thought Greg, *unless they're completely stupid*. They got lit up: the entire barracks of fifty cadets unloaded everything they had. The attackers never even got out of the cars. They burned down with the assailants still inside them.

The Georgian Legion was heading to Lviv, in the far west of the country. Greg saw no reason to leave Kyiv. He stuck with the experienced Australian, who liked the Ukrainians he had been working with since Hostomel. Greg stayed to translate and got the Australian into the recon unit's ranks. Then he packed up to go to his apartment and collect more gear. He had a machine gun in his backpack. Every block or so he hit a checkpoint, was put on the ground, and searched. He got home, took a day to collect his things, and went with a few friends to join a civilian militia that needed medics. There were no taxis or vehicles available anywhere. He walked fourteen kilometers with his kit to join his next unit.

The new unit sent Greg to Moschun on March 7, just after Ginger arrived at the border. He was told to pack up. He got his med bag and was issued with another AK-47, a new one that hadn't been fired yet. He had no idea where it shot, and didn't have time to zero it. *Well, okay*, he thought. *I'm happy I have a gun this time. That's already a step up.* He had a shitty, janky vest, basically a sheet of plastic-wrapped metal with rubber backing tucked inside. *I think it's more for something mental, I don't know*, thought Greg.

There weren't enough medics to go around, so Greg and the other medics were attached to different units in turn. Their first rotation was to relieve another unit that had been thrashed by artillery on the outskirts of Moschun. Greg climbed onto the bus and was dropped off at the edges of the suburb. They hadn't made it more than two houses in when the artillery started crashing around them.

No one was killed, but there were some wounded. Greg had his first combat casualty: a massive 6′ 6″ unit leader built like a football player, someone tough to move even for the 6′ 5″ Greg. *He has to weigh 240 pounds of muscle*, thought the medic.

A big piece of shrapnel had gone through the man's arm. His bicep was torn away; the arm was broken. *Brave as hell*, Greg thought, as the man stood up and walked out about one hundred yards. Greg and another medic helped him into a hole. The walking wounded and almost everyone else, as Greg put it, "fucked off." There were just two other medics, a few guys who kept their cool, and the wounded unit leader.

They put a tourniquet on him and bandaged him up. They put him on a stretcher and started to carry him out through the nearby woods. An Orlan drone was following them. They kept just about one hundred meters in front of the creeping artillery that was exploding behind them as they ran with the big man on the stretcher.

A kilometer later, they came to a road, found a vehicle, and hotwired it to take the wounded man out. They drove to Horenka, the next town under Ukrainian control.

"Okay, good," Greg was told after they handed over the casualty. "We're going back in."

The plan was the same as before, just with a different unit for the medics. *A bit of chaos*, thought Greg, *but orders are orders.*

On the way, they started getting hit with accurate artillery. They were pulled back, and the plan was to assault Moschun the next day. But all the backpacks were still at the point of bombardment. Greg's gear, including his socks and snacks ("all the important shit"), was in his bag, so he volunteered with three other guys to go in a van and pick up the backpacks.

The place was completely bombed out. Houses and cars were on fire, and shell holes were everywhere. *Oh*, thought Greg, *interesting.* The leadership told them to find a basement to hide in, which they did. They discovered canned pickles and tomatoes, which were delicious. For the next two hours they were bombarded by 152 mm artillery. At around 11 p.m., they heard on the radios that everyone needed to switch their armbands from yellow to blue. "Enemy was seen wearing yellow armbands," they heard. "Anyone seen wearing yellow armbands after midnight is an enemy."

They looked at each other while the basement rocked from the artillery. *Where the fuck are we supposed to get blue armbands at this time?* They found a blue Louis Vuitton shirt in the house, cut it up, and turned it into armbands.

The next day, the unit got rotated out, but the medics were told to stay in order to be attached to the next unit. They would go into the village in the afternoon.

While they were waiting, Greg saw a few guys around a tractor. "Hey, anyone know how to drive this tractor?" they asked.

"I can drive a tractor!" responded Greg cheerfully. He got in and drove it to a different part of town for them.

As he walked back, he came upon an officer screaming at his soldiers for losing a tractor. *I had no idea that was not their tractor! How could I know?* thought Greg, sliding past.

That evening they were told they would hold an observation post on the flank of Moschun itself. Greg and another medic friend were the last men in line for the vehicle. Just as he was about to step in, Greg looked to the right and saw the vehicle next to them explode from an artillery round. Everyone leapt out and headed towards the only available cover: a bright teal building that bore the sign of the Jehovah's Witnesses. They hid behind it as the artillery exploded around them. Greg could feel the pressure from the shelling begin to cause a concussion. Shrapnel struck the teal walls overhead, and then subsided. Everyone had survived. *You can give it to the Jehovah's Witness church for protecting us*, he thought.

The orders remained the same. They got back into the van. *A few more holes, less windows*, thought Greg, but it still ran. They drove to the outskirts of Moschun, then walked in, looking, as he put it, like "military hobos," with mismatched kit but prepared to fight.

They were spotted, and soon Grad rockets were falling around them. Two helicopters came in and strafed their section of town, killing no one but wounding two men. They tucked into a two-story, red-brick house. The mission was forward observation: to look out and call for artillery at any Russian advance.

Next to them was a position held by the 72nd Mechanized unit. Greg watched as they just kept getting smashed. Everything hit them: mortars constantly, Grad, artillery, helicopters. At one point he saw a jet drop a bomb on the position. *Crazy*, he thought.

The next morning, the medics were told that the infantry unit was getting rotated out, but that they would stay in order to serve as medics for the units that would be rotating in for the next week. It was freezing. There was no food; he and his medic buddy split a can of beans. *Okay, well, whatever*, Greg thought.

The new batch contained a very, very eager commander, who decided that the best way to be a sneaky forward observer unit was to dig trenches in front of the enemy. "I don't know what the fuck was his idea," Greg said later. They did it, and got spotted. Greg shoveled, expecting to die at any second. The building was smashed that night. *I have no idea how we're alive*, Greg thought. The building in front of them was leveled. *They must have thought we were in that building, or they're horrible shots.*

The next morning, the unit was rotated out. The medics stayed. Greg was not sad to see the man he identified as "that idiot" go.

For days they supported the infantry units that came to them, and treated whomever they could. One man was brought to them with shredded legs. They were nonexistent; it looked like they had been through a meat grinder. One arm looked the same. Greg was told that his patient had lain out on the battlefield for two days before getting picked up. When he was brought to the medics, he was smiling at them. *No idea how that works*, Greg thought. *I don't know how that works.* It had been $-17°C$ at night. *How did he survive?*

He saw more shredded bodies, and many, many traumatic brain injuries from the pressure waves caused by the artillery that kept exploding all around them. One man had a case of mutism, another was incontinent. Both were neurological injuries. This was shell shock, as though straight out of World War I: a far cry from the psychological PTSD so heavily diagnosed among the American military over the last twenty years. Most of those cases were nowhere near artillery, because most of their enemies didn't have any.

Shelling gave him ninety percent of his work as a medic. Bullet wounds, he thought, were relatively straightforward. But stopping the bleeding from shelling could be another job altogether. This was the scariest, he thought, because it simply took flesh away. The medics had only backpacks with them. But a piece of shrapnel could take entire chunks out of people. A missing section of thigh could eat up an entire bandage supply. Greg found himself lining the space next to the bleeding with combat gauze, and stuffing the rest with bedsheets, clothes, anything he could get his hands on in order to tamponade the hemorrhage.

On the fourth day, they saw a bunch of Russian infantry move in, and called in their mortars to halt the advance. As the Russians pushed forward, the order came to shoot when they got within one hundred and fifty meters: close enough for accurate rifle fire. One man shot early, wounding a Russian at a good two hundred meters, but giving away their position.

Greg was upstairs. The medics, as the longest short-term residents, knew the place best. His position had once been a little girl's room, with pictures and paintings on the wall. It made Greg sad: she was gone and he was in her place. *Because some dumb-asses decided to come here*, he thought.

He watched thirty Russians sprint across a field three hundred meters away, too far for a good shot. That night the village was hit with white phosphorus shells. "White phos" gained notoriety during the Vietnam War, when the GIs called it "Willie Pete." It is an incendiary explosive that can burn almost anything. It can also be strangely attractive. *It was really pretty*, Greg thought, *until half the village started burning down.*

The next morning, his unit was told that they would all be rotated out, because they were anticipating a big Russian advance. Thirty seconds after they ran out of the back of the building, an amphibious BTR rolled up to their position. They fired an RPG in return. Greg looked back in time to see the little girl's house being demolished.

They took cover for Ukrainian Grad rocket launchers to hit the Russian positions in the village, which also managed to strike the little girl's house again. *Thank you for that*, Greg thought. The medics picked up a few wounded along the way. Greg noticed a few dead men who had been "splattered" by artillery. *That wasn't very pretty*, he thought. *Guts everywhere and stuff*.

They were driven out, got a shower, and slept. Greg was given a few days off to recover from the concussion he'd gotten during the artillery barrage at the Jehovah's Witness building.

After two days, the Ukrainians blew up a dam and flooded the Russians out, forcing them to retreat around Moschun. Greg's unit was sent to the edges of Irpin. For the next several days, he dug in and sheltered from artillery while Ginger, Dan, and Tex fought in the suburb with the Legion teams.

The medic decided that he was sick of watching people getting blown up in trenches. *I would kind of like to go shoot Russians*, he thought. *You don't get to do that too often in a trench*.

He put in his paperwork to transfer out of his Azov civilian militia ("just people, led by old vets," as he put it, not professionals, and not the hardcore who ended up in Mariupol) and into the International Legion. Somewhere along the line a disgruntled officer took offense at this and implied in his own paperwork that Greg was trying to run. This landed him in the brig for two days. Soon another officer, who knew the work the medic had done in Moschun, sorted it out.

Greg switched over to the Legion in Kyiv and was added to Alpha Team. That was how he ended up standing in front of the surprised Ginger.

"This is Greg," Eric continued outside the barracks. "He's going to be our medic. He's a real swell guy. He said he'd help us around, give us rides around town if we need it. He's got an apartment in town if you guys get a little too fucked up and need a place to stay; he said you're more than welcome to crash on the couch." *What the fuck?* thought Ginger. *Right on, dude*. Greg promptly took them into the city and dropped them off. "And then we gallivanted," said Ginger. A few days later the infantryman would help Greg sight in his new rifle at the range. The medic carefully placed a piece of masking tape on the top of the stock, where he wrote out an abbreviated range card in permanent marker.

4

BEHIND ENEMY LINES

They had been told that they were being sent back to Kyiv to meet their new commanders, and were eager for a change. Since Vadym's promotion, they had had only a temporary unit leader. Each Legion team had a Ukrainian officer to serve as commander and liaison with the Ukrainian Army for the foreigners, and now they needed a permanent one.

The next morning Ginger was standing around bullshitting, smoking a cigarette outside the barracks. A car pulled up, and a tall, handsome man in his mid-thirties stepped out. He wore a Boonie hat and carried a .308 semi-auto rifle. *Real nice, real Gucci,* Ginger noted. He was clean, clean-shaven, and practically smelled new. *Like out of a magazine. Oh great. Here we go.* Ginger turned and looked at the officer's partner: a short man with a beer belly, a shaven head, and a giant bushy black beard, who looked like a Ukrainian Santa Claus. *Oh my God, look at this. We've got a fuckin' junior lieutenant and a fuckin' white supremacist hand in hand about to run this fuckin' team. This is fantastic.*

Everyone was talking shit. The tall officer said, "Everybody get in formation."

Ginger looked up. He had one boot on, torn pants, and half a cigarette in his hand. No one even had proper civilian clothes anymore, and in the infantryman's estimation they all looked like dogshit. "Get in formation!" *What the fuck?* They all looked at each other. *No fuckin' way.* "Do you guys know what a formation is?" *Holy fuck. Alright. Slow down there, buddy.*

Everyone formed up. "In the United States, do you guys smoke in formation?" *Oh, I'm gonna fuck this guy up,* thought Ginger. They all looked at each other, laughing, and put their cigarettes out.

The short man translated for the taller officer, whose English was slight. Out came a whole lecture on looking and dressing the part, and being professional. Ginger was still picking out blood from under his fingernails and hawking black mucus from the back of his throat because of all the cigarettes. *Who the fuck is this guy talking to right now? This is madness.*

The shorter man was called Symon. He was an old hand: a former member of SBU-Alpha, the elite Ukrainian special forces group. Symon was a crusty soldier who had been fighting in the Donbas since 2014. He had recently left the army but joined again when the war broke out. The beard earned him the call sign "Pirate," and, combined with his seen-it-all demeanor, it made him look much older than he really was, which was closer to thirty.

The tall handsome man was Oleksii Chubashev. He had ended up in the Ukrainian special forces by an unusual route: television. A professional reporter, he had a TV show called *Recruit*, which was famous in Ukraine, in which he filmed the selection process for the unit. It wasn't part of the initial plan, but he made it and became a full-fledged officer in the special forces. He eventually returned to civilian life but maintained a public relations role, with a popular YouTube channel. He was famous; people would stop him on the street to say hello. Well trained, he was also still untested.

Oleksii was smart enough to realize that the men he was commanding had far more experience than he did, so he would elegantly cede the tactical floor to them, reserving the technical administration of the unit for himself. He was an idealist, having rejoined the army after the Russian invasion. Greg saw Oleksii scolding the men one day for littering cigarette butts on the ground. "What the fuck? You guys are willing to die for this land, but you're not willing to respect it enough to clean up after yourselves." Greg, who admitted to a certain fixation on neatness, didn't mind. Ginger, still in bed one morning when Oleksii came in and harangued him for an empty water bottle still sitting on a table, found his manner less charming, especially when Oleksii called him a "dirty American."

But they all loved the man and thought it was hilarious. They genuinely liked working with him: he was smart, charismatic, and a true believer in the cause. He was also a kind person who was always willing to go the distance and leverage his own connections, once linking Greg to personal friends in important places who were able to ship in supplies. *Oh wow*, thought the medic.

Greg served as Oleksii's driver. The older man was from Kyiv and had never learned how to drive. Greg drove a lot and, as a fluent Ukrainian speaker, was the logical choice. Greg still had his Azov-style discipline, *yes, sir* this and *no, sir* that. Oleksii was always after him. "Greg, you've got to stop this *yes sir, no sir* shit. That's line infantry. This is special units," said the officer in the passenger seat. "I appreciate the respect, but I don't want this top-down hierarchy; you guys all bring something to the table."

A cool pep talk, thought Greg as he drove. "Yes, sir! I'll do that, sir."

"That's what I'm talking about!"

Oh shit.

They road-tripped down to Mykolaiv, a port city on the Pivdennyi Buh (or Southern Bug) River, west and slightly north of Odesa, close to the Black Sea. The men called their new home the roach motel, but it was really housing for workers in the shipyards. They overlooked the port. There was a rail yard, a bunch of cranes, the shipyards, and the water; the warehouse for a big Ukrainian steelworks was visible from their windows. A three-story building, it also had a bomb shelter in the basement, with a series of rooms in which they stored their weapons and explosives. The first floor housed Oleksii's kitchen, a guardroom, a place for a concierge, and a few rooms, but most people crammed into the rooms on the second and third floors.

Personal gear from the previous occupants was all over the place. There was old food in the mini fridges; clothes and other items were stored as one would expect. Cockroaches were everywhere.

Apparently disliking one another to the point of inseparability, Ginger moved into a room with Rob, the nearly fifty-year-old Craig, and a British para named Alex. They were relentless. Each morning Craig, whom Ginger would torment by calling "Grandpa," would rise by 6 a.m. and begin making coffee. Alex would roll over and start cussing. "Craig, ya fuckin' cunt! Go back to bed! It's six in the morning, mate! What are you doing?"

This would wake Rob. "Alex, you fucking little bitch, just go back to bed, leave the man alone."

"Rob, you fat bastard," Ginger would groan from his bed, "would you just stop causing problems, man? We get it. It's first thing in the morning and you haven't eaten yet. Calm down."

This would go on for an hour, until they were all so pissed with each other that they'd leave the room. *A nonstop cycle*, thought Ginger. *A lot of fun.*

They heard that they were going to be doing maritime work. *Ah, this is going to be right up my alley*, thought Dan. "Which it was," he admitted later, "but not in a good way."

Their target was the Kinburn Peninsula, which sits opposite the basin where the Pivdennyi Buh and Dnieper rivers dump into the Black Sea between Mykolaiv and Kherson. From there the peninsula runs west towards the city of Ochakiv. It forms the small, western-most finger of the larger spit of land that runs below Kherson, to Mykolaiv's southeast.

It was a beautiful place: a nature preserve in peacetime. It was also sandy, boggy, swampy, and home to a prodigious number of mosquitoes. It was unfriendly to armor. A Ukrainian maritime unit had been crossing the Black Sea to do reconnaissance there, trying to see if they could pin down Russian troops or even find a way to flank. The foreigners were going to jump into that role and see if they could pull Russian forces away from Kherson.

They were given Zodiacs by the 73rd, the Ukrainian maritime unit. Dan had been the "Zodiac guy" for his whole career in the SEALs. Zodiacs are small, rubber, light infiltration boats, designed for swift insertions. They look very cool.

I hate Zodiacs, sighed Dan. When he left the SEALs, he thought that at least he'd never have to see one of these again, but here they were. The design that made them light and fast also meant they were prone to breaking down. The engines, the fuel lines ... something always went wrong. "I always suggest that we *don't* use them, but some officer always wants to use them," he explained.

The Zodiacs performed as expected. On their first trip to the peninsula, one of them broke down. *In the SEALs we would have tanked this*, thought Dan, but the Ukrainians simply hooked the working boat up to the broken one and towed it to their insertion point. There were no spare motors. There was only one driver. The navigator was his smartphone.

They landed. It was a three-day search and recon mission, trying to get the lay of the land and see if they could find Russian activity. They worked their way eastwards. On the last night, they moved towards a beach that was much further east, hoping to use it as a future landing spot. They were picked up off the new beach, and taken back to Ochakiv, the closest port on the Ukrainian side. Another boat broke down, and they were towed the rest of the way.

By now they had collected enough men to split the teams up even more. Their former second-in-command, Prym, took charge of a new team, christened Charlie, made up of former French Foreign Legionnaires. They landed on one of Alpha's newly scouted beaches to do a follow-on search and recon (S&R) mission. The 73rd started up some trouble for the Russians, causing the enemy to begin a westwards sweep of the peninsula. They came out in force and lit the forest on fire with flamethrowers. Charlie Team moved back, towards the far end of the peninsula. Charlie evacuated the civilians who wanted to leave the peninsula, and came back across the sea.

In Zaporizhzhia Alpha Team had picked up a Ukrainian-speaking Green Beret medic. His name was Dmitri. Born in Ukraine, he emigrated to the United States with his parents when he was young, eventually joining the U.S. Special Forces (also known as the Green Berets) and serving overseas. Now Dmitri was connected through friends to another former American special operator who wanted to join them. The team discussed it, agreed, then promptly asked the new guy to bring them a few specialized items: kneepads for Dmitri, helmet counterweights for NODs, and a small helmet task-light.

His name was Riever. Quiet, around thirty, with brown hair and eyes and a strong jaw and hands, he had the classic country boy turned soldier vibe (as Dan put it, "you know a good soldier when you see one"). Valedictorian of his high-school class, he had gone straight to the elite 75th Ranger Regiment, the unit made famous by the film *Black Hawk Down*, and served several combat tours in Afghanistan, quickly making sergeant. A former member of his platoon's weapons squad, he was intimately familiar with the heavier of the guns available to a light infantry unit. After leaving the army he had gotten into overseas defense contracting and had begun earning his undergraduate degree at a well-respected U.S. university. He toggled between deployments and school. When the Russians invaded, he was nearly finished. He handed in his work for his final semester early and skipped his own graduation to fight in Ukraine.

When he arrived at the International Legion's sorting school, the gymnasium was loud. The soft-spoken colonel interviewing him looked like a quiet professor in fatigues. *This country has turned into a military overnight*, Riever thought, eyeing the older man. "You're probably going to die," the Ukrainian said. "Are you okay with that?"

"Yes, I have a background," the Ranger said, gesturing at his paperwork. He had brought copies of his DD-214, his U.S. military discharge forms.

"Well, I don't know what all this is," said the colonel, looking at the form, which bristled with awards, combat deployments, and schools ranging from Master Breacher to Ranger School to the SERE survival school, "but this is pretty serious." After some back-and-forth, the Ranger was sent to Kyiv, to sign his International Legion paperwork and join Alpha Team in Mykolaiv.

After much disorganization and waiting, Riever was finally sent to the International Legion's incongruously located office in Kyiv. The two surly girls working in the office (they had been ordered to be mean, for obvious reasons) helped him get his paperwork sorted. He signed on the dotted line (which was actually solid), a three-page, two-columned contract for the International Legion, with Ukrainian text on the left side and English on the right. You signed on both. This gave him a green book, the Ukrainian Army's pay-book and official identity document, and the right to draw a weapon. He headed to the armory, which to a soldier looked like Aladdin's cave but was devoid of the useful stuff. There were stacks of FNC rifles but no mags. There were stacks of .338s, and piles of AK variants, with mags.

He was handed a new CZ Bren 2, an old Soviet-designed Makarov pistol and one box of ammunition to go with it, and two rifle magazines. *Bro, are you fucking kidding me?* he thought. *Two mags?* He eventually browbeat the man he called the "arms room troll" into giving him more rifle mags from the troll's own personal stash.

Thus armed, he could no longer go back to his hotel, so he was sent to the converted girls' dormitory barracks, where he eventually ran into the questionable Pole who ran the place, a man Riever called "the king frog of this little toadstool."

"Who the fuck are you?" asked the king frog soon thereafter, eyeing the American.

"I'm with Alpha Team," responded Riever, which ended the conversation. He searched his room, finding notebooks full of a schoolgirl's beautiful, neat handwriting and a leather jacket that was probably someone's pride and joy. *Hopefully they can find it all when the war ends*, he thought.

He stayed the night and bore-sighted his rifle. He never thought he would love anything as much as he had loved the SCAR he carried in Afghanistan with Ranger Regiment, but the Bren was beautiful. A military history nerd, he knew Bren for its light machine gun, which the Brits had carried in World War II. That was the sort of gun that commanded affection, as in the story of the dying Cameron Highlander at the Battle of Blackpool in Burma, who had whispered to his retreating comrades, "Gi' me a Bren. Leave me. I'll take a dozen wi' me."[1] His model was an assault rifle, with a better stock than the SCAR, clean and crisp with good sights, even if the trigger was a little long. His Makarov, the "Mak," had the cutest little round-nose bullets.

Together with a big American who had fought in Irpin and was in and out of the team and a British para (called British George for specificity), they drove south to Mykolaiv after a few difficulties in getting gas. They stopped for hot dogs, Riever eyeing a convoy of pontoon bridges and a few burned-out tanks along the way. It was beautiful country. He also saw a fox and fields of farmland but with war in the background. He kept his Mak on his hip as they drove, the rest of their gear stacked and ready.

When he arrived, Dmitri told Riever that he needed a mosquito net to wear on missions. The Ranger went down to the local sports store and bought a Boonie hat with an attached net. He was put on the next mission as the .240 gunner. Three days later, they went out.

Now that the Russians had moved, and had burned so much of the peninsula, their old scouting information was no longer good. Alpha was tasked to go back for a redo: starting at the west and clearing east. They re-set for another S&R. They went out in force, taking almost everyone they had. The first S&R had been light: only the pros, the most experienced soldiers, moving fast. This time they rolled heavy, hoping to set up an ambush.

The mosquitoes were like nothing they'd ever experienced before: a constant, thick, 24/7 cloud. The men on the team had served and worked all over the globe. Not one of them had ever seen anything like it. You would literally breathe them in through your mouth, they were so thick.

Dan looked around, keeping an eye on everyone. *There are guys who've been to Ranger school looking at me like this is the worst day of their life*, thought the SEAL. *This is biblical, plagues-of-Egypt stuff*.

It seemed impossible. Aside from this unlucky group of men, how could there be enough for this many mosquitoes to eat? They decided that it must have been the result of the Russian arson: the forest fires seemed to have blown the mosquito population of nearly the entire peninsula to this spot. *I've been in Africa, Central America*, thought Greg. But nothing compared to this. *Awful. Horrendous*. No one could sleep, and in the daytime they couldn't move, so they were stuck "getting raped by mosquitoes," as Ginger put it.

The first night they were meant to hike out, British George went down hard. Everyone was covered in mosquito bites, but he was having an allergic reaction of some sort: swollen, red, puking, and dysfunctional. British George was as tough as they came, a former para and a paver in civilian life who looked like a stronger Tom Hardy turned boxer. Someone later produced a video of him in a bar fight in Odesa. He got into it with another man and started walking towards the guy, arms down by his sides and relaxed. The other guy hit him, hard, in the jaw. British George just kept on walking, grabbed the guy in a suplex around the waist, picked him up, and threw him to the floor, where he methodically and brutally beat him to pieces. He had won his military fighting reputation in the early days of Irpin, where he deafened himself by firing rockets from a room without ear protection, and volunteered to drop his kit and sprint a kilometer with an NLAW anti-tank weapon to a position so as to hit a BMP that was hammering his team. But the mosquitoes had effectively poisoned him, and he had to be evacuated.

They tried to move to a different location and link up with the rest of the teams, and swapped British George with a man they called Baby Scott, who had been left behind. A twelve-kilometer march was shortened, because two of the guys fell out two kilometers later. Greg carried someone's rifle, and even picked up some of Riever's extra ammunition, to lighten the heavy load of the .240 gunner.

They found an old Russian patrol base and set up another ambush, but no one came, possibly courtesy of the mosquitoes. Riever once pushed forward with a few men, including Greg and Tex, but they couldn't find the Russians.

They got loaded up on the Zodiacs. They weren't what Ginger had been expecting, because he thought that the 73rd was going to pick them up in their LCUs, a sort of D-Day-style landing craft for ferrying marines around.

The rest of the team who hadn't been on the op, plus Symon, came in their own three rigid rubber boats. As they approached the beach, one ran out of gas about a thousand meters out. *Already a shit show*, thought Ginger. There were fourteen guys on the beach, three boats just showed up, and they were trying to load everyone into two boats so that some of them could be loaded into the third one, which was out of gas. *Oh my God, here we go. This is where the bullshit starts, and it will continue to go until it comes to a climax and we all die.*

Six men jumped from one boat to another in the middle of the Black Sea in full kit. They filled up the gas tank with their reserves, and took off. The first twenty to thirty minutes were miserable, Ginger thought, but everything seemed otherwise okay.

One of the Charlie Team men, a Hungarian, was driving. "Hey, where's the LCU?" Ginger asked. Everyone assumed that they were being ferried to the bigger boats for the long run across the sea. "It's over there, over there," responded the Hungarian.

They kept going. "Feeding us this lie," said Ginger later, "that nobody knew was a lie because we didn't know that they didn't know what an LCU was."

Two hours later, Ginger said to the driver, "Dude, *where* is the LCU?"

"We are going here," said the Legionnaire, pointing to the map on his phone.

"Dude, that's Ochakiv!" exclaimed Ginger.

"Well, what's that?"

"That's a port, man! An LCU is a boat!"

"Oh no, we're going all the way." Ochakiv was thirty-two kilometers away over open water.

Everyone was soaking wet. The boat was full of water, up to their knees. *Dude, this is going to be fucking horrible*, thought Ginger. *I hate the water, I hate being on the water. I was in the army, I wasn't in the damn navy.*

The water was freezing. The air temperature was freezing. Everyone was numb.

Ginger's boat ran out of gas, again. The three boats met up. The men used red-light flashlights, signaling—they had no radios. They were still in Russian-controlled waters. The other two boats had no extra gas, so they started to tow Ginger's boat. All three boats were full of water.

They had swapped their original Zodiacs for boats that had been given to them for free. A slight upgrade on Zodiacs, these inflatable RHIBs had a center console but were also rubber boats. All of a sudden they went from ankle-deep water in one boat to knee-deep water. They were taking on more water than they could pitch out.

The driver's side sponson on Dan's boat had been, unknown to them, failing for hours. They were starting to sink. They stopped, meeting up again, floating in the middle of the Black Sea.

They had finally leveled up in terms of gear: now they had decent NODs, expensive guns, everything they actually needed to be operational. *We're gonna lose it all*, Dan thought. *It's gonna get deep-sixed right now.*

"We're going down!" Ginger heard some of the men in the other boat say. Symon put on a life jacket. "You got more?" someone asked. Symon said, "No. The commander must survive." *What the fuck?* thought Ginger. Everyone started laughing.

Dan stood up. "Any of your good gear, take it off. Hand it to one of the guys in the boat that's floating. You can swim; your gear can't. Get ready to get in the water."

An incredulous voice floated out of the darkness. "Is he fucking serious?"

"If you can't swim, get off this boat right fucking now. If you can swim, if you're a strong swimmer, strip your kit off and get on my boat," said the SEAL. All of them just looked at each other. Everyone went silent. *This is actually it. We're going to die in the Black Sea. We're still five hours away*, thought Ginger. *We aren't even at the halfway point. Even the sea stopped making a noise for a second, the waves just stopped. This is like something straight out of a movie, the climactic this-is-it speech. Holy shit, man.*

Riever, standing in Dan's boat, started handing over his gear. He took out his mission phone. The International Legion didn't have the same sort of formal family notification process he was used to from Ranger Regiment. He'd made a special lock screen for his phone, a black background with white writing. It said "In case of death please notify" and listed his longtime girlfriend's name and number, and then his father's. He handed it over to one of the former Marines, and asked the other man to call his girlfriend if he didn't make it.

Everyone started throwing their gear into Greg's boat, next to the medic and the recently delivered Baby Scott. By the time they were loaded up, neither of them could move their limbs. NLAWs, ten machine guns, rifles, everything: hundreds of pounds of equipment had nowhere to go but on top of them. It took Greg an hour to wiggle one arm from underneath the pile. *If we're going to drown, I can literally do nothing*, he thought. *I have never been this close to certain death, and there is not a Russian in sight.*

The boat started nosediving into the water as they cruised forward. *They're getting literally waterboarded*, Ginger thought, watching. His boat was being towed, taking on water, while everyone on it tried to use their helmets to bail out. They were completely waterlogged. *An absolute nightmare.* Greg and Scott joked that this was going to be like the ending scenes of *Titanic*, with the pair of them holding hands as they went down.

They linked up again. The two broken-down boats were stuck. They only had one more chance: Symon's boat quit them, barely floating, to return to Ochakiv and get tanks of gas to bring back. This left two boats full of people in the Black Sea: no radios, no cell-phone reception, no food, no warm or even dry clothing.

A man named Tom had gotten custody of Riever's Makarov. He took it out and shot a round into the air, randomly. Guys started laughing; Ginger thought it was hilarious. Eric, who had introduced Ginger to Greg, went white in the face. *He looks like a ghost*, thought Ginger. *The whitest thing I've ever seen in my life. He's so white he's glowing.* "Eric, are you okay?" he asked.

"Dude, I want to go home," said Eric.

"Okay, we broke Eric," said Ginger. "Good job, Tom, you broke Eric; he's fucked up."

"He was fucked up anyway!" protested Tom. "Dude's a pussy!"

It's just one thing after the other, thought Ginger.

Eventually Symon returned, with gas. They made it back to Ochakiv, towing the sinking boat.

5

WHEAT FROM CHAFF

They lost almost everyone. *People's souls just fell out of their bodies,* thought Ginger. *This was the third mission we'd ran out there, it was a very slow op tempo, dudes just weren't happy there. We weren't doing a lot, and what we were doing seemed absolutely ridiculous.*

Eleven guys went home for good after that op, and another five or six went elsewhere in the country or home on leave. It humbled a lot of people, and a lot of people simply left. Bravo disappeared. Dan was put in charge of Alpha. Now he had Ginger, Dmitri, Riever, and Greg as his team. Tex was temporarily borrowed by their former SWCC (special warfare combat crewman and maritime vehicle expert), who called his two-man team Delta.

Riever looked around, finally able to keep track of who was who in the aftermath of the exodus. In addition to Alpha and Delta there was Prym's Charlie Team. It consisted of Marti, a tall Hungarian former boxer with an imposing set of tattoos, including some on his neck and back and more on the backs of his hands; Mykola, a Ukrainian PKM machine-gunner who had the odd habit of some-times driving on the wrong side of the road; and Loup, a nearly silent, darkly handsome young Georgian sniper who had defected from the French Foreign Legion in order to finally get a chance to kill the Russians, who had been oppressing his native country for so long. "We're just holding Loup back," one of the Americans said to Riever before the exodus. "If we let him go out east, we'd find him after a while with all of the Russians dead and him wearing nothing but a necklace of their ears."

They were looking for other work, chasing intelligence, trying to set something up. Dmitri was in touch with a Ukrainian unit that was talking about raids in Kherson. Someone suggested getting on Tinder, posing as women, setting their location to the peninsula, and seeing if they could catfish a few Russians in order to get better location information. Symon was working his contacts with the Ukrainian Security Service, the SBU.

Finally, the Ukrainian leadership decided that they wanted to go bold: they wanted to hit a compound on the peninsula that senior Russian officers used for rest and recuperation. It was a forty-kilometer insertion involving their center-console RHIBs. Dan was pleased: it felt like a real mission. They'd done the planning, had the intel, had worked through everything. It was all done right. It was also just going to be cool.

Alpha came up with the raid plan. They had everything down to a T: time hacks, rehearsals, the whole nine yards.

As they were working to finalize their plans for the compound raid mission, they received two new men. The first was George, a Canadian veteran of the French Foreign Legion in his mid-twenties. Nearly as tall as Greg, he had dark hair and a lumberjack's beard and kind eyes, giving a gentle feeling to a man who had deployed in some of the world's uglier places with a unit famed for its toughness. He spent six years in that Legion, then went back home to Canada. When the Ukrainian war broke out, he was working in security for a sensitive infrastructure installation.

"I at first honestly didn't even want to come here. Of all the people I'm going to fight, I really didn't want to fight the Russians, because they fight dirty and don't respect the rules of war," George explained. "But I really should help. Ukraine needs help. Everyone helps out in their own way, whether it be through media exposure or donating money or whatever. My way is to donate my experience, which is military experience. I'll go donate it physically in person on the front lines," said the Canadian.

A friend had convinced him to join something called the Norman Brigade, which was a militia group working in Dnipro. He put his job on hold and planned on helping out for two months. It didn't work out; the group was unfunded, poorly armed (there were not enough AKs to go around and the main feature was an actual World

War I Maxim gun), not linked into the Ukrainian Army, and generally ineffective. *Enough is enough*, thought George, *we've accomplished nothing*. He took everyone who wanted to go, a group of nearly two dozen, across the country to Lviv. *I came this far*, he thought, *it's been a shit show till now, but I'll still find a way to help*. In Lviv he walked into the school and joined the International Legion.

Most of the men whom George had brought to Lviv went to First Battalion, the inexperienced section of the Legion. He and a few others went to the GUR special teams. They went to Kyiv, where George signed his Legion contract on May 15.

George was about to head out to Zaporizhzhia with a team when several of his men were nabbed by an SBU unit, run by one of the Ukrainian officers who had briefly led Alpha Team in Irpin. The remainder interviewed for another team: Alpha. He was redirected to Mykolaiv instead, where he was added to Charlie Team as a French-speaking former Legionnaire.

A Ukrainian maritime unit came through and warned the Legion teams about the PDM mines that the Russians had been using to protect the beaches on the peninsula near their positions. The multiple-wire-tripped antipersonnel mines were hidden underwater. They would destroy their RHIBs and kill everyone on board if they hit one. The men would have to swim in and clear the approach first.

Riever had always been interested in swimming missions, but he'd never been formally trained for it. Even as kids he and his younger brother, who wound up as a Green Beret, would practice for swim missions together; they'd practically grown up in the water. He decided to offer to help Dan. He expected to get shot down.

"Hey, Dan," said the Ranger, "I know this is silly, and I haven't done any formal training on this, but I have done over-the-beach swim-ins. If you're going to do this, I'm capable, I'm happy to go down to the water and I'll swim, and you can teach me how."

"Yeah, okay," said the SEAL, "that works." Riever had expected traditional gatekeeping, to be told it was really hard, and so on. *Really?* "If you say you can do it, I believe you, that'll do," Dan replied.

What Ginger referred to as the "diver clearing the beachhead thing" came up, so he felt, relatively late in the planning process. "You guys are fucking insane!" protested the infantryman.

"What? No, dude, I'm trained for this shit. This is easy. That's easy work," said the SEAL.

"What? No! That's fucking madness. You're just gonna swim up and try to de-mine a beach ... with a fishhook?"

"Yeah!"

Riever was still pleased to finally get a swim mission. *Riever's dumb ass*, Ginger sighed. "Well, you guys fuckin' have fun," he declared.

"Ginger, you're coming too," insisted Dan.

"No, I'm not! I am not going out on that. No way."

"Well, you'll be backup if something happens."

"I'll be backup, if the backup gets fucked up. I am not swimming into a minefield! I don't even like being on these boats. You want me to swim through a minefield? Get out of here!"

Riever found Ginger's protestations amusing. Like everyone else, the Ranger knew that Ginger was rock-solid. If they needed him to go, he would go.

They built the target package, set up their training, and started collecting gear. They bought Ukrainian Chuck Taylors and swim fins at a store called The Epicenter, which was heavily sandbagged but still open. It was a combination of Target, Best Buy, Walmart, Home Depot, Bed Bath and Beyond, REI, and Cabela's, all rolled into one. The Epicenter was the epicenter. Riever loved it. You could buy a crowbar, a toilet, a mission burner phone, spray paint, and a war belt all at once. One day Marti bought sheet steel and made targets. *A great institution*, Riever decided. *Really wonderful.*

Dan taught everyone his system for close-quarters battle, or CQB. They zeroed again, did a few range days, and trained some more. When they got back, Riever would use the system Dan had taught him for cleaning saltwater from his gear, filling the bathtub and dunking everything in it before hanging whatever could hang on a clothesline strung across the room.

They did rehearsals for the compound raid itself. They had it all figured out and kept getting more information as they went. There was a local man in Mykolaiv who had worked on the compound, and he provided additional layout details. They had imagery, drone flights, and pretty decent intelligence.

For the swimming portion, Dan taught Riever how to rig a harness to hold his swim fins, different strokes to keep his head (and NODs) out of the water, how to run 550 cord through the grommets of his shoes in order to link them to a carabiner to help with switching to fins, and how the brackish water off the peninsula would affect buoyancy. They talked about tricks like putting sections of closed cell foam behind their plates and magazines in their swim kit in order to add buoyancy; there were so many iterations and possibilities. They experimented with lights to see if they could visually locate the mines in the Black Sea's water. They did practice swims, finishing with a three-kilometer swim when their boats broke down again on a different exercise.

They had a long section of 550 cord and a big loop of metal that they'd found at the hardware store. Dan ran the metal loop through the 550 cord. He and Riever would each take one end of the cord, Dan would whip the bolt out like a sling, and they would drag-line it in. It was slow, but it worked. They could clear in a triangle towards the beach. If they snagged a mine with their line, they would be dead instantly: they would never even know it. If the mine was outside their wire, they stood a chance of locating it with their feet and pulling back. They also had waterproof lights that they could use to visually check underwater. They had no plans to try to defuse the mines; it was too complex. If they found them, the mission would be aborted. In the worst-case scenario, they would sacrifice two men to protect the rest.

They planned the approach for a miserable piece of beach which they thought the Russians would not have been able to reach in order to lay mines. It was out of the way and not close to any roads, but if they went in there, they should be able to land the RHIBs safely. Then they could break trail through the reeds into the woods and approach the compound on foot. Then they would signal back for the boats to come in, and the rest of the teams would join them while Dan and Riever changed into their assault gear. They planned to arrive at midnight.

Even while they practiced and trained, life in Mykolaiv went on. They found a local gym that was still open. Everyone worked out, but Marti and Dan were particular regulars, once trading videos of some very serious-looking boxing workouts back and forth on the group chat. As the weather warmed, Dan reverted to his preferred state: shirtless. Everyone finally got a look at his elaborate, naval and Celtic-themed back and arm tattoos. His nod to convention when out shopping in Mykolaiv was to add a simple black t-shirt to his jeans and Chucks: effortlessly cool.

At the roach motel, someone had scrounged a PS4 and a monitor. Riever and Ginger played the version of *Call of Duty* that had the Welgun, the experimental British sub-machine gun developed by the Special Operations Executive during World War II that was notorious for jamming. They would set it on zombie mode and try to develop as many game-beating hacks as they could.

They became converts to shawarma. Riever would also walk to the corner store and buy sausages and cheese and a loaf of bread. Dan never went on missions without a sausage in his pocket, which he could be seen gnawing on at intervals. Greg in particular loved the fact that the SEAL had fully converted to the eastern European-style foot-long salamis.

With him George had brought an older American former Marine named Michael who had served as a tanker. Now close to forty, Michael was a machine-learning specialist, programming "our AI overlords," as he put it, in a big corporate job overseas. His company gave him a volunteer's sabbatical. His wish to go was complicated by legal issues: as an American expat, he and his family lived on his skilled worker's visa, which normally would not allow one to leave one's paying job for more than thirty days without facing deportation. There was an exception that applied: volunteering for an international humanitarian disaster, which would allow him to be gone for up to ninety days.

"Yup," said his attorney, "this is an international humanitarian crisis and you surely are going to be volunteering, so it seems like this qualifies." The attorney was a kind man who also promised

Michael that, should the worst happen and Michael be killed, he would represent Michael's wife and children in court and petition for them to be able to remain in their adopted home.

Michael had ended up in the Norman Brigade after the International Legion accidentally rejected him for his visa-imposed time limit and the Georgian Legion rejected him for the fact that he was married to a Russian woman who had emigrated to the U.S. at the age of fifteen.

On the train out to Dnipro, he met a Russified Ukrainian couple who were going to pick up their elderly father. They had been revolutionized by the invasion: they swore never to speak a word of Russian again. They were amazed that Michael was there, and that he wanted to help Ukraine fight. They were very kind and prayed over him as he left the train, an experience he found very touching.

"There were a lot of countries that were sending weapons and sending ammunition, but it was important to me that the Ukrainians knew that there were people who were willing to actually stand with them. And that there were people who were willing to put their own safety on the line, and that we were not going to just watch as the Ukrainians died to protect us and basically Western democracy, which was the way that I saw that," he said of his decision. "And Ukrainian women and children were being killed, and Ukrainian men—and women, to be clear—were fighting and dying, and the collective West was sending money and weapons, which is not nothing. But there is not enough money in the world that makes up for the blood being spilled on our behalf. I didn't think that we were there to save them, because I think they were doing a really good job of saving themselves. But it was really important to me that they knew that they were not alone. And I think most of them did feel like they were alone."

But Michael's experience with the Norman Brigade was as disappointing as George's—they had not helped. He left with the Canadian, taking the train to Lviv.

Michael walked back into the school with George and the rest of their former team. In the hall he encountered the same colonel, sitting at the same child's desk, who had told him before that the rules precluded men who had a time limit on their potential service.

The colonel looked up and peered at Michael. "I know you," he said.

"Yes, sir, you do!" said Michael. He explained that the last time they had spoken he had been turned away by his ninety-day limit.

"Well, that's not the rule anymore," declared the colonel.

"Great," said Michael.

"You're in, here's your handshake, you're going into the GUR special teams," said the colonel.

Michael had been jaded by his experience in Iraq. He was just a kid then, but he had expected that he would be able to help people. To see women and children who were so clearly frightened of him, who so clearly did not want him to be there, had been sad and disappointing and startling. Twenty years later, he was finally signing up to do the thing he had tried to do all along: protect people who needed his help.

He had been particularly moved by a political cartoon that he saw at the outbreak of the war: Russian missiles traveling towards a group of Ukrainian women and children, standing in a line looking fearfully at one another while a group of much larger figures, labelled with Western flags (all of them drawn as marshmallow men), hid behind shields with the NATO logo on them. *I need to stand between the Russians and these women and children*, he thought. *I could not live with the shame if I didn't.*

Every Marine is a rifleman, goes the saying, and Michael had come to fight. But he was aware that, all things being equal, his machine-learning skills were better than his soldiering ones, especially at his age, and, since there were no Abrams tanks in sight, his true military specialty. At this juncture, helping a high-speed team with their intel was probably more useful than being a regular rifleman elsewhere. "I did not stay because I was a high-speed special forces soldier or marine," Michael declared. "I stayed because I was a machine-learning scientist who had done business intelligence analysis and knew computers." That he could read the Cyrillic alphabet, and could understand just enough Russian to help out, made him even more valuable. He was accepted as the unit's new intel guy and was happy to take the role.

Michael settled in to help with the detailed planning for Dan's new mission to raid the peninsula's rest-and-recuperation compound. Michael spent each day in the office with Oleksii, working through the computers and software and intel, listening to the officer's notorious Duolingo practice which he invested with what the American called "*extreme* enthusiasm." It was Michael's job to put everything into the mapping software, to get everything on ATAK, to get the waypoints set, mapping the buildings and diagrams, and the like.

The day of the mission, they did the op brief: the target was the same, nothing had changed. They got the loadouts for the boats set. Everything was squared away and ready. *Everything's looking really good*, Ginger thought. Alpha and Charlie loaded up, but the latter had no room for the recently arrived George, who was left behind with Michael and Oleksii.

As soon as they reached Ochakiv, Oleksii got a phone call. At the same time, they realized the smoke and sound they could hear was the Ukrainians blowing the shit out of something on the peninsula. You could see the fire from the port, forty kilometers away.

Oleksii started swearing on the phone.

"What's going on?" the men all asked.

"Watch this: mission's canceled," said Ginger.

"Shut the fuck up, Ginger," said Dan.

"It's canceled, bro, I'm telling you."

Oleksii got off the phone. "*Pizdets! Blyat!*"[1]

"What, man? What?"

"The 73rd hit our target!"

"What?"

"Yes, they fire MLRS at our target. They blow the whole thing up."

You are shitting me, thought Ginger. *No. This was going to be badass! A nighttime raid on a compound … it was going to be one for the history books! A forty-kilometer, over the Black Sea movement, two teams take out a compound and then bounce. And the 73rd smashes it with MLRS.*

"Well, you guys are going anyway," declared Oleksii, "so figure out what you want to do. We're already here, we did all this work, you guys are going over there. So figure it out."

"We'll just go over there, do a BDA [bomb damage assessment]," said Dan. "Maybe that missed, maybe they smashed it, maybe we can get intel, set up an ambush on them trying to leave. We'll figure something out. Let's go."

Their SWCC, who was driving one of the two boats, had briefed them that it was a forty-two-kilometer journey. Moving at twenty kilometers an hour, they expected a two- to three-hour ride.

At the five-hour mark, they were at the halfway point. They weren't moving as quickly as planned. They stopped while everyone refueled, ate a bit, and had some water. In the dark Symon had forgotten to turn off his bilge pump, so his battery died. They were about to take off when the commander said, "Wait, wait! No power, no power."

The SWCC did a battery swap. He took the battery out of the working boat, used it to start the dead one, took the battery off while it was running, and put the dead one back on so it would charge—all in the middle of the Black Sea. That took an hour. As soon as they restarted, they saw something in the water.

The SWCC said, "Ginger, you got eyes on that boat out there?"

"Give me a direction." Ginger scanned. "Yeah, I've got a big one."

"Can you see what it is?"

"I can't, but it's big."

"Is it ours?"

"I have no idea."

Both boats slowed down. Everyone got online, and they crept past the giant gunboat. *Dude, that was nuts.*

An hour later they saw another one. *Dude, where are these coming from?*

They checked in with Symon. "Did the Russians move their fleet in here?" These were technically Russian-controlled waters, but they had never had intel on Russian gunboats in that operational area. These were well-armed cruisers: guns front and back, anti-aircraft, the works. *What the hell, man?*

Dan decided to allow the mission to go on. They could still get there with enough cover of darkness. But every so often, he would give an update: we don't have time for this, so here is the new plan. Finally, they got down to brass tacks: they only had time left to go in close and run in with white light under the water, moving slowly.

Then finally, about a thousand meters from the beach, just before they were about to start the attack run, Charlie's boat, ferrying over two hundred pounds of explosive, broke down. It just wouldn't run. They could see the compound burning on the peninsula. They tried to manually feed the boat gas with a pump. The driver cracked: it had been too much, and everyone was exhausted. Ginger watched as the SWCC trolleyed the motor out of the water and started whaling on it. *He is revving the absolute dog piss out of this motor*, Ginger thought.

Okay, thought Dan, *I have to call it. If I keep pushing past this, it's irresponsible at this point.* He tanked the op.

Riever stood next to him, looking at the beach. "That was my chance," he said, half joking. "That was my one chance to do a combat swimmer op. I was going to talk shit to every SEAL I ever meet." He was just as relieved as he was sorry; clearing mines with a dragline is not healthy.

Everyone tried to get the driver to stop. Prym looked terrified. "Mate, enough. Please, stop. We need to go." He put the motor back in the water, and they started to tow back. They were moving five kilometers an hour. They got to twenty-seven kilometers away and halted in the middle of the Black Sea. The boats just stopped. It was nearly morning.

Symon was on his phone. "Symon, what the fuck is going on?" everyone asked the commander.

"We wait," said the Ukrainian.

"For what?"

"We wait here for ride."

"Who's coming?"

"I don't know. Someone."

What the fuck, dude? Just give us some information, man. He's fucking with us, thought Ginger. *He likes fucking with us.*

Hours later, they saw a gunboat in the distance.

Holy shit, that's a big-ass ship, Ginger thought. *Is that coming towards us?*

It was, armed to the teeth.

Prym stood up. He put one foot on the front sponson of the boat and sighted down the optic on his rifle at the gunship. *Like it's George Washington crossing the damn Delaware*, thought Ginger. *Picture freaking perfect.* Everyone started laughing. Prym was still aiming at the ship.

"*Blyat*! Prepare for the combat, *suka*!" exclaimed Prym.
Everyone cracked up.

"What are you talking about?" asked Ginger.

"Ginger!" insisted Prym. "Ginger! Prepare the NLAW!"

"Prepare the NLAW for what?"

"To shoot the boat!"

"Prym!" shouted Ginger. "What are you talking about?"

"Mate, I am serious! We must fight!"

Everyone else was still laughing, sleep-deprived and exhausted as they were. There was no realistic way to fight a gunship with an NLAW; they were already well within the ship's range. Prym was having none of it. *He's seriously gonna fight a battleship with a CZ Bren and a fuckin' RPG*, thought Ginger. Riever watched the pirate Symon out of the corner of his eye and caught a glimmer of a grin forming on the other man's lips before it disappeared. *Okay*.

"Dude, that thing's like three thousand meters away and it could kill us right now, you're not even gonna stand a chance. We're tied to each other on Zodiacs. None of our boats even work. What do you want to do here?" Ginger laughed.

"Greg!" said Prym, "Get your PKM! Get ready to shoot at them!" *A medic with a PKM*, thought Greg, who called the gun a Pokémon for fun; *that makes literally no sense*.

They finally saw the Ukrainian flag after it was far too close for comfort. *Oh man*.

"Ah!" said Symon. "Our ride's here!"

Yeah, thanks for that, thought Ginger. *Really appreciate that*. It turned out that Symon had called the Ukrainian Navy. He had sent them a Google Maps pin, via Signal. And then they waited.

They climbed up onto the battleship, which towed Alpha's broken boat; Charlie Team beat them back to shore in their boat, which, freed of the dead weight, had restarted. The Ukrainian crew were laughing at them. "You guys have a rough day?" they joked. "Yes, we've had a rough day, man," Ginger responded.

The crew brought them coffee and fresh packs of cigarettes while they dried out on deck. Ginger had a crashing, pounding headache. He looked up to see the sun rising over the gun of the ship. He took a photo and set it as his phone's background.

Oleksii laughed at them as they got off the gunship. Everyone loaded their gear into the trucks for the drive back to Mykolaiv. They were all exhausted. They had been on the water for over eleven hours, cold, wet, and miserable. Greg stripped to his compression shorts, pulled his headlamp down around his neck, and climbed into his truck with the Green Beret Dmitri, who ditched his shirt. Neither bothered to buckle their seatbelts as they rolled out.

Ginger looked around. "Hey, where's Greg and Dmitri at?" But the other men had already left.

Greg started off down the road, driving through green fields of young sunflowers. Suddenly, they were rolling—off the road, making at least two revolutions, possibly three. He smacked his head on the ceiling as it caved in. Greg passed out briefly. When he came to, the truck was upside down in the field. He and Dmitri crawled out through the destroyed windows, covered in cuts and scrapes and blood.

Then, as he put it, "the most Ukrainian thing happened." Almost as soon as they had crawled out of the truck, picking glass out of their wounds, an old man in an old Soviet Zhiguli pulled up.

"Hey! What's up, guys? You need help?" asked the man.

"Uh," said Greg, looking around. "No, I don't think you're going to help us!"

"Would you like some fresh milk and eggs?"

"Yes, please!"

A few minutes after Greg left, just as Ginger was about to pull out, Oleksii came running up to the Jav gunner's truck. "Hey, I need you to go to this point," he said, indicating on his phone.

"Why?" said Ginger, still exhausted.

"Greg flipped his truck."

"What?"

"Yeah, Greg crashed his truck off the road. It flipped."

"Just now?"

"Yeah."

"Oh my God! It's just nonstop in this country! When one thing happens, it's just a freakin' shit show," Ginger exploded.

They drove up the road. Off on the side, upside down in a beautiful green field of baby sunflowers, was Greg's truck, hand-painted with a very cool green camo pattern. Rockets, weapons, and landmines were everywhere—on the road, in the field, all over.

Greg and Dmitri were standing on the side of the road, drinking their warm milk, straight from the cow. They were covered in cuts and blood; Greg had a gash on his left temple, and Dmitri a good one on his right arm. Greg was still in nothing but his compression shorts, barefoot, though Dmitri had kept his cargo pants and boots on.

Ginger walked over and pinched Dmitri's nipple. "Now you're havin' a real bad day, aren't ya, buddy?" he asked.

Greg and Dmitri stood for photos, Greg grinning like a lunatic, Dmitri still looking dazed, the former with a water bottle filled with warm milk, the latter holding a carton of a dozen eggs. Everyone flipped the truck back over, its top caved in and all the windows busted. Greg slid in, ducked his tall frame down, started the ignition, then leaned out of the driver's-side window to drive—the crushed windshield was useless. Riever told him that the truck was fucked, but Greg insisted that he knew someone who could fix it. He drove it off down the road, hanging out of the side. *Awesome*, thought Ginger. Oleksii took a video as Greg rolled away.

Charlie went out on one more mission: a land-based sniper recon, further east, close to Kherson. They were fairly close to a Russian base, which meant that artillery and grenades and gunfire tore into all the surrounding woodlines. Charlie had no choice but to stay in one of the woodlines, though they avoided overlapping with the Russian fires.

6

JOURNEY TO THE END OF THE WORLD

The Westerners had pushed their Ukrainian officers to do something better with them almost the entire time they were in Mykolaiv. "We're being wasted!" Ginger would argue. "We're wasting money, we're wasting equipment, we're wasting bodies—people are leaving because they don't want to do this shit. Send us on a different mission. Why are we doing this? Why are we crossing the Black Sea in Craigslist boats?"

In the meantime, all eyes had been on Severodonetsk. "Let's go to Severo!" the men would say. "Absolutely not," the Ukrainian officers would respond. "We're not going to Severo." The city was close to being surrounded. Anyone passing into the deep pocket around Severodonetsk and its Ukrainian-held neighbor across the Siverskyi Donets River, Lysychansk, would be within Russian artillery range from three different directions. The Russians were about to close the pocket. Anyone caught within it would be surrounded.

Symon was former SBU-Alpha. He was experienced, elite, and burned out. He had done that sort of fighting for years. He did not want to go to Severodonetsk. One of his close friends had just died in the city. "You guys want to fuckin' fight in the trenches? I'll put you in the fuckin' trenches," Symon would say. "But *I* don't want to fight in the trenches. I did that shit for eight years and I don't want to do it anymore."

"Okay, yeah, I get that," Ginger would say.

For three days after the last disastrous maritime mission, they had been looking for ground targets to hit. If Symon did not want to go east, the Westerners did not want to go out again on fruitless maritime missions. They found work towards Kherson, hitting ground targets with Javelins and running sniper missions. They were in the midst of building a target package when word came in for a meeting at 1900 hours.

Out on their op, Charlie Team were called back to base, halfway through their planned six-day mission. *Weird*, thought George. *All the way to base? Whatever.* They packed up everything in the pouring rain and ran back to where they'd stashed the vehicle.

They were an hour's drive away. On the road, they debated why they'd been recalled.

"We're going to Donbas," predicted Prym. "To Severodonetsk."

Everyone crammed into the briefing room that night. Ginger looked around. *Super weird*, he thought, watching the officers. Symon and Oleksii seemed cagey, very uncomfortable, and definitely not very happy.

"Okay, listen, guys," said Oleksii. "Tomorrow, at 0900, we leave."

"Awesome!" said Ginger. "Where are we going?"

"Severodonetsk."

The whole room became quiet. Ginger and Tex looked at each other slowly across the room. Then they exploded: "*Yes!*" The men were laughing. Dan messaged Dmitri: "It feels like Christmas morning!"

Symon and Oleksii looked angry. *They're mad that we're happy*, Ginger realized. *They know that we want to go there and we're going to want to actually scrap.*

"Tonight, you pack everything," said Oleksii. "Clean everything. Tomorrow, we load trucks to fight."

"What do you mean?" everyone asked.

"We're gonna load a bunch of shit on the back of a truck. All your personal belongings. Anything expensive that you don't want stolen or destroyed or left behind. All ammo, fuel, and big rockets go on the main truck. Then prepare yourselves and your vehicles to fight."

"Wait, what do you mean, prepare the *vehicles* to fight?" They had no infantry fighting vehicles or other armor, only light-skinned trucks and a van.

"We're going to Severodonetsk. We very well may have to fight to get to our position from the trucks."

Ginger watched Oleksii closely. His face was very, very nervous. It was exciting. But it was a grim bit of news. The whole International Legion had been called to Severodonetsk. It felt like a last stand.

Only combat equipment, they were told as they packed. *I don't know how many times I've heard that, then we get there and I really wish I'd brought my hot water kettle* ... Dan thought. He indulged in few comforts but was attached to his electric kettle. He packed it with his Zapo mug, the one with the little girl with Mickey Mouse ears on it. He carefully wrapped the mug in a t-shirt and put it in the safest part of his pack.

Michael packed up all the intelligence gear, including the computers that had access to his intel feeds and mapping software. They would go back to safety in Kyiv. He was keenly aware that he was about to drive into a pocket, and that he was getting close to his visa expiration date. *Of all of the reasons that you should be worried about getting entrapped by the Russians*, he told himself, *missing your visa expiration is probably not the worst*. It still weighed on him.

Greg, organizing stacks of gear, was pissed. Medics are responsible for a lot of material. *They could have told us literally in the morning to pack and we're leaving the next day*, he thought, *but no. The commanders packed all their shit!* It took him until 3:30 a.m. to finish. He called his family and warned them that they might not hear from him for a few weeks. He called his best friend, who could tell exactly what was happening even though Greg didn't refer to it. The medic didn't usually make phone calls like that.

Each truck was loaded with rockets, at least two per person, plus a box of hand grenades. There were five extra loaded mags per person, about twenty full loaded mags per man, plus five thousand rounds of loose ammunition. Every truck had a machine gun. There were landmines. The Mazda had a Carl Gustaf rocket with sixteen rounds. The flatbed was almost overflowing. Riever took a photo of Ginger as the infantryman tossed one more pack in the back, tucked against the spare tire.

Dan, Riever, Ginger, and Dmitri got to drive the truck that was always referred to as the Black Mazda. "It's the smallest, the most uncomfortable," Dan declared of their little vehicle, "but it's been the most reliable."

The four gathered in front of the tailgate for a photo: Dmitri on the far left in dark sunglasses, Ginger flashing obscure Cleveland gang signs, Riever resting back against the tailgate on his elbows,

Dan standing confidently with his arms at his sides. No one wore a shirt.

"Well," Dan quipped, "at least they'll only need one picture for the memorial!"

Riever texted a copy to his girlfriend on Signal. "We are off on our road trip to the end of the world," he wrote. As always, he didn't tell her where they were going. He also didn't mention what Dan had said.

Riever headed to the squat toilets just before they left. He heard Oleksii calling his name. The commander was holding an infrared (IR) laser, new in the box. He handed it over and explained in his broken English that it was a loaner. "You give it back when war is done," he said. *Dude, that might be a while*, Riever thought, gratefully accepting the laser. The officer headed back to the trucks.

Outside, Tex approached Oleksii with a wad of cash. A few weeks before, Tex had needed a watch. Oleksii was a Garmin rep, so he helped the American get a new Garmin smartwatch. It was tricked out with all the latest: GPS, a map, a compass. But the Legion's pay system was malfunctioning again, and Tex didn't have any cash, so Oleksii bought the watch for him. "Listen, man, when you get this money, you pay me back, okay?"

Their pay had just come in, and Tex wanted to settle up. Oleksii took the money and counted it. He looked at the money, at Tex, and back at the money. He handed the cash back to the American.

"When we get back from this," Oleksii said, "we'll talk about it."

Tex was confused, but there was no time. They were getting in the vehicles. The American kept thinking about it as they headed east. *Why would you say something like that?*

Ginger drove the Black Mazda as they set off. It was a beautiful, sunny afternoon in Mykolaiv. But the atmosphere was thick, nervous, almost eerie. You could feel the tension in everyone. *Well, this is it*, seemed to be the feeling. *This is gonna be our last one, so let's have fun. Let's make it a good one.* It was a long drive. Thoughts like these ran through everyone's mind on replay.

Here it was: the opportunity to fight in one of the biggest battles of the war, possibly one of the biggest battles since World War

II. This was what they had all trained for. *This is what we do. This is what you're supposed to want to do*, thought Dan, *but this might be it*. He had been on so many missions over the course of his career, and had always felt pretty confident. Now, he wasn't so sure. *But this is like the guy in the landing craft going into the beaches, or the dude in the plane about to jump into Normandy. They did it. I've got to be able to do this sort of thing.*

Greg thought that if any of them made it out, it could only be on foot. They knew that they were driving into what Dan called "the far back corner of a huge encirclement," and that being taken prisoner by the Russians wasn't an option. Marti had taken to carrying two bullets tucked into his helmet. Someone asked him why. "This one is for Loup, and this one is for me," came the answer.

It was a long, circuitous drive. They couldn't take the direct route. Part of it was occupied by the Russians. Other parts of the highway had been mined, some were closed, some had been hit by artillery. They patched together a route from side roads and short sections of highway, taking the long way around, with Oleksii and Symon in the front truck to lead them. The day dragged on. Some of the trucks broke down and needed small repairs, which they did on their own. They stopped in a few places, eating hot dogs and joking nervously. Nearly twelve hours in, they approached a small city.

They had seen very few young people out east at all, and very few of the famously beautiful Ukrainian women in particular since any of them had arrived in country. Now, suddenly, there they were. It was as if they had entered the twilight zone. The road turned into a long main drag, with bars and restaurants on either side. They had forgotten that it was a Friday night. The place was full of people. Ginger's eyes bulged. He thought there must have been three gorgeous women for every regular human on the street.

Bad bitches all dressed up and just smoking hookah! he thought, leaning out of the window. They wore heels, skirts, tight jeans, lipstick. They looked amazing, confident, defiant, as if the war wasn't even on. *We're four hours from one of the biggest war zones on the planet*, thought Ginger, *and you're just walking around in your stilettos, dressed up and shit …*

77

Chock to the brim, thought Dan. "We've got to come back *here* if we survive!" the SEAL declared. "Screw going to Kyiv! Let's come back to this place!" *Wow*.

The men were dressed in full combat kit, rifles in hand, their truck beds full of ammo, rockets, and landmines. Everything else around them looked like the Sunset Strip. All frantically checked their phones: where *were* they? One truck nearly rear-ended another as they rubbernecked. Was this happening? Had they died in the warehouse after all? *Unreal*, thought Ginger. *It's like a glitch in the matrix*. They didn't stop. *Leaving the city of broken dreams*, he sighed. It turned out to be Kryvyi Rhi, the hometown of President Zelensky.

They drove into a military fuel point, full of tanker vehicles and everything else. Then they kept going. It was five or six in the morning when they stopped for a break in Bakhmut, just outside the pocket. The city was almost empty. They stopped outside a big, municipal-looking building. "Gear up," came the order. They put their combat gear on, buckled their helmets, and prepared to fight their way in.

As the sun came up, Greg was driving one of the trucks, an assignment that got him some ribbing given his accident. "But did anybody *die*?" he demanded indignantly, insisting that everyone else was "being babies" about the rollover.

After one last top-up of the gas tanks, they began the final leg of the journey. There was barely a road; they were bumping over what felt like open fields. Maybe it was just a track. It had been bombed out so many times that it had laid the foundation for what might have been a road, but Ginger couldn't tell. He had switched into a little Volkswagen utility van, pulling a trailer and driving for Mykola, who needed a break. He could hear the artillery in the distance as his truck bottomed out its suspension and he struggled to keep the little trailer from jackknifing. They were crawling; they could have walked faster than this.

Coming in the other direction were broken-down tanks and convoys of medical vehicles. Everyone kept pulling over to let them pass.

In his truck Greg shifted to the side to let a massive vehicle go past while he and George debated what it was. Michael, a former armored fighting vehicle identification instructor, had spent hours drilling them. "It's an armor recovery vehicle," the tanker confirmed from the back.

"Is it pulling a tank, I'm assuming?" Greg asked, looking over.

"It's pulling something," George answered. "Goddamn, that's a fat ass."

Greg waved to the other driver as the massive hulk went by with a T-80 tank.

As they approached Lysychansk and Severodonetsk, an enormous refinery came into view, with half-a-dozen tall, thin smokestacks interrupting the open skyline. It was serving as brigade headquarters, and the Russians were bombing the living daylights out of it.

"That was a pretty big fucking explosion," George said, turning his camera on.

"I think we're just hearing delayed explosions," said Greg. "Yeah, the whole infilling in light-skinned vehicles in the daytime ..." he continued, as George laughed. "Just something about it ..."

"You don't understand the plan, man!" George ribbed. "It's all according to the plan! Well, fucking ..." He reached up and pulled and released the charging handle on his rifle.

"Well, it is what it is, guys," Greg said.

"I don't think that's gonna help, man," said Michael from the back.

"It makes me *feel* better," George chuckled.

"On the left there is a ravine down there," Greg said, "so if something happens, we'll run to there."

"We're not even in fuckin' Luhansk yet and they're shelling the shit out of this. Jesus H. Christ," muttered George.

"You do realize we have to be, like, standing around the vehicle unloading it ..." Greg continued.

"*Shh*, one thing at a time," laughed George. "First we'll concentrate on actually getting there."

In front of them was an enormous industrial plant, attracting constant Russian fire.

"That was a *massive* fucking explosion," said George, eyeing debris flying what looked like two hundred meters into the air. "You see how much dirt that kicked up?" *Was that a missile? Would they really shoot a missile at a patch of dirt?*

"If that was artillery, it had to be something *huge*," responded Greg.

"Might've been one of the 220 rockets," Michael added from the back.

Another hit. "That one landed over there," George said, pointing left.

"Right where we're going, guys!" Greg said.

"We're driving through that shit? Fuck," George replied as they rumbled over the dirt track.

"I'm loving this plan," said Greg quietly.

"At a fuckin' breakneck pace, too. Goddamn. Whose idea was this again?" George quipped as they passed a random civilian in a Lada.

"I like that he's just nonchalantly driving around a battlefield," said Greg.

A nasty shell burst nearby. "*Yeee*," said George.

"I do not like this," said Greg quietly. "I've been under artillery before, and that sound … I don't like. Moschun," he said of the town where he'd looked out for Russians from a little girl's bedroom and then watched her house get demolished as he egressed, "brings me back to Moschun."

They entered a residential neighborhood, heads on swivel.

"Look at this guy. He's no helmet, no fuckin' frag vest," George said, noticing a soldier close to the road.

"Staying in this house …" Greg replied, looking around.

"It's normal," cracked Michael.

"Well, this house doesn't look too normal," said Greg, eyeing a bombed-out building, "unless they're redecorating."

"It looks perfectly normal for a house in Ukraine these days!" laughed George.

"They have redecorated! Maybe they're throwing an apocalypse theme party," Greg said. Everyone laughed. "Maybe that's what it is, guys!"

A bit further down the road they saw a group of soldiers sitting and eating. "Okay, so these guys are just chilling here eating soup," said Greg. "I think we're okay."

"See, this is a lesson I learned in Iraq," said Michael.

"Observe the locals? Except maybe don't do what they do …" replied George.

"Yes, except maybe they're slightly *less* crazy than the Ukrainians," laughed Michael.

"We are the ones who came up with the 'this is normal' phrase, so you know ..." responded Greg.

At one point Greg looked up to see the truck in front of him being sandwiched by flying saucers. *Good thing George is up here keeping me awake*, he thought. He was hallucinating from the lack of sleep after his late-night packing job. *Bizarre. I'm so tired.*

Their little convoy approached the spur of a railroad. A few train cars sat on the rails. The convoy halted. "Dude, what's going on?" asked Ginger. There was artillery landing all around them, in the treelines, the road, the railyard. "Mykola, this is it, we're not even going to make it to Lysychansk."

"No," the Ukrainian laughed. "I don't think so."

They watched two enormous missiles hit brigade headquarters at the refinery, a few kilometers behind them now. The sound was as if it was right next to them. The ground shook. *Insane*, thought Ginger. *This is gonna be the real fuckin' deal.*

"Do you think Oleksii's scared right now?" asked Mykola.

"Hell yeah, I think Oleksii's scared right now," said Ginger. "I feel like I'm gonna shit the bed and I'm still in the truck." *Just trying to keep our minds busy with this petty conversation*, he thought as they started moving again, *as we drive through an active artillery zone.*

In the Black Mazda, Dan, who had shifted into the tiny backseat, missed everything. He'd gone to sleep.

They finally reached battalion headquarters in Lysychansk. It was a large hulk of a building, a one-time school or office building. Now it was full of people coming and going, to the extent that George thought it felt like a train station. Armed guards stood at the doors. Legionnaires came in and out, leaving on missions and debriefing on their return. Every thirty seconds or so, an artillery shell landed nearby, shaking the building.

They ran into a Brit whom George recognized. The Canadian knew him from Dnipro, and they sat down to talk. Next to George, Ginger and Dan eavesdropped.

The Brit was full of news, none of it good. An International Legion team had gotten smashed in the city two days earlier by something like a TOW missile or maybe a mortar. It had been led by a man named Yuri, who had been one of the original Ukrainian commanders in the Legion when the war first broke out. Some of the men knew him from Irpin and Zaporizhzhia. On his team were several other men George knew from his days in Dnipro. Yuri was dead. Others had lost fingers and limbs. The day after, another team had gone on a body recovery and had also gotten chewed up. Two guys died from friendly fire after a three-hour gunfight. The guys on the Brit's team who hadn't died had left. The refrain they heard from the Ukrainians was consistent: if you don't want to be here, you don't have to be here. But if you don't want to be here, you have to go home.

"If you go in there," the Brit warned, "you're going to get killed."

And here we are, with the only English speaker in the headquarters building telling horror stories, thought Dan, frustrated.

"It's like *Saving Private Ryan* on steroids," the Brit continued.

Shit, thought George. *I guess it's been a good run.* "Ginger," George said, surprised to hear himself say it, "we're all going to die here." It felt like an inescapable last stand, as if he was watching a movie, but it was happening to him. *Well, I'm going to do my job*, one half of him thought. *It's the only fucking thing on this earth I know how to do, so I'm going to do it.* The other half thought, *Oh God, this is terrible! Why are we doing this?* It was like being on autopilot with a sort of backseat driver baked in.

Dan was just frustrated. They did not need this. *Again, if I'm ever in charge*, he thought, *I'm going to make sure that anyone who doesn't want to be there gets their own bus and goes straight back. And they don't meet anybody who's coming the other direction.*

The commanders went to search for a safehouse in the city. The headquarters officers gave the rest of the team mats. They ate some MREs and passed out on the floor.

They had parked their trucks with all their gear under the trees and took turns guarding them. A Kozak personnel carrier pulled in as Riever was on watch. A young Ukrainian kid with a mohawk was serving as the driver. He gestured to Riever and said hello, then showed the American a makeshift holder for his AK-47 that he had fashioned from wire and attached to his belt. It stuck out perpendicular from his body, allowing him to fast-draw the gun and, crucially, to carry it that way while driving. *Cool*, thought Riever, *I've never seen anything like that!*

The Ranger was relieved and went inside for his turn to sleep. When he woke up, the place was crawling with every unit and weapon that you could imagine. Across the hall he noticed a small, fine-boned, almost elfin young man, with blond hair and perfectly bright blue eyes. He was wearing Salomons and Cryes, with a war belt. *He's Western*, Riever thought, *he looks just like a Ranger private.* The other man looked back at him, two Westerners making eye contact in a foreign war zone. Neither man said anything.

7

THE SAFEHOUSE IS NOT SAFE

The safehouse they had been assigned to by the staff officers was the basement of a private home in Lysychansk, next to an underground garage that could fit two cars. The concrete floor was covered in an oriental-style rug in a brown and taupe theme, with a small table on top. A light hung in the middle of the ceiling. Their stuff was stacked everywhere, with a miniature arsenal against the wall in the garage. A Ukrainian flag hung on the wall in the basement. The house, like the others on the street, had a nice small yard with a walled garden. They loaded all their gear in.

They were close to the only bridge that was still standing between Lysychansk and Severodonetsk. In peacetime it was a green, leafy, charming neighborhood. Soon they had new neighbors: a Ukrainian mortar team who moved around and shot at the Russians all day and all night. They were so close that the outgoing fire hurt the team's ears in their basement.

Just perfect, thought Ginger.

For George it was a recurring theme. Somehow the mortars always managed to find him. *Okay, thanks, guys.*

The mortarmen could "shoot and scoot." The Russian counter-battery, arriving a few minutes later, always missed them. But the shells usually landed very close to the safehouse. *Our safehouse is very not safe, that's for sure*, Ginger decided. Not long after their arrival they learned that battalion headquarters had gotten hammered just after they left it. The building was almost entirely gone.

The house had been used by a unit before them—a police unit, by the looks of it. No one knew who they were exactly, but they'd left a lot of stuff lying around. In one room there was a set of someone's personal gear: fatigues, a jacket, and some odds and ends. It looked like a dead man's personal effects. Marti picked up a perfectly good GoPro and programmed it to turn on and off with voice activation in English. Greg found a patch from the "Bob Marley Volunteer Defense Squad" with a weed leaf, a skull, and crossed joints, and promptly stuck it on the front of his plate carrier. Riever found a few mint 1972 burlap AK-47 ammo pouches. They smelled, like all Soviet gear, of the preservative Cosmoline. But each pouch had two cells, which had been designed to hold four AK magazines apiece. Riever wired them together with a clothes hanger, added some straps from his own kit, and turned them into a custom backpack and rocket carrier.

Someone found a Kevlar armor panel and laboriously cut it into sections to fit in the sides of his kit, offering some frag protection. Several of them grabbed big black velcro panels with "Police" written in Ukrainian in reflective letters, and Riever found an ex-British Army knit sweater with big shoulder patches and epaulettes which he wore constantly from then on. It replaced an old sweater he had from his father's U.S. Army days, for which Symon gave him grief because of its deteriorating condition. "Ah!" said the pirate when he saw the new version. "You've upgraded!" Everyone tried not to think about why the police unit had left so much good stuff behind.

They discovered crates of French MREs as well. "You can talk a lot about French fighting spirit, but they make really good MREs," Greg said. They came in tin cans, with alcohol fuel pods. One of them had two Bavarian sausages. They were the tall medic's favorite.

In Ukraine they'd had an accidental tour of NATO MRE offerings. Dan decided that the French ones tasted the best, that the American ones were the most tactical, but that the Canadians had cornered the market on the ideal intersection of taste and practicality. Everyone except Riever agreed that the German version was best left to humanitarian rations. Guys would start to go through the rations, picking each component, and spend an hour designing and cooking a "perfect" meal.

"Michael, we need to do intel stuff!" the former tanker heard almost as soon as they'd finished getting their stuff in the door.

On my phone? thought Michael. *You told me to send all that stuff back!* They didn't even have a laptop with them. Michael spent the next several days hand-loading intel data onto mission phones and an Android tablet, using the Ukrainian equivalent of the American ATAK. *Now I'm really the IT guy,* he thought.

Dan pulled out his Mickey Mouse girl mug and his kettle. *Combat gear only.* Symon had packed his hookah. Marti had packed his TRX exercise bands, on which he rapidly set to work in the garage.

They started their guard roster and settled in for the night. Loup had first guard duty. He was sitting in the doorway, looking out. Riever, half asleep, walked past him to pee in the bushes. There were no utilities in the bombed-out city—no electricity, no water, nothing.

The artillery boomed, then everything lit up. Streamers of fire floated down a few blocks away with an insidious hissing instead of an explosion. Riever turned to Loup with his eyebrows raised. "*Phosphor*," said the Georgian. Inside, Ginger heard him but couldn't understand what he'd said. "White phosphorus, mate!" said Prym. *No*, thought Ginger. *Wow. This is a good day one.*

The whole block behind them was on fire, much like Greg had seen when he was in the little girl's red-brick house in Moschun. It was so bright you didn't even need NODs in the backyard. Smoke was everywhere.

They were surrounded by the Russians on three sides, which meant that they were within range of three different artillery lines. The fire was constant. There was nowhere that was safe from the gunners, and it was hard to get used to it.

The shower at the safehouse consisted of a water bottle or bucket and your choice of bush to tuck behind in the yard. George was bathing one day when two or three shells went screaming over his head and exploded nearby. Metal started falling from the sky in shreds. *Man,* George thought, *I should really finish my shower and go back inside before I get more of a* metal *shower.*

Ginger would sit inside listening to the artillery shells whistle overhead and think, *Oh, that's incoming.* Then he'd listen to the angle of the next whistle and think, *Oh, that's outgoing*, before he realized, *Oh, no, we're just being shot at again from a different direction*, when the boom landed just outside. *This is crazy.*

One day Ginger and Riever were listening to the rounds as they drank canteen cups of MRE coffee and took long, luxurious pulls from their cigarettes. The whistle and booming were constant. Then they heard a whistle and a metallic ringing *crunch*. They both laughed. A dud round had just wiped out someone's car or metal shed. Two more times came the thuds and smacks of duds. They cracked up. In a humor-starved world the sound of the shells smacking down like meteors was just too funny. "Bad batch of rounds," said Ginger, giggling. "You fuckers had one job."

There's nothing you can do about artillery. They became desensitized, to an extent. There was one particular spot, about a thousand meters down the street, that seemed to be a constant target. *I don't know what that is*, George thought, *but they really don't like it and they don't want it to be there.*

"Dude," Ginger said to Riever one day as they sat listening to the shells trying to kill them, "artillery is weird in the way that every time you hear it, it puts you on edge. You can power through it, but every round that hits kind of shaves away a little bit of the sanity and humanity that keeps you calm and conditioned under pressure. And the closer those rounds get, the bigger the chunk of sanity and humanity that it cuts away."

Artillery makes you revert to a carnal instinct, a flight or fight response. There is no way to turn off the reaction to the whistle of a shell. Your eyes are wired, all of your senses are heightened, and you start to count. If you get past three, you're going to live: it's going past you. But once they get in close, the mind starts to do something different. Fear of death, of uncertainty, and above all of not being able to do anything starts that shaving away of the soul. "People who are afraid of bullets, I've never understood it," Ginger said. "You can shoot back at these guys! But artillery ... what are you going to do, take a badminton racket and smack the rounds back at the Russians?" The powerlessness chips away at you. *Man, there's nothing I can do*, Ginger would think. *I'm just gonna light this cigarette and stare at this window.* Men either break or revert to basic survival instincts, find a hole, and power through.

Artillery takes a toll on the brain as well. The pressure waves, especially if you're sheltering underground, can be intense. You can feel it in your head, your chest, your bones. "It creates so much pressure that it feels like you're being sat on," Ginger complained. "It feels like someone's knocking you on the head with a rubber mallet."

Almost everyone on the team had had multiple concussions from the pressure already. Ginger once got caught in an artillery barrage in Zaporizhzhia. They had sheltered in a small cellar, something straight out of *The Wizard of Oz*, for several hours while they received effective fire. When he came out, the light hurt his eyes, he had a headache, and couldn't eat anything: classic signs of a mild concussion. Some of the earliest members of the team had gone home because of more serious concussions.

Tex, George, and Greg pulled the first trash duty. They loaded the bags into the back of the truck and set out to find a gas station dumpster. They threw some kit over what they were already wearing; it was too hot outside for more. It was just a fifteen-minute ride, but it was still an active war zone. The artillery was everywhere, as usual. When they arrived at the gas station, it was completely bombed out. They tossed their bags, drove back, and found Marti blasting bad Euro techno in the garage.

Tex and Greg started dancing as Marti picked up his phone, and George sidled out of the way. Greg was still in his partial kit of helmet, plate carrier, and rifle over shorts, t-shirt, crew socks, and Crocs. Tex was killing it: fancy feet, Elvis hips, a natural. A few feet away, Greg, bouncing on the balls of his feet in his Crocs, was fully committed to his own version of the Robot.

Their presence attracted the attention of other members of the neighborhood. Soon several moved in. There was a truly tiny, adorable, giant-eyed kitten, whom they named Matador, after the rocket. There were two full-grown cats. One Greg christened an "evil motherfucker," but he adored him anyway because he reminded the medic of his cat at home. There was also a cute mutt of a dog, who looked like a corgi crossed with something with a Labrador-like tail. The four-legged population kept increasing the longer they stayed. One day Tex found a hedgehog in the yard outside and brought it in too, while Loup fashioned a grenade necklace for one of the cats and let him run around the neighborhood with it. *A red-blooded Ukrainian cat*, Ginger thought, *he's ready to go.*

The animals in Ukraine broke Michael's heart. You saw them everywhere, and they always looked at you so expectantly. *Are you my new person? Will you take care of me?* the eyes always seemed to say. They were first-world pets, now living feral in apocalyptic conditions.

Soon another team moved into the house next to them. Led by a Ukrainian Canadian who had been an officer in the Canadian military and happened to live a few hours from Greg's parents in Canada, they called themselves Black Team. There was the officer, Artem, a very serious-looking young man with dark hair and eyes. There were two Americans, the aptly named Big Max and the former Marine officer Samuel. There was one Portuguese man, Pedro. And there were two Brits: the young, blond, blue-eyed, elfin Jordan, who had just finished his enlistment with The Rifles in March, whom Riever recognized as the Westerner he had seen in headquarters. There was also Doug, a slightly older former Royal Marine with dark hair and bright blue-green eyes.

They traveled light. Greg counted five men, a few MREs, and two rockets. But they wanted to assault Severodonetsk with Alpha and Charlie, so here they were. They had been planning to join a Ukrainian unit. "But they said we had a few weeks," Doug explained in an impossibly rich baritone that sounded like an opera singer marinating in Scotch, "so we just came down here for the scrap!" From anyone else it would be bravado, but from the Royal Marine it was just fact. *One of the bravest fuckin' guys out there*, Riever would decide later.

Greg declared them all "good dudes," and soon everyone had settled into what Ginger called "a fuckin' frat boy block. It was retarded." Everyone piled into Alpha's basement to bum the WiFi off the Starlink and to smoke Symon's combat-essential hookah.

8

A LITTLE NIGHT RECCE

On their second night in town, Alpha Team was tasked with what Ginger called a "crawl, walk, run" operation. They would have to cross the bridge into Severodonetsk, get the lay of the land, connect with units on the front line, and probe across into the Russian lines. Then they would propose missions based on where they thought they could be most useful. Alpha rolled light: just Dan, Dmitri, Riever, and Ginger. A few members of Charlie and Black Teams went along to observe.

Jordan drove them in an uncooperative armored car over the bridge. *It's crazy this thing even holds vehicles*, Ginger thought. There were fifteen or twenty burned-out cars all over the bridge. There were holes in the structure. The guardrails had been knocked off. The houses around and below it were on fire. *This is like driving the highway straight to Hell. Like no man's land into Hell.*

They were dropped off short of the front lines. A guide helped them make their way forward and connect with their assigned unit: another International Legion team called the Mexicans. They crawled through gaps in fences and snaked through a heavy industrial area. The whole city was covered in broken glass and rubble. Dan entered the building to find a host of Brazilians and some Portuguese. Ginger noticed some Colombians and maybe a handful of Spanish speakers. *There's not a single Mexican on this team!* he thought. Still, the team went by the name of, and was known by others as, the Mexicans. *Okay, what the fuck.*

With them was one good ol' boy, a Texan with an ancient Dragunov sniper rifle. "I'm the only motherfucker who speaks

91

English in this building!" he declared. He was very grumpy but happy to see Dan. The SEAL thought that he looked like the kind of guy who would *not* want to be holed up with a bunch of Mexicans.

The Mexicans were holding a small house on the front line. To their left was a Ukrainian special operations unit, and to their right was a Ukrainian Special Operations Forces (SSO) team. This formed one sector. There were dozens more across the front line.

Within two minutes of their arrival, gunfire exploded from their side: a fully automatic, unsuppressed burst from downstairs.

Ginger threw his helmet back on. He and Riever took up position at the door.

That's got to be Prym, thought Dan.

"Dude, I'll bet that was fuckin' Prym," Ginger said.

"Yeah, I'll bet you it was," said Dan. Riever just shook his head.

The Mexican commander was pissed, swearing and shouting. "Now they're going to return arty fire!" he snapped.

Prym came up the stairs, shouting back at the Mexicans' commander. "*Suka, blyat!* That was me, that was me, everything is fine."

"Why are you fucking shooting?" demanded the commander.

"I seen a Russian!"

"Where?"

Prym took out his map. He pointed at a ten-story building two blocks, perhaps three hundred meters, away. "He was on top of the building!"

"It's probably just a cat, Prym. You're shooting at cats!" Dan snapped. "Why would there be a Russian over there?"

"Mate, I saw him, I saw him!" Prym protested.

The Mexicans' commander was still pissed. "Stop acting stupid! We've been here for five days and we haven't had any issues."

Dan stayed to talk to the Mexicans. Ginger and everyone else ("the peons," said the infantryman glibly) went downstairs to pull security.

The SEAL turned to the Texan. "Have you guys gotten into any firefights or anything?"

"No, man," the other American replied. "There's shooting down the street, and we get mortared every night. But we haven't gotten in any firefights."

"Have you seen any Russians?"

"No. We've been here a whole week and it's been nothing but fuckin' mortars every night landing on us."

Okay, Dan thought. *This must be a fairly quiet section of line.*

Alpha examined the front line. The line wasn't straight. In between them and the next sector the line doglegged around a single building. Its status was unknown. It was perfect for Alpha on a night op: they could clear it and let the Ukrainians bump up to hold it and make the line flush.

Dan took Dmitri and Artem to translate and went to the Ukrainian special operations (SOF) unit next door. He needed to deconflict and coordinate with them, and to reach the friendly units in the next sector. They didn't want any blue-on-blue and have men killed by their own side when they went to clear this building.

In the Mexicans' base, Charlie Team saw a civilian-looking car roll down the street, right in the middle of the combat zone. "We wanna fuckin' kill these guys!" the men on Charlie insisted. But they were in civilian clothes. Driving literally down the front line, they were most likely spotters for the Russians, Donetsk People's Republic (DNR) members willing to abuse the rules of engagement. They had to let them go.

"You can't do that," the Ukrainian officer told Dan when the SEAL offered his plan. "We don't have comms with the guys over there. If you go out there, they'll shoot you. A new team just showed up there today, and they don't know any of us."

What? Dan thought. "You're telling me we can't fuckin' operate because you can't communicate, and some dumb-ass will shoot me if I go walking over there from the side of friendlies?" *We're finally here, we're finally in the city, we've got NODs, we're ready to do night ops, and we can't do it because these guys won't talk to each other and they're not deconflicting?*

The Ukrainian SOF officer promised to call up the chain of command. But clearance would take a few days.

Okay, fuck it, thought Dan. *We can't go left or right of our sector. All we can do is go straight ahead.* Based on the fact that they hadn't taken any fire, hadn't gotten into any firefights, and hadn't seen any Russians, it was a good bet that at least the next block was clear. *We'll go over and confirm that tonight.*

He briefed the rest of Alpha on the new plan. They would bump straight across and clear the big, tall building in the next block. It had a commanding view and would let them get eyes on the rest of the area. It would be an easy, low-risk recce.

Dan told the Mexicans' Ukrainian commander. "Okay," said the officer. "I'll tell the Ukrainian SOF and SSO," the other neighboring units. He explained the boundaries of the other sectors. "Don't go further than this, and this," the officer said, pointing on their maps. "Those are other sectors and I can't deconflict those."

They confirmed times for the crossing: one o'clock in the morning. Drop-dead time was 3:30 a.m. "I'm on it," the officer confirmed.

Dan, Dmitri, Riever, and Ginger tucked into a stairwell. They'd been taking artillery since they arrived. The Mexicans had security, so they decided to bed down until they went on the op at 1 a.m. They lay down on the landings.

The artillery started getting closer. It was going past them. Riever was at the top landing scanning out of the window with his thermal. Every time one flew over, Ginger could hear Riever duck on the landing above him.

Ginger started laughing. "Dude, you alright up there?"

"Those are getting close!" Riever responded.

"Yup," Ginger said.

"Should we go downstairs?"

"You know what, man, don't worry about it," Ginger said. "They do this thing. They drive up and down the forward line with mobile artillery, and they just smash random spots. They are just trying to keep people awake, to keep 'em scared."

"Oh, okay," Riever replied.

A few seconds went past. "And it's fuckin' working, dude!" Ginger concluded as a shell landed right outside. Everyone started laughing.

"Fuck this," Riever said in exasperation. He moved down to Ginger's landing. The artillery started getting closer and closer. Riever began laughing. A shell ripped just over them. It hit the building southwest of them, 150 meters away, shattering a window in their stairway.

No one said a word. They got up, put their gear back on, and started walking down the stairs. They found a workshop room in the basement, laughing. *Are we really going to do this? What happens if the artillery is this hot?*

Another round came right over the building. It landed directly in the back parking lot. It blew the rest of the windows out, including those in the stairwell where they'd just been. The van and trucks that had been parked there were now a twisted, burning steel pit.

"Yeah," someone said. "We're going to have to do it anyway." Everyone started laughing again. They dozed for a half-hour. Then it was time to go. They reconfirmed the plans: standard emergency procedures, actions on contact, the usual.

Dan radioed to Prym. "Did the Mexicans' commander deconflict?"

"Yes, mate," replied the Ukrainian. "You're good to go."

Dan got Artem online. They would have direct radio communications with Black Team. Alpha would laser when they came back across, and Black would confirm. They went out the back door.

They crossed the street and passed through a blown-out section of wall. They got into Dan's target building. It was empty, and they couldn't get to the top because someone had blown up all the stairwells: probably the work of smart Ukrainian sappers as they retreated to the current front line. There didn't seem to be anyone around. They kept moving, slowly and carefully. After a few hours they had cleared a whole city block, including what might have been a Soviet-era library. They found an auto shop with stacks of brand-new tires. *What the fuck*, thought Riever, *we are running trucks with mismatched tires and no spares, and here's every tire we need in no man's land.*

They found a four-story building: perfect for reconnaissance. It was locked. No one wanted to risk a demo entrance, which would give away their position. Ginger looked down the street and saw another overhang. He walked down and found a wide-open door, right into the basement.

Someone had clearly used it as a fighting position before. There were sections of drywall smashed out by hand in the walls, to allow people to crawl from room to room. Riever looked around. Ever since he'd been old enough, he'd read stories about the siege of Stalingrad. Russia has claimed credit for the brave defenders there, but Russians formed barely half of the 62nd Army that fought in the city itself. Many were Central Asian; others, including several generals, were Ukrainian.[1] Soviet fighters in Stalingrad had created ratholes in building walls just like these. It had become standard military practice in U.S. Army field manuals since then: you chop holes in all the interior walls so you can move from room to room easily. This one was a maze. You could look through a doorway but see holes that would lead to entirely different rooms. *Super sketchy shit*, thought Ginger. *Creepy.*

On the first floor they found plastic paneling and big panes of glass everywhere. A sniper, or perhaps an infantry squad, had used the building as a hide. The stairwells and floors were littered with things that would make noise: the stairs were blockaded with furniture and panes of glass were lying on the stairs, making it impossible to move quietly, and providing warnings that someone was coming. At the top, the doors were barricaded. The building was clear. They were the only ones there.

Riever and Dmitri stayed on the third floor. Riever set up on the east side of the building, looking out of a window with his thermal. He had eyes on a compound that they thought was the home of the mobile mortar team, the one that drove up and down the front line all night, smashing everyone. It was an excellent candidate for their next op. They started to build a mental target package.

Dan and Ginger climbed up to the roof to see if they could get a better view. The roof door was barricaded. Someone had tried to seal it shut with random material. One lock had a twisted-off wire tied through it.

They got it open and climbed onto the roof. The view was commanding. *The Ukrainians need to bump up to this building*, Dan thought. *This building can control a lot of territory.*

The city was on fire. Mortars and artillery went off in the distance. Under NODs, everything glowed, like the Northern Lights. *It doesn't look real*, Ginger thought. *It doesn't feel real.* He could see every star and every constellation. Rockets flew through the night. Drones whizzed across the sky. Everywhere you looked there were missiles falling from the heavens. *Surreal.*

"Ginger," said Dan, "there are only a handful of men on the planet who will ever see something like this." It was very beautiful but also very, very dark.

The SEAL had grown up on the *Terminator* movies. His favorite scenes were the "future war" sections, where robots had turned most of the planet to rubble and the human resisters fought a rear-guard battle. He used to watch those sections before going outside to play as a kid. But this looked like Armageddon, and it was real.

It was getting late. Dan could see the sky turning just a bit lighter. He and Ginger came down from the roof. They had seen a main supply route past the compound that Riever was examining, confirming their suspicions: it was a solid target. They packed up and began to move out.

They moved carefully, approaching their sector. They went through their previously cleared areas easily. There was one final street to cross. Then they would pass through a small driveway between the Ukrainian SSO position on the left and a small, red-roofed building on the right, turn right, and continue up the small alley towards the Mexicans' position.

Dan radioed to Artem. "Hey, we're coming across."

"Yep," the Black Team commander confirmed with an IR flash. "You're good to go."

Alpha started walking across. They moved casually and non-tactically: there was no reason to startle anyone, even with Artem's confirmation. They patted their own heads as they walked, the International Legion's internal, friendly-identifying deconfliction signal. Dan went first, then Riever, then Dmitri, and finally Ginger at the tail.

On the Ukrainian side of the road, Dan was almost to the right-hand side of the wall that formed a corner between the SSO position on the left and the driveway that they needed to walk up on the right. They heard a window break.

Oh, no, thought Riever. Everything happened at once. Dan dived towards the wall, the Ranger just behind him. Dmitri made it across, tucking into their left, around the corner of the wall.

But Ginger, as last man, was still in the middle of the narrow street. He looked up. He saw an SSO soldier smashing a window with the butt of his rifle. *No fuckin' way. This guy's gonna fuckin' shoot me.* He kept up his deconfliction signal. His hand wasn't even on his weapon. The guy kept smashing. *This is it. He's gonna shoot. If you run right now, you're gonna die.* With icy, unteachable calm he thought, *There's no way he actually sees us. He heard us crossing the street. He might have seen my shadow up against the wall. There's no way he's got that much of an image of me that if I jump on the ground he won't lose me right now.* He dove to the ground.

Ba-ba-ba-ba-ba-ba-ba!

The friendly dumped a full, thirty-round AK-74 mag out of the window just as Ginger hit the ground. Everything went blank.

Riever started first, almost immediately after the window broke, screaming the only words he knew in Ukrainian as he turned towards Ginger: "*Slava Ukraini! Slava Ukraini!*" Dmitri was shouting in five different languages. "Friendlies! Legion! Americans!" There was no answer from the SSO. Riever saw sparks flying all around Ginger's body on the ground, dancing off the pavement like a child's sparkler on the Fourth of July.

All Dan saw was a lump in the middle of the street. *He's dead*, the SEAL thought. *He got cut in half by whatever it is just fired at us.* Everyone was shouting. "Ginger! *Ginger!*"

Ginger had his head on the ground. He could see the sparks from the bullets flying around him.

The lump started moving, crawling towards them. *He's still alive!* thought Dan. *God, he's bleeding out. I'm going to need to run out there and grab him.*

The friendly stopped shooting: his magazine was empty. Ginger heard him go to reload. He leapt up and ran to the wall. "I'm good! I'm good!"

Dan let out the breath he hadn't realized he'd been holding, and felt a huge wave of relief break over his body.

"Are you okay? Ginger! Are you okay?" demanded Dan.

Ginger didn't respond. He had the thousand-meter stare.

"Ginger! Are you okay?" insisted Riever.

Suddenly, the infantryman clicked in: raging, livid, pissed. "I'm gonna frag him."

Everyone stopped. "What?"

"I'm gonna frag him. Let's throw some frag grenades over the wall and fuckin' kill these guys."

"Whoa, whoa, whoa, whoa, whoa!" exclaimed Dan. "No, no, no. We can't do that."

"Yes, the fuck we can!" Ginger snapped. "He just tried to kill me!"

"We can't be doing that!" the SEAL said.

"Dan," Ginger said, calmer now, "I'm going to throw a frag grenade over this fuckin' wall."

"Dude, stop," Dan said. "We can figure this out."

Ginger stopped. He drank some water, leaning against the wall. But now they were stuck. The SSO still weren't responding. If they moved, they would be exposed to the friendly line of fire. The only way to their position was right past the SSO.

Dan called Prym on the radio. "You need to get the commander on the radio and tell them to let us through."

"You're good, you're good, mate!" Prym responded. "They won't shoot you, just come!"

"They *just* fuckin' shot at us!" Dan snapped back.

"Mate, okay, I will handle," said Prym. "Give me a minute."

Ten minutes went by. Ginger was getting antsy. "Dude, just let me kill these guys and we can fucking go. We have no other option!"

Dan called Prym again. "The sun's coming up! We're pinned down by friendly units and we don't know if the Russians are going to get attracted by all this mess."

"Okay, mate," said Prym. "You can come, they will not shoot you. But go really, really fast."

"No! Fuck you, you come to us," said Dan. "I want to see you walk over to their building, talk to them, and come get us."

"Okay, mate. Where are you?" They described their location. Silence.

"Prym, where are you? We're sitting ducks out here!" radioed Dan.

"Where are you? I cannot see you."

"That's because you have to go outside!"

"No, mate! It is not safe!"

"But you told *us* it was safe!" Ginger exploded. "You told *us* it was safe!"

"Okay, mate," said Prym. "Wait one minute. I need to go deconflict."

What? thought Dan. *You told me it was okay to come, but now that I need you to come, you need to deconflict. So obviously you weren't certain that they wouldn't shoot us.*

Artem came over the radio. "Guys, don't fuckin' move anywhere. They haven't talked to the other Ukrainian commander at all. They have no idea that you're out there. Stay put. I'll try to handle it."

Great, thought Ginger. *This is fantastic.*

"Dude, we gotta do something," said Riever. Now they had been stuck for at least twenty minutes.

"I *know* ..." said Ginger.

"We're not fuckin' fragging them!" Dan and Dmitri said at the same time.

"Then follow me," said Riever. He turned behind them and ran to the small, red-roofed building that sat on the opposite side of the driveway. He'd had time to judge that the way to the door was just out of the line of sight of the SSO. He checked it. The building was clear. "We're good, we can get through here! Let's go."

They moved through and came out on the other side, clear of the SSO team. Prym was there, finally out of the Mexicans' building. "*Blyat!* Hurry up! Let's go, let's go!"

They got inside the Mexicans' building. Prym said something that Ginger couldn't hear. The American exploded. "Prym! What the fuck is wrong with you?"

"Mate! What are you talking about?" Prym replied.

"Did you or did you not deconflict with the guys on the right side?"

"Yes, mate! I told you we did!"

"Do you fucking know what deconflict means? Because it doesn't mean shoot your fuckin' teammates. It means the exact opposite."

"If you guys weren't such fucking cowboys, and if Dan wasn't trying to be such a superhero all the time, none of this would have happened in the first place! You should've just stayed here, you shouldn't have gone out there," the Ukrainian responded.

"It was our fucking job to go out there! And you stayed here like a bunch of pussies, and we got shot out because you didn't do your fucking job. And then you left us out there for like thirty fuckin' minutes." Ginger was furious.

"Ginger," said Prym. "Do not fuck me. I am serious. Do not fuck me." He kept repeating what he'd said, agitated.

"What does that even mean?" The Americans looked at each other.

"Seriously, mate. Just don't. Don't fuck me."

What does he mean? "Ah, okay?" said Ginger. And that was the end of it.

Ginger kept pacing around the Mexicans' building, asking people for cigarettes. He was out. Irpin, Zapo, even the Black Sea: *I've never, ever in my life been so close to dying.* He was shaking.

"Ginger, you just wanna hit this?" Dmitri held out a blue raspberry e-cigarette. The infantryman had called them "doucheflutes" and every other foul name in the book. *Those are for pussies, those are for losers, they're for hipsters, blah blah blah*, went his refrain.

"Yeah," Ginger said, "you know what, I guess." He took it and started chain-smoking. Sitting on the ground, he probably hit it three hundred times in a row.

When they got back to their basement, Dmitri handed him two more. This started what he called his "horrible addiction" to e-cigarettes. They began to call the tubes "combat sucks," since you could smoke them without giving your position away if you covered the small LED with your finger.

They exfiled in their Kozaks. Ginger walked into the safehouse and saw Oleksii. "You guys are gonna fuckin' kill me before the Russians do," he bitched.

"What?" said Oleksii.

"The fuckin' Ukrainians won't stop shooting at me, apparently! Apparently when I show up to places, the Ukrainians decide *I'm* the bad guy," Ginger continued.

"What happened out there?" the officers asked.

Everyone told the story. After nearly drowning in the Black Sea, the friendly fire incident was just another item on the list. *And now I have this perpetuating nightmare of me almost dying at the hands of this Ukrainian douchebag who I never even got to punch in the face*, thought Ginger later.

After some sleep they sat around smoking hookah in the basement. Alpha pitched Symon on another night operation. They would go by themselves, deconflict on their own. They wanted to go after the mobile artillery unit they had spotted from the high-rise.

"Fuck yeah!" said Oleksii, who took them to battalion headquarters to prep.

As soon as they arrived, the mission was canceled. "No, we're planning large offensive tomorrow," the staff officers said. Alpha and the rest of the teams were going to be rolled in.

Symon and Oleksii briefed the teams on the new op. They set out the map, friend or foe identifiers, and started to explain. They would cross the river, link up with the Georgians, then push forward into contested territory and hit a target building. They would leave at four in the morning. It was already 10 p.m.

The line was simple: we need all hands on deck. But if you don't want to go, you don't have to go. Michael was torn. He knew he wasn't a scrapper, and he worried that despite his habit of running up and down the stairs in full kit in Mykolaiv, he was still out of shape. He had joined this team to do intel work, and he was very good at it. But he had come to Ukraine to fight the Russians, and he hadn't yet.

Ginger pulled him upstairs. "Dude," said the infantryman, "there's no pride, there's no nothin'. You have a family. You have two young daughters; you have a wife. You shouldn't make this decision lightly. If you don't want to go, you have a job to do anyways. You're not a scrapper. You don't have to go. If this is a pride thing, you need to stop."

"It's not a pride thing," said the thoughtful Marine. "I know I'm not the most fit dude to fight, and I'm scared I won't be able to keep up."

"Then don't go," Ginger said flatly. He told stories about urban fighting in Irpin: jumping over walls, evading a BMP, long days out on their own. This was serious. "Because we don't have time to look after you."

"Really?" said the tanker.

"Yes."

"Okay," Michael sighed. "I think I needed to hear that."

Everyone prepped kit and went to sleep. At 4 a.m., Symon went to headquarters for final confirmation. He came back only to declare that they were on standby. Hours went by. They started to get antsy. Then they began to assume that the mission had been canceled. Finally, at 8 a.m., the trucks pulled up. Black Team went first, then Charlie.

9

NO MAN'S LAND

George followed Loup out of the gate in bright early morning sunshine. The Kozak was still running, the driver standing by. They loaded their rockets into the back compartment. Michael came out and shook George's hand.

"Be safe, man," said Michael.

"I'll try, man, thanks!" said the Canadian.

Charlie Team crushed into the seats. "George!" said Prym, patting a seat. "Put your ass here." George sat wedged against the right-side window. *Finally, an armored vehicle*, he thought, tired of riding in Craigslist trucks. Then he started to inspect the welds, which looked suspiciously handmade. *This is the sketchiest armored vehicle ever. Will this thing really stop a bullet?*

Their driver took off, bouncing down the shelled and mortared residential roads, still lined with leafy greenery, trees, and shrubs. Prym and Symon shared the front passenger seat. Behind them, George could hear them all talking in Ukrainian.

"Yes!" Prym said, suddenly in English, "my darlings."

The vehicle became quiet. "GoPro," Marti ordered his camera, "stop recording."

Ukrainian joking and chatter picked up again. The very young driver turned to the right. Then the road veered right once more. Before them suddenly lay the smokestacks of Severodonetsk: the looming industrial city, smoke coming now from artillery and not industry. They were nearly at the bridge, the only one left.

Beside Prym, their driver crossed himself reflexively. He didn't let up on the gas. The greenery turned abruptly to pulp. George saw the road yield to the bridge, now easily visible and even more intimidating in the daylight. Burned-out cars and trucks littered the sides, one lane now barely passable and not necessarily in the middle. What was drivable had holes in it. The trees that grew at the edge of the river were snapped like twigs at their tops, roots still firmly planted, looking like something out of no man's land in Flanders. The Kozak shook violently. The driver held onto the wheel with both hands as it leaped back and forth. They passed what looked like an armored personnel carrier, tipped on its side, which seemed like it was about to fall off the bridge to their right.

Then they were on land again. The driver said something to Prym in Ukrainian. Both men laughed. They sped along, with huge smoke plumes from artillery hits rising in front of them, not much further into the city.

The Kozak stopped at a three-story apartment building: bright blue, with red-trimmed windows. Pieces of siding that had once been the roof lay crumpled in the overgrown yard. Charlie Team unloaded and found Black Team guarding the perimeter. Symon conferred with Jordan next to the long side of the building. "What's up, guys?" said Prym, checking the corner. "All is good?"

The blue building was an abandoned Ukrainian position. The door was blocked. Loup paced along the building's exterior. "In through the window?" he asked in French. "*Oui, kurwa*,"[1] replied Prym, but the window was stuck. They finally entered through the other side of the building, after detouring around a long concrete wall, with shell holes and pieces of roof littering the way. An artillery shell streaked in and threw up a huge black smoke cloud a block or two away as they walked inside.

It was an apartment building, or it had been. While the Ukrainian officers huddled on the first-floor landing of the stairs, studying their smartphones loaded with combat maps, George went into the basement with Marti.

He turned on his headlamp. In the basement were crates that looked military and hopefully were useful. Pulling one open, he was surprised to see French grenades. *Hey!* he thought. *I know these.* He started to unpack and prep them, screwing the ignition tops into the teapot-shaped grenade bodies' explosives.

Marti appeared in the doorway. "I'll leave the Russian grenades," George muttered to himself in French as the two men debated where the firing they were hearing outside was coming from. Marti wanted the French grenades as well. "Yes," said George. "They're smaller, don't have a shitty fuse ..." he continued, unwrapping more. "French grenades, French rations ... I feel like I'm back in the Legion!"

Alpha arrived at the same time as two Georgian medics who were going to serve as guides to their target location. Everyone jumped out of the truck. Greg had been stuffed into the back storage compartment, where Charlie Team had put their Matador rocket launchers. Someone had to let the tall medic out; there was no handle on the inside. The driver peeled out. Prym was there to meet them, impatient. Behind him, Loup suggested going in through the window, concerned about their overhead. Prym pounded on the same window that Loup had tried to open before. Oleksii walked up, tossed his backpack through the window, and began to climb in. They held security for one another as they clambered in, rockets, men, and material all passing through the small window. Prym climbed in last. He handed his rifle to Loup and pulled a tall bookcase across the window, blocking it.

From the blue building, the Georgian guides led them on a circuitous route, trying to avoid exposure and Russian shellfire. They hopped from building to building, crossing the industrial edges of the city. Soon they came into one of the Georgians' own stronghold positions, a massive repair shop for trucks and large vehicles. They gathered in one of the bare rooms on the side of the building, with a floor above it for shelter from the shelling that they could hear outside.

The Ukrainian officers conferred with the Georgian unit leader, an older man with a greying beard named Otar. Dmitri hovered on the edge of the conversation, then walked over to translate for Dan, who leaned over Otar's shoulder to look at the map. George sat on the floor. Someone found a massive jug of water and passed it around; they checked radios. Riever moved into the big hangar room, holding security. Marti helped Oleksii balance his NLAW as the Ukrainian lifted it to his back. Loup, always in front, double-checked the maps on his own mission phone.

Artillery boomed again. They had to wait. Prym dropped his sunglasses. "*Suka, blyat,*" he muttered under his breath, reaching down to pick them up. "*Suuuuuuka!*" he squealed, earning a nervous chuckle from Artem, who was sitting on the floor next to him. Fast, repeated booms that sounded like Grad rockets erupted outside.

Prym offered the water around. "George!" he called. "I have my own," the Canadian responded.

"Yes, but save yours," chided Prym.

"But then I have to carry it!" retorted George. He turned back to Prym. "I found French grenades in the basement."

"Yes!" said Prym. "I gave one to Artem, and have one myself and gave one to Symon."

"I have six in my bag!" laughed George.

A new explosion boomed just outside. "Oh, yes!" sneered Prym, with a mocking nervous laugh. "Ooooh, yeah," he crooned to himself in a sing-song voice as more crashed nearby.

They began to move out, Loup in front, the big SAW sitting in his hands like a child's toy, and his back carrying a massive pack of ammo and his other preferences, such as fishing line for tripwires. Even with all his gear he still moved as if the balls of his feet had springs, like a big cat. They passed through the big open shop room, full of working bays. A large pile of firewood lay opposite the door that Otar swung open for Loup. "Friendlies to the right!" went the call down the line, in French and English. The artillery boomed in the background.

They moved through one industrial courtyard, then through a hole in a concrete wall, and into another compound. The telltale whistle came overhead again. Everyone knelt next to whatever cover was closest. George found himself next to a huge concrete cube as the artillery landed, closer this time. They started to move at a jog. "Well, hurry up, I guess," the Canadian called to Alpha Team, coming up behind him.

They turned into a new park. On one side was an old Soviet-style two-story concrete building, with all of the windows blown out. On the right was a series of parked eighteen-wheelers, one labelled "Annecy" and "Bordeaux" on the back door, another strange French connection.

George was making his way around a pile of oil drums when the pace sped up again. The men in front of him ducked into a two-story brick building, where Mykola held the door. George entered just as another shell whistled over him. Riever came in, right on his heels. They crammed into a tiny entry chamber: this was the way to the basement. "GoPro, stop recording," said Marti to his camera as they went down into the dark.

There were no lights in the basement. Men shifted around, trying to find places to sit. There were a few Ukrainians down there; this building was their position.

"We've been getting shot at by a tank all day," they complained. "Do you have anything that can kill it?"

Yeah, buddy! thought Ginger, who carried an NLAW. *I'm gonna go get to kill a freakin' T-72 on the first firefight!* They decided to wait it out in the basement. Killing the tank was more valuable than hitting their initial target building. Their officers went up to confer with those of the Ukrainian unit. Everyone else sat in the dark, hydrating against the oppressive heat.

Oleksii came running down the stairs. "Ginger! Ginger! Get the NLAW!"

Ginger slapped the battery on, ran a test as he sprinted up the stairs, and handed his rifle over to Symon. He ran up to the third floor. He walked in to find a bunch of Ukrainians, including Prym, communicating with one another at high volume.

"Prym, what's going on?" he asked, looking around.

"There is a tank down the street!" Prym exclaimed.

"Then why are you guys fucking screaming?" Ginger asked.

Prym stopped. "I don't know mate! We're just talking ... we're trying to find it."

Okay, thought Ginger. He pulled up against the wall, picturing these guys getting smashed by a tank because they insisted on standing in the window.

The tank never showed up. Ginger packed it in and everyone moved out.

Otar led them to the door on the opposite side of the building, working the creaking metal bolt back and forth to unlock the door.

Loup slipped through, with Charlie, Alpha, and then Black following. The bright daylight was startling after the darkness of the basement. A fire from a new shell hit burned just to the side of their path, behind a small outbuilding.

The approach had brought them to the edge of the industrial section of the city. Before them was a wide open space, covered now in scrubby brush and downed power lines. Marti stepped carefully around a big shell hole, rifle up and towards another huge pillar of black smoke to his left. Several power lines lay across their path. They stepped over several and ducked under another as they got closer to the main road. "*Encore!*" shouted Marti as another shell whistled over them and crashed with a boom nearby.

George ran across the deserted main road that marked the edge of the forward line, and turned left to move up the road, behind the big Hungarian. He passed a narrow but severe shell hole, perhaps four feet deep, on his left. Ahead on his right he could see another enormous plume of black smoke. In front of him, Marti started to jog towards a looming building set right up against the road. As George turned through a big gate, he heard cheers. It was the Georgian base. They had arrived.

Ginger saw a Georgian he knew from his Irpin days. "Ginger, brother!" the man exclaimed. "Look what we found!" On his knees in the corner, wearing fatigues, blindfolded and facing the wall, was a prisoner.

"No fucking way, dude!" Ginger exclaimed. "You got one?"

The prisoner had been walking down the street. The Georgians had spotted and grabbed him. He didn't have a weapon, but he did have a Russian military ID and a Ukrainian military ID. The face on both documents was his. They suspected he was DNR, a member of the breakaway pro-Russians in the region. His story kept changing. First he admitted to it, then he said he was just a civilian. *A civilian in an industrial area wearing camo*, thought Greg. *That doesn't make sense.* The prisoner couldn't name the street that he lived on or any other basic identifying details. The Georgians took the prisoner back behind the forward line and turned him over to the Ukrainian Security Service. Alpha, Charlie, and Black prepared to move up.

Ginger, Riever, and Dan moved forward to clear the overwatch building, just up ahead and to the right of them. As they entered, they saw a series of combat packs neatly stacked against the wall.

"What the fuck?" asked Ginger.

"Yeah," said the Georgian guide. "This is where the SSO got hit."

Their original mission had been to support an SSO unit that had taken this building. The SSO had gotten smashed by a tank: this had been the reason for the delay that morning. Five were killed, three injured. This was their gear. One flight up, on the floor, walls, and everything else, was their blood, splattered everywhere. *Horrible*, thought Ginger, looking around. On a table was a huge suppressed Barrett .50 cal, with a Schmidt & Bender scope on it. *Fuckin' nice!*

They knew that Loup, Charlie Team's sniper, could make excellent use of that gun. They packed up the Barrett and carried it back to show to the Legionnaire.

Loup lit up like a Christmas tree. Greg watched the sniper systematically check every component on the rifle, ensuring it was useable and undamaged. *Like a kid in a toy store*, thought the medic. He realized that it was the first time he'd ever seen Loup smile. Loup grabbed a bench from the rubble, flipped it, and mounted the bipod legs on it, building a stable platform, and tucked his body cross-legged into the small space in the corner behind the gun. He reached forward and dragged the bolt back. The dust in the gun made a slight grinding noise as the bolt slammed home on a high-explosive Raufoss round. Loup nestled in behind the scope and began scanning the apartment building looming to the south, watching for half an hour while everyone planned. But Loup was set to carry the SAW for this mission. The Barrett would go on loan to Black Team, who would be positioned in the overwatch building where Alpha had found the gun.

Meanwhile, Black Team had assembled in their overwatch building. Riever went across, brought the Barrett in, and asked who wanted it. Big Max eyed it. *Oh my God.* He wasn't a sniper, but he had fired a Barrett .50 before. "I'll take it!"

They moved to the end room, a second-floor office with salmon-pink walls and a mediocre painting of a bay horse hanging skew on one wall. They found a table that was perfectly situated to rest the massive rifle on and point out towards the target building: probably the spot where the last man who had shot it died.

Big Max sat down in a dead man's last seat, popped the caps on the scope, and began scoping the target building.

In front of Black Team on their overwatch lay the objective, already part rubble, like everything else in Severodonetsk. There were a series of buildings, almost all of them only one or two stories high. Most were made of concrete, and they were messily rather than systematically arranged, as if a giant child had played with them like Lego blocks. In between the buildings stood concrete walls taller than a man, obscuring the view and potential lines of fire from the ground. Vehicles of various descriptions were parked, in most cases permanently, in the intervening dusty courtyards between the buildings.

From their vantage point, Black Team had a good view of what appeared to be a standard Greyhound-style bus, bombed out and worse for wear, parked about twenty meters away from and parallel to Alpha and Charlie's next objective, a fifty-meter-long warehouse. The bus sat in front of an ill-kept island of scrubby bushes, tall grass, and concrete rubble.

George exited the Georgians' building behind Marti. To his right was the huge, black-roofed hangar. Just in front of it, smoke rose from a new artillery hit. Another plume ascended not far beyond. Charlie Team stacked up in the breezeway that bisected Black Team's building. It must at one time have served as a repair station for vehicles. As in the hangar of the previous Georgian stronghold, the breezeway held a small trench in which a man could comfortably stand and work on a vehicle's undercarriage, instead of using a hydraulic lift. George took a position on the right edge of the breezeway, Marti on the corner opposite him.

Riever led Alpha in from the Georgians' building, followed by Dan, Dmitri, Ginger, and Greg, the tall medic shouldering the large aid backpack. He ducked into the doorway on the right side of the breezeway that led to the staircase and Black Team's position. Oleksii ran in, carrying an NLAW in his right hand like a briefcase, closely followed by a chuckling Tex with his PKM machine gun. Greg inspected the trench. He turned, looking behind them.

"I don't like the look of that building up there," said George to the tall medic, glancing at an ominous structure looming up behind them from the next block to the southeast. At least six stories high, it could provide a perfect vantage point for a Russian sniper.

At the mouth of the breezeway, Prym gestured to his team to move up.

"You stay here," he said to George, holding him for the tail position.

Alpha, led by Riever, sprinted across the open two hundred feet of no man's land and past an abandoned BMP into the next warehouse. A booming crack, more like a rocket than artillery or a bullet, rang out to their right, towards the Russian line. Inside, Alpha began to clear the building.

The rest of Charlie Team moved out. "You're last, *kurwa*," said Marti to George with a nod.

Everyone else moved across in the fast, low, bent-knees tactical gait.

"Okay, okay," said Prym to George. "*Allez, allez!*"

They sprinted to the insulation warehouse. A moment later they were joined by Mykola and Loup, who had returned from final preparations with Black Team on the second floor of the breezeway building. Loup checked an abandoned BMP in the road, the Georgian running back easily in the heat. Now they were all in contested territory.

The "insulation warehouse," as it came to be called, was a long concrete barn of a building, about fifty by two hundred feet. At each short end were broad metal doors wide enough to admit heavy machinery and forklifts for industrial loading. The space was mostly wide open. So was a ground-level chunk in the back wall the size of a Volkswagen, blown out at some previous point in the fighting. At each end there was a loft which ran the length of the short side of the building, above the doors, probably twenty feet wide. On the east side of the loft walls, facing their target building across the courtyards, were big windows made of small squares of frosted glass blocks. Along the top of the east side of the building ran a series of high windows, and a big window looked on to the ladder that led to the loft on the north end of the building. Otherwise, it was just a box.

They broke through the back door with some wrenches that were lying around, planning to move forward and clear the block. As they opened the door, they saw something that was not visible on their maps: a concrete wall, with wooden shipping pallets stacked haphazardly against it, directly in their path.

Symon and Oleksii checked their maps. Should they breach it, or try to go back out and around, in front of the forward line?

Humans have fought in cities for as long as they've bothered to build them, but fighting with modern rifles among closely placed buildings still has a very recent feel to it. The U.S. Army published its first manual on urban fighting only in 1944, and that was a short pamphlet which referred to "combat in towns."

Urban combat is complicated, frustrating, and unnerving. There is no such thing as simply crossing a street or sticking your head out of a window to get a better look at something. Urban combat is a 3D puzzle, where the line of control is not static and is almost never straight. The enemy is usually difficult, if not impossible, to see, and you have to guess at his angles of fire from buildings that might not be visible to you yet.

Imagine the task of trying to leave your front door to visit a neighbor across the street and two houses down if your neighborhood became a combat zone. You can't go out of the front door, because the house immediately across the street now has a machine-gun position in the window. You might be able to use a side door if you could quickly move from cover to cover. But if the house next door had enemy in it—which you can't confirm—you would be a sitting duck. Even if the houses immediately surrounding yours were empty, the big Victorian down the street could have a sniper on the third-floor windows, or a tank might be parked at the end of the road waiting for someone to cross. Where exactly was the corner window positioned in that house? If the enemy were up there, would he have a clear shot if you went out the back door, or could you make it to the treeline without being seen, hoping the treeline wasn't mined? Urban fighting is a strange mix of cover everywhere and nowhere. Movement is restricted, and visibility is poor. The enemy could be in the next room, and until you open the door, you could have no idea.

As the Ukrainian officers planned a route, everyone else tucked up to await further orders. Ginger, Dmitri, and Riever held security on the back, northern door. George sat pulling security on the southern door of the building, the one through which the teams had entered and which Black Team could see from their office overlook. From the interior of the building, the left-hand side of the big metal double-door was closed, in order to provide cover. They left the right-hand-side door open, to provide situational awareness. George sat just short of the open door with his Bren ready, but he saw no movement.

Suddenly, three shots flew by his head and slammed into the door. George leaped backwards, raised his rifle, and dumped half a mag in the direction of the shots. There was no response.

They waited. George sat in the door, his left shoulder to the left-hand door for cover, though it was pockmarked with holes from some sort of projectile. Marti stood a few feet away, further into the building.

A grenade burst against the door. George felt the wind in his face as it hit the target and exploded.

What? he thought, briefly confused. *That's a grenade!* He leaped up and dumped a whole magazine on full auto in the direction of those shooting the grenades.

In Western armies, soldiers are often taught that grenades have a danger radius of up to fifty meters. Grenades kill and maim by fragmentation, sending small bits of metal flying in all sorts of directions, causing bad wounds across (theoretically) a large space. No one standing close to a grenade should be unharmed or even alive, or so the doctrine goes.

George was untouched.

"Grenade, *kurwa*," said Marti.

"Take the shot!" said George as the big Hungarian moved towards the door. Marti fired three shots, quickly.

"I'll take it," George declared coolly in French, aiming around the door in the direction they assumed the Russians were shooting from and dumping half a mag.

Suddenly an enormous volume of fire poured just past the door. There was nothing but noise. "*Ah, kurwa!* Contact!" shouted Marti, moving back from the door. "*Kurwa!*"

"They exploded two meters that way," George shouted to Prym in French over the noise as the Ukrainian stepped towards the door. Another grenade exploded just outside. "*Voila,*" said George. Prym ducked back inside.

"*Kurwa!*" spat Marti.

"Loup!" screamed Prym in French to the Georgian, positioned on the southern loft with his SAW. "*Look! Right! Look right and see what it is!*"

"Can you say in English what you see?" shouted Dan down the warehouse as the shooting subsided.

"*On il y a*—oh, *blyat*," sighed Prym. "We didn't see anything. We just contact from there. They shoot us!"

"They shoot the door!" Marti shouted to Dan, in English. "What we see, *kurwa*," grumbled the Hungarian, walking towards George at the door.

"They're fucking shooting grenades at us!" George clarified, as more gunfire rang out beyond the door.

Prym approached the door, trying to find the angle. "It exploded only five meters that way," said Marti, pointing. Another explosion boomed. Prym leaned out and shot. "Shoot!" shouted Marti, in French. From down the warehouse, Mykola, on top of the other loft, shouted that nothing was happening. "Who do you think is shooting then, you?" Marti exclaimed, in French.

More shots came towards the door. "Ah! Mykola shot that one, huh?" Marti snapped in French. George leaned out and took his turn.

"Loup!" shouted Prym to the Georgian. "*Allez!* Go to work!"

"Fuckin' shoot back!" called George, in English.

Two hundred rounds went streaming out of Loup's SAW, filling the warehouse with noise. He aimed towards the bushes just beyond the bombed-out bus, twenty-five meters in front of them.

Badass, thought Ginger. Loup on the gun looked like something straight out of *Rambo*.

From across the warehouse floor, Greg was tall enough to catch sight of Loup's face as he unloaded into what was assumed to be the Russian position. The Georgian was working the big SAW continuously. He was grinning, again.

Okay, cool, thought Greg. *Scary man.*

Below him, Marti approached the door as the Russians shot back. George tried to shout to him over the din. The Hungarian turned back. "No, no, no," he chided himself, chuckling.

Prym approached, ducking out quickly. Tex came up behind them with his big PKM machine gun. "Do you see anything?" asked the Texan.

"Be very careful!" George called to him in English. "They're fucking shooting grenades and landing right next to us."

Tex checked Black Team's location and the suspected Russian position. "It's down the street to the left," George said.

The big Texan stepped out of the door, alone, and pulled the trigger. The machine gun misfired, sending up smoke and a *thunk* that sounded like a mortar dropped into its tube. He ducked back inside to fix the gun.

"It's not far, is it?" Prym asked Marti in French.

"Not at all," replied Marti. "Not at all."

Loup called down for Prym. "In front of the building," said the Georgian, gesturing to the bushes directly in front of them, rather than the spot further up the street and to the right that they had been aiming at. "I saw movement."

"In *front* of the building?" said Prym. "Okay, okay."

Prym hustled to the opposite end of the building, translating Loup's information for the others. "That way?" asked Greg in Ukrainian as he pointed, confused. Were there two Russian positions now?

Black Team came over the radio. "There's movement in the bushes in front of you," they warned. Doug had seen someone sneaking around near the bus.

No fucking way, thought Ginger. How could they be so close?

Greg turned to translate for the Americans.

In their office, Black Team peered across the now explosive courtyard.

"Anyone got eyes on?" called Doug, his velvet British baritone echoing across their rooms.

"Negative," replied the former Marine officer Samuel, standing in the window with binoculars.

Black Team opened up with the Barrett .50 cal that Loup had left, the American former Marine Big Max laying rounds into the bushes. Doug fired over the top of Big Max, who was tucked into the former office desk in the window.

Later in the afternoon Doug would see a Russian spotter in a window, probably the source of the Russian artillery that crashed near their overwatch building. Big Max saw the man standing at the heavy concrete window sill. The Russian's entire torso was exposed. Big Max nestled the crosshair on the enemy soldier's head and began the trigger squeeze. He had no idea where the rifle was zeroed, but at this range it should be no issue. Two hundred meters was point-blank for the big fifty.

The shot broke, and the concussion of the round raised the dust from the floor as Big Max got back on target. He looked where the Russian had been standing. The base of the window was gone, right where the man's pelvis had been. The concrete sill was now destroyed right where the Russian had been standing. *I shot that dude in the dick*, he thought. They didn't receive any more accurate Russian artillery after that.

Presumably the Russians had seen Alpha and Charlie cross and thought they could sneak up on them. The grenades had been a risk. The first one shot at George was a bouncing model, designed to project further before it exploded. The grenades didn't kill anyone, but they did give the Russians away, even as they moved from their original position and into the bushes.

But once the Legion teams knew they were there, that small Russian team found itself in a classic L-shaped ambush. The enemy was trapped between the short and long legs of the L, unable to escape fire from multiple directions. The Russians had failed to realize that Black Team had been left as an overwatch. The movement in the bushes stopped: Black Team would never see anyone leave that space.

Loup and his SAW still manned the loft near their entrance point. Prym sent George up the ladder at the north side of the building, to take up a position that was nearly straight across from their target building itself. From his loft, the target building was forward and to the left, the bombed-out bus to the front. Then there were the bushes behind it, and the wide open ground in front of the target building.

Some of the little square frosted window blocks in front of George were blown out. Even without the broken panels, his tall form, bristling with combat gear, was silhouetted against the glass. He couldn't see much, but whoever was out there could probably see him. George stationed himself towards the left side of his window, shoving around the peach-colored insulation pallets in order to rest his rifle in a shooting position.

Below him, a huge round exploded a foot above Marti's head on the far wall. In response Mykola blasted with his PKM out of the first-floor window which looked onto the ladder. *He can't possibly see what he's shooting at*, Riever thought, annoyed. *You're just making noise, Mykola.*

"Hey, Mykola, stop," the Ranger called, gesturing. "I'm going to go up the ladder." He confirmed with the Ukrainian, then stepped forward and began to climb, holding the slim side-rails that covered the last few feet as he went, hoping to get a visual on the shooter.

He was just pulling himself up with the handrail that covered the last rungs when a loud and dramatic *slap* pierced the air, with no report: a suppressed Russian sniper rifle, probably a VSS. Below, Ginger watched a bullet crash through the big first-floor window that looked onto the ladder, and strike just beneath Riever. Someone had that ladder zeroed.

Hey! That guy was shooting at me, Riever thought. "Did you see that shit?" he chuckled to Ginger. On the loft, George just stared at him. *Well, okay then, you do you, Mykola*, the Ranger thought.

"I think they're in the building right there, dude," George said. He barely knew the other man; they hadn't overlapped much yet. The Canadian pointed to a building just past the hangar to Black Team's east. The ladder sharpshooter and the grenade launchers were not coming from the same place. The angle of fire was too different.

At the other end of the building, Alpha sent two RPG rounds and Tex's PKM fire into the suspicious bushes and towards the original target building, with support from Loup on the loft above and Mykola at the other end of the building.

"Well, light 'em up, I guess," George said as he and Riever fired from the loft. The building filled with noise. They took up staggered positions, Riever in front, George a few feet behind and to the right.

"George!" Prym shouted up to the loft as the noise subsided. "Do you see something?"

"No, just explosions," said George. "But I heard when they were shooting ... I think it might be that building there," he said, pointing towards the building to Black Team's right, past the big bus hangar.

"Loup!" shouted Prym, running back to the other side of the building. "Can you see anything to the right?"

The Georgian peered out of his window. "This one here?"

"Maybe, maybe," said Prym.

"Okay," said Loup, looking back outside.

Heavy gunfire exploded again from the Russians: someone had a PKM in the original target building. The rounds hit the inside of the upper walls near the original entrance. "They're fucking hitting the inside of the buildings!" George shouted. He watched a round throw up a huge *pfft* of concrete dust on the back wall, just underneath the high windows.

"Prym, get down!" shouted Tex, under the southern loft. The volume of fire was enormous and sustained.

"Loup! Loup! Move down!" screamed Prym. "George, lie down! Lie down! George! *Lie down!*"

Riever and George, on the northern loft, were pinned by the sharp-shooter's bead on the ladder. George hit the deck. "Get outa there, dude, Jesus Christ," he muttered, watching Riever, still aiming out of a broken frosted window square, trying to find where the Russians were shooting from. Both men lay belly to the floor.

Marti, near the southern door, nearly got hit again. Gunfire boomed; shouting in multiple languages filled the building.

"GoPro, stop recording," said Marti.

George turned his head to the right and looked down the length of the warehouse. Armor-piercing PKM rounds were flying in one wall and out the other. He watched the bullets slowly walk down the warehouse towards him, just at his head height. He had nowhere to go.

The volume of fire was still incredibly loud. At the entry door, Charlie Team yelled to one another in French while everyone tried to get a visual. Symon shouted on the radio in Ukrainian. Upstairs, the only guys with decent angles were pinned down by Russian fire.

"Riever!" called Dan. "Do you have a visual?"

"No," called Riever.

"No, but they're hitting the fucking ..." George ducked down again, hard, as more rounds splattered off the ceiling above him.

"Riever!" shouted Dan again. "Hey, man, I wouldn't be up there!"

"Yeah. I'm stuck where I am," Riever shouted back. "They have the ladder zeroed."

"What?"

"They have the ladder zeroed!"

"What?"

"We can't go up and we can't go down."

"We can't go down the ladder," bellowed George, "or they'll shoot us!"

Then, just as suddenly, the bullets stopped their long walk down the building towards George. Downstairs, Marti and Tex started triangulating the bullet impacts on the interior walls.

"You okay up there?" Dan called to the men in the loft.

"We're fine; don't worry about us," Riever replied.

"No, we're *not* fuckin' okay!" snapped George at the same time.

"I think it's the same building as Black, but further up," said Dan, indicating the same building George had guessed at a few minutes before, to the southwest of their target building.

Boom! went a Russian rocket, striking the wall not far short of the southern door.

"Ooh yes, baby, *kurwa!*" sneered Prym at the miss.

Prym heard snaps from behind them, to the west. "*Blyat!*" he shouted. "*C'est* friendly fire!" He raced across the huge open hole in their back wall to confer with Symon and Oleksii.

"Fuck, we're getting friendly fire now too?" exclaimed George, still belly to the loft floor.

At one stage Russian fire had gone through their building and into the forward line. The Ukrainian National Guard soldiers manning the line behind them then started shooting back, without deconflicting first. The insulation warehouse was taking two direct lines of fire.

"Tell Symon to get out of there," Riever called to Dan, gesturing for the Ukrainian officer to get out of the sniper's line of sight from the first-floor window.

Mykola approached the hole in the back wall, cupping his hands to his mouth. "*Suka!*" he shouted, yelling in Ukrainian to the men behind them to stop shooting.

"You good, Riever?" George shouted to the other man.

"Yep," said the Ranger.

"They have a bead on the ladder?" called Dan as Oleksii got on the radio to Otar, the Georgian, trying to resolve the friendly fire to their rear.

"Yeah, through that window," said Riever.

"They're hitting the tops of the buildings and the back walls as well," called George. "The fucking bullet impacts are up here."

"I don't think they can really *see* you," Dan said, poised on one knee and measuring angles of fire to the warehouse in his head. "I think they can see that door and the top of this building."

Tex approached the opening in the back wall, his own PKM hoisted at hip level like a gunslinger in an old Western.

"Tex, be careful. Don't shoot, *blyat!*" shouted Prym, rushing towards him.

"It's friendlies?" asked Tex, in a mix of relief and astonishment.

"Friendlies, yes!" said Prym.

"They're fucking us up, man!" Riever exclaimed.

Tex shook his head and went back to his position.

Another boom shook the warehouse. Then another. "Go down, guys!" screamed Prym.

"It hit the bus," called Greg, peering outside. The Greyhound in front of them had taken a rocket.

George called down to Tex. "Hey, Tex! How's it going down there?"

"Nothin' special," replied Tex.

Prym walked down to the southern end of the building. "*Kurwa*," said Marti, gesturing to their own forward line. "It's them who's shooting?"

"Yes," said Prym. "*Blyat*. That direction is also *blyat*," he continued, pointing towards the direction of the original Russian fire.

"Yes!" said Marti. "They think they are being shot at by them and so they're shooting back."

"Two *blyat*," sighed Prym.

"Yes, there are two *blyats*!" replied Marti, as both men laughed. Loup stood next to Marti, silently.

In their overwatch position, Black Team nearly got smoked by friendly fire as well: one of the Georgians mistook them for a group of Chechens and sent a rocket through their window, giving Doug a concussion and knocking out his hearing for more than an hour. For ten minutes the men in the overwatch position thought the Russians had flanked them, until they realized the almost deadly mistake.

10

URBAN JUNGLE

In the lull George and Riever came down, taking their chances on the ladder. Jumping in kit with rifles onto the concrete floor was out of the question. They went down very, very fast, hoping the sharp-shooter wasn't looking. He wasn't.

Riever went to help call in Ukrainian artillery rounds on the target building while George moved back to the point of first con-tact. Four rounds were lobbed at the original Russian target building from behind the Ukrainian front line, but none hit the target. From a spotting position in the insulation warehouse, Riever and Prym called in measurements, trying to correct the rounds that were landing frustratingly short of the target building. As Ginger put it, "Ukrainian artillery is a lot like Russian artillery ... but the volume of fire is a lot less."

In the overwatch office, Black Team could see the rounds landing on the open space in front of the building. *Whoooooom ... crump. Whoooooom ... crump.* The rounds landed with a sickening thud, pancaking the ground as they exploded, sending up huge billows of dirt, dust, and explosive. But the target building was still standing, with the Russians tucked safely within it.

Doug briefly dashed across the road to confer with Charlie in the insulation warehouse: which building to the east did he think the Russians were in? Black Team would go out and clear it. They had two rockets, which they now prepped to take out the grenade lob-bers' initial right-side position. Samuel and Pedro crept down the steps, rockets in tow. They paused in the breezeway.

"Ready?" said Samuel. "One, two, go!" They ran together, for-ward and to the right. Samuel moved past the disabled BMP and shouldered his rocket. Marti stood just back from the door of the insulation warehouse, ready to cover them. "They're firing the missile," he said in French to George. "Black Team is firing their fuckin' Matadors!" the Canadian shouted to the other English speakers.

Samuel took a knee. *Boom!* A huge cloud of black smoke exploded in the tree-line in front of what they assumed was the southeastern Russian position, past the hangar next to Black Team's building. He ducked behind the BMP.

Pedro took a knee and fired. *Boom!*

"Let's go!" called Samuel, as they ran back to their position.

Ginger moved to check the lock on the back gate that Alpha wanted to use to push forward. He suddenly heard a low, rumbling growl. Then came a series of repeated booms. It was a tank: but whose? Both the Ukrainians and the Russians used similar tanks, and while there were certain models (T-64s for the Ukrainians and T-90s for the Russians) that only one side had at this stage in the war, they mostly overlapped with their large stocks of old-school T-72s, a design first developed in the late 1960s.

Tex and Ginger both lined up at the door, eyes on the tank.

Tex shouldered a Matador. "I'm gonna fuckin' shoot this thing! Is it ours or not?" he demanded.

"I do not know. We're waiting on confirmation. Don't shoot," said Symon in his bored voice, trying to contact the other Ukrainian units on his radio.

Fuck that, dude, thought Ginger, prepping his NLAW and hoisting it to his shoulder.

Generally speaking, tanks shoot three kinds of ammunition. The first is a kinetic energy round, or basically a very, very large bullet with a heavy penetrator at its core. The other is a high-explosive anti-tank round, whose shape charge at the very front uses hot plasma to create a small entry hole. Through that deceptively small opening, as one wit once said, "all the good news rushes through, causing alarm and despondency to those on the other side."[1] Their anti-tank rockets worked the same way. The third is simple high explosive, like a very high velocity artillery shell. None of the options were good for the occupants of a building whose walls had already proven susceptible to standard armor-piercing bullets.

Ginger almost had sights on the tank. He did not want to end up like the SSO team that had been hit that morning.

"It's ours, it's ours!" came the call. *Oh my God*, Ginger thought, putting the NLAW back down as the tank went to work. *What the fuck?*

"Hey, you guys, be careful, just in case!" Tex called to Marti and George by the southern door.

Boom! went the tank.

"I hope they know we are here," Marti declared loudly in English, doing his usual boxer's shake-out of his joints as he walked away from the door nearest the tank, "and that they don't want to shoot this fucking building!"

The tank aimed again at the right-side Russian position, the one from which the enemy had tried to shoot George in the door.

Boom! Boom!

Invisible behind its own grey smokescreen which matched the drab clouds of the afternoon sky, the tank unloaded on the Russians. A brilliant flash of orange and yellow singed the air as the rounds flew out of the barrel. From somewhere to the left, what had been someone's pet dog ran for cover, rushing out in front of the parked tank and up the street, parallel to the forward line.

The tank left to reload. Like the dog, they were alone again.

The original target building seemed to be the main base, but the tank and artillery fire had not been able to destroy it. They could not assault it head-on, or they would be cut down by the PKM gunner or caught in a pre-set ambush in much the same way the initial Russian attackers had been. The only option was to keep the Russians busy shooting at their men in the insulation warehouse while another group moved around to flank.

The French Legionnaires were left in the warehouse to do what, as Greg said, they did best: just all-out "fight them." Meanwhile, Alpha Team would flank through the maze of buildings that they had been attempting to navigate before the Russian attack began. They would move north and then loop back east, trying to come at the Russians from the rear and side of their own stronghold position.

Riever pulled from his back the red crowbar that he had bought in the hardware section of the Mykolaiv Epicenter. Fitting it carefully, he broke the flimsy lock on the gate that Ginger had been inspecting before the friendly tank arrived. Alpha flowed through the opening.

Beyond the gate was another small courtyard. At its far end was a stout building. In a previous life it had been some sort of cross between a garage and a car wash, but now it was locked up. Their wirecutters wouldn't work. Riever tried with the red crowbar again, but the locking mechanism was too strong. They had some old Russian C4 plastic explosives but didn't have enough time to build a breaching charge: they needed to get through fast to flank for Charlie.

Alpha moved around, looking for a point of entry or a way past. Riever checked the angles. Flanking to the only available side would leave them exposed to fire from the target building.

"Well, we can't go back and we can't go forward, so we're going to have to go through," said Symon. The only option left was a bad one in the semi-enclosed space of the courtyard: blowing the door open with a rocket.

Riever's attempt to use an M72 LAW failed, though, as they later realized, it was simply operator error: he had been pressing the wrong button. Someone loaded an RPG round into a launcher instead.

There was very little space for cover in the courtyard. The rest of the team formed a dogpile in a scrubby set of bushes along the side wall, out of the way of the backblast. They tucked in tightly, expecting pressure and flying metal from the round.

The doors blew open as the rocket fired, one set of hinges nearly gone. *Those are blown to fuck*, thought Ginger. But nothing else was: no one had even a scratch.

On the ground, Ginger started laughing hysterically. Fifty meters away, Charlie and Black were in a full-on firefight with the target building. Here he was, lying in a scrum of dudes in a dogpile while someone blew doors open with a rocket in a semi-enclosed space while a LAW of questionable status lay on the ground, all so that they could move through a single building. *Fuckin' unreal*, he thought.

Everything inside Alpha's newly blown-open building was locked as well. The only way to the rest of their sector, on the other side, was through what had once been an office window. It was already broken.

"That's a tiny-ass window," Ginger grumbled. He went first, accidentally catching a piece of kit on the jagged frame. He crashed to the ground outside, an NLAW still strapped to his back. His landing zone was covered in window glass.

Inside, the rest of Alpha heard a florid variety of curses explode as Ginger bitched, picking the glass out of his hands and kit, and trying to get himself up again.

"Ginger!" hissed Dan through the window. "Shut the fuck up!"

"I'm *sorry!*" retorted Ginger, hot, sweaty, bleeding, and showing signs of their 4 a.m. wake-up. "I'm just fuckin' mad, dude! This is such bullshit, I *hate* this shit!"

They were in another compound of buildings. Each had to be cleared, even the small storage sheds. As they worked, they occasionally heard bursts from the PKM machine-gunner fly over their heads. He could not see them, but he had some sense that they were moving towards the Russian flank. Every so often, the machine gun would rattle, and bullets would fly across the tops of Alpha's collection of buildings.

One single-story building was open on one whole side, leaving them exposed to the southeastern Russian position from which George had first been shot at in the door. Another looked better. The angles on the building were promising. If they could get the right window on the second floor, they should be able to target the PKM gunner directly.

Alpha entered the building. It was a warehouse, not so different from the one Charlie was still fighting from. Most of the building was a two-story-high room, but there were a few offices on the second floor, connected by a catwalk. They climbed up, heading towards the Russian positions.

Dmitri moved out on the catwalk first. After a few steps he nearly went straight through the floor: it had rotted through. There was no way it could hold the whole team while they tried to find a way through.

Symon took Dmitri, Ginger, and Greg to try in another building. Dan and Riever stayed behind. Maybe there was another way around the rotted floor. If they could get a good position, it was worth taking the chance in order to be able to target the PKM gunner directly. Each man stepped carefully, looking closely, searching for angles.

From a window just beyond the rotted floor, Dan could see the plume of smoke from the PKM's muzzle every time the Russian fired. *If I could just lean out a few more inches*, Dan thought, *I would have the shot*. But the floor wouldn't hold. He couldn't get the angle.

The bullets generating the muzzle flashes that Dan was tracking were aimed at Charlie.

George was back up on the northern loft on Prym's orders, trying to spot Russian positions through some of the broken sections of the frosted glass cubes that formed the window. Suddenly a burst of fire exploded the little glass cube next to his head: the Russians had seen his silhouette. The Canadian flattened himself to the floor. He looked up and saw the bullets pinging off the ceiling and the girders.

"Can you see anything?" the rest of Charlie called up to George.

"No! I can't," he called back, "but the bullets are passing just next to my head."

The volume of fire was immense. George considered the geometry.

Maybe, he thought as he lay with his head closest to the windows and his feet towards the back wall, *I should move*. If he lay as he was, perpendicular to the incoming fire, his head would be hit first. It was covered by his French Foreign Legion helmet ... but it was still his head. *Maybe I should move sideways, parallel to the windows*, he thought, *so that my bulletproof plates will cover me. But then they could still possibly hit my head*, said his own internal counterargument, *and also the rest of me*.

George's GoPro was pinned under his body, filming the sandy, taupe-colored floor of the loft. He remembered the nervous Brit talking about *Saving Private Ryan* at headquarters. The penultimate scene of the movie ends with a dropped camera staring into the lifeless eyes of the character played by Tom Hanks. George carefully reached up with his gloved hand and turned his camera off.

"George! Come down!" came the call from below.

"I'm coming down!" replied George, leaping up from his spot of inadequate cover and dashing towards the ladder on which Riever had nearly been shot hours before.

As quickly as he possibly could, George moved down the ladder. It was a rapid combination of stepping and sliding. His rifle, riding on its sling over his shoulder and neck, snagged on the ladder, *bang-bang-bang*, and caught on the small handrail that connected the ladder to the loft as he went.

"Fucking cunt!" muttered George as he dashed out of the narrow alley between the ladder and stacks of insulation, the one in front of the sharpshooter's window. Mykola, alarmed, put out his hands: *slow, slow*.

Kneeling on the ground, safely within the cover of the long wall of the building, George argued with his teammates. "That's not a good spot to be in front of that window. He's shot exactly there twice. He knows," said George, breathing hard.

A few minutes later Prym wanted him to go back up to the loft a third time, to look for the angles of Russian fire again. George had spent six years in the French Foreign Legion. The loft was not particularly valuable real estate from either a strategic or a tactical perspective. But the French Foreign Legion, and its veterans, prized toughness above almost all else. This was a unit that had once trained its men to handle the worst-case scenario of getting run over by a tank, by simply running them over with tanks (in those days, if you arranged yourself properly, you'd survive). French Foreign Legionnaires had been some of the last holdouts at Dien Bien Phu. They had fought hard during the Algerian War of Independence. They had also produced plenty of the men who rebelled against France when Algeria was granted independence, men who formed part of the OAS which tried to (and very nearly did) assassinate President Charles de Gaulle. This is why all officers in the Legion today come from outside its ranks ("You try to kill the president *one time* ..." George would joke).

Once, stationed in a remote corner of French overseas territory, George had a personal encounter with Legion toughness. His team leader then was a bully, the kind whose preferred entertainment was torturing the new guy until he deserted. George was not the deserting type, and there was nowhere to desert to anyway. After months of torment, he decided that he had two options: fight or flight. He chose to fight. The good-natured, kindly Canadian went to the workshop, took a crowbar off a shelf, walked into his offending team leader's room, and beat the shit out of him. The other Legionnaires thought this was a perfectly acceptable response. It also became a calling card. When George arrived at the office for his honorable discharge years later, the clerks looked up and said, "You're the crowbar guy!"

"No!" George snapped back at Prym. "If you told me to sit in the middle of the street, I wouldn't do that either."

After they prepped the Russian position with their Matadors, Black Team had moved out to try to clear the position. They climbed into the giant bus hangar that adjoined their right flank, fragging all the rooms. It was a big, creepy structure, ultimately little more than a giant awning over a wide array of buses. The roof looked like some sort of girded metal, painted black. They cleared it. They pushed into the building next to it, fragged all the rooms, and kept going. They got up to the top floor. Big Max and Doug cleared it and could hear gunfire echoing from the next building. *Oh, fuck*, they thought.

They went back outside to try to flank around the back. There was a gate to the street, with a big lock on it. All the windows and doors on the backside of the building were barred with rebar, locks, the whole nine yards. Black Team didn't have any breaching charges to assault through the defenses, and the only other approach was open to the target building's line of fire. *Well, they don't have a way out either*, they thought. Black Team would keep an eye out, but their position seemed secure. Black started to egress quietly, moving back towards their overwatch position.

Across the block Ginger stood with Greg, Dmitri, and Symon outside the open building with the high windows, alongside the long, tall concrete wall that blocked them from the target building. Suddenly there was small-arms fire from the opposite side of the wall. They could hear voices just on the other side. The Russians did not seem to realize that Alpha was right next to them.

No way, thought Ginger. *This is great! Let's dump a bunch of fuckin' grenades over the wall.*

They tucked up against the wall, very, very quietly. Each man selected his grenade.

Their grenades were a hodgepodge of different makes and models. They had both old Soviet-style RGO (defensive) and RGN (offensive) grenades. The defensive model had a larger fragmentation radius. Both would explode on impact so that the enemy could not pick them up and throw them back. The Westerners had collected other versions as they went as well, like the French teapot grenades that George had found that morning. Alpha also had some curious lemon-shaped grenades with Portuguese writing on them.

"I looked them up!" Riever had said to Ginger as they packed. "They're a Portuguese copy of a South African copy of an American M26."

"Dude," said Ginger, "that's the most *Forgotten Weapons* thing I've ever heard."[2]

Ginger, Symon, Greg, and Dmitri threw simultaneously, in intentionally different directions, trying to spread out the radius of the grenades' blasts: four overlapping fields of fragmentation at close range.

Boom! Boom boom boom! All of the grenades exploded at once. Then everything stopped. Silence descended on the block. Even the PKM gunner stopped firing.

Fuck yeah, dude! We must have gotten two or three of 'em, Ginger thought.

Then the Russians guns opened up again, a massive volume of sustained fire flying over their heads from the PKM. *Oh yeah, one of those grenades definitely killed somebody.*

The sound of the renewed fire was enormous even inside the insulation warehouse.

"Alpha?" asked Marti.

"I think that it's Alpha who's shooting," replied George. "Or I hope."

He sat on the floor, just beneath the edge of the south-side loft. The concrete dust was settling all around him. Early in the fight, even Mykola had given up and pulled his gaiter over his nose and mouth. George's back rested on a poorly tiled pillar, one which had previously been dedicated to holding up a piece of cardboard, scrawled with graffiti and pasted with magazine images of two bikini-clad, suggestively posing women. The modern pin-ups had fallen to the floor, ignored.

Marti, standing in front of George, shouted down the warehouse in order to be heard above the din. "Prym! Is that Alpha who's shooting?"

Another huge volume of fire flew past.

"That passed just next to us," George said.

"Prym!" called the Hungarian again. The other man had the radio. "Is that Alpha who's shooting? Who's shooting now?"

"It's Alpha, usually," called Prym.

"Okay," said Marti.

The fight had been going on for more than five hours. Charlie had one SAW, one PKM, and the assault rifles of the rest of the team. Most of the fighters from all the teams carried disposable rockets of some sort—NLAW, AT-4, or Matadors, depending on stock. But Charlie, locked for hours in a gun battle with a bunch of Russians who were probably sitting on top of an ammo dump ("like cheat code levels of ammo," as George put it), was running low on regular ammunition. George had brought extra magazines. He started distributing them to the rest of the team.

In the U.S. Army, a standard combat loadout for magazines in a standard infantry team is seven. The CZ Bren 2's magazine carries thirty rounds; that would give each man 210 rounds apiece. Exactly how many mags to carry is a long-standing debate. Different combat zones have dictated their own conditions, even for highly specialized, elite units. The men in MACV-SOG, the Special Forces soldiers who operated clandestinely across the border in Laos and Cambodia during the Vietnam War, carried as many as twenty mags. Those men were sent to collect intelligence and hunt hardcore soldiers of the Vietnamese People's Army, and might have to survive for days or weeks at a time, alone. During the recent war in Afghanistan, by contrast, it would not have been out of place for a squad leader to carry three mags on his kit, with one more in the rifle. The volume of fire there was significantly less.

But neither in Vietnam nor in Afghanistan did American soldiers face the volume of fire that Alpha, Charlie, and Black met with in Severodonetsk. MACV-SOG had some very hairy missions, but at the end of the day they did have the option of being extracted by helicopter. The jungle can be friend or foe (as one British genius of a jungle operator put it, "the jungle is neutral"). Those properly trained could use it to their advantage in terms of cover and concealment, and the men of MACV-SOG were experts. But they were not facing enemy tanks in the jungle, and for the most part they did not have to worry about projectiles much beyond standard mortars. The jungle simply made it too hard to move anything big.

Likewise, in Afghanistan, Coalition forces did not face anything like combined arms from their opponents. Americans have always liked air power, and have always assumed that air power can drop you anything that you need (it can also shoot the bad guys by leveraging gear like flying thermal ISR and A10 Warthogs). As in Vietnam, the heavy stuff was on the Americans' side. But as the Russians were finding, the war in Ukraine showed that air superiority was a harder thing to achieve than might be expected.

Now the teams on the ground found themselves in a very different situation from what any of them had ever been in before. One of the major strengths of a special operations unit is speed: it can move quickly, silently, and get into places that other units can't. But you can't do that if you need to carry a lot of heavy ammunition. For these fighters in Severodonetsk, ten mags was the minimum. Now they were being faced with a special operations mission in what had become a conventional unit's position—but without the conventional unit's come-up-from-behind supply chain.

"Are they coming in here?" George asked, sitting against his pillar under the southern loft.

"Okay, they're crossing," Marti said, watching Black Team return to their original position. "They're going back. Prym! Black Team is crossing there, they're going back."

Heavy Russian fire opened up again. Prym called down to Marti to confirm Black Team's movement.

"*Kurwa*," muttered Marti.

Prym shouted at George in warning from down the warehouse: there was another suspected tank outside.

"Who shot at me? Who shot *at me*?" George demanded. Mykola moved to his right side and set up his PKM on its bipod. "They hit just there," George said, pointing at the wall across from him. Prym and Oleksii went back and forth on the radio in Ukrainian.

Symon, Ginger, Greg, and Dmitri approached a long, thin warehouse that could bring them flush with the concrete barrier wall that separated them from the target building's courtyard. As in the insulation warehouse, there were windows that ran along the top of the building, just under the roofline. If they could get up higher and see out, they might have a shot at the target building. But there was no floor beneath the windows.

Greg suggested a ladder. There was none in sight, so he went to look for one. The odds seemed poor. But soon he was back, carrying a ladder about fourteen feet high. Like many of the buildings, the ladder was damaged. One long side was missing a surprising amount of material on the supports. It was rusted and twisted everywhere.

"I'm not fuckin' going up there," declared Ginger, giving the ladder a long and doubting look.

"I'm going, it was my idea!" retorted Greg.

"Alright, dude, have fun," said Ginger.

They placed the ladder under their preferred angle of fire. Up went Greg, hand over hand, to the top of the ladder.

The ladder was just tall enough for the tall medic. He could shoulder his rifle for a shot. Beyond him was the target building, which looked like an old Soviet administrative building or school. The windows were barricaded, and there were trenches in front of it. He looked for an angle. There was a big, bushy tree blocking the way. The ladder creaked.

"Can you see anything?" shouted his teammates from the floor below.

"I can't see shit!" Greg shouted back in frustration. "There's a tree right in the damn way!"

"Can you get a shot off at *anybody*?" Ginger asked.

"Well, maybe if I sat here long enough," replied Greg, shifting on the rungs, "but I think this ladder is going to break."

"Yeah, probably," said Ginger, eyeing the missing chunks of the long edge.

Greg came back down.

Marti had an idea. "I think," he explained to Prym, who was prepping his Matador, "that they're crossing this street to pull back." He gestured towards the southeastern Russian position. The open street between it and the larger, main target building was wide. The huge volume of fire may have been meant to cover their egress, which might still be ongoing.

"Okay," said Prym.

Mykola shouted to be careful of the backblast deflecting off the open metal door. Shots fired past the door.

"Two hundred meters, *kurwa*," Prym muttered, adjusting the range on the Matador. More fire crashed just outside. "Oh, *pa pa pa pa!* That's good, that's enough already," he exclaimed, stepping further inside. "We must go further out," he said to Marti. Another crash rang out.

Prym dashed forward through the door, with Marti following to give covering fire with his rifle. Prym aimed at the southeastern Russian position. *Boom!* went the rocket. They raced back inside.

"Hey!" Marti cried in delight. "Well done! *C'est bien*, Prym."

They talked back and forth for a moment, debating their situation.

"Alpha is going to get into the building across from us," said Prym, gesturing to the big target building with the PKM gunner inside.

Dan and Riever linked back up with the rest of the team. Greg had found an irregular space at the far side of the warehouse where he'd propped up the ladder. He went to show the SEAL. Concrete blocks were rubbled and jumbled in what had a messy but also somehow man-made appearance; it had once been a standard exterior wall. Riever caught up with them, and they started to dig.

Some of the rubble was real. The rest turned out to be an attempt at cover. Beneath the concrete was a very small hole at the base of the wall.

"A rathole," said Riever.

The Ranger and the SEAL could see light through it. If they squeezed, they could get through.

They checked the maps on their mission phones, looking for a route. Straight in front of them was another street, one held by the same sort of National Guard unit that had accidentally fired at them earlier. They had no comms with the guardsmen and no other ability to talk to them. But they did not need to move forward; they needed to move to the right. They checked that direction. They saw another wall, one with concertina wire strung across it. The only route would expose them to Russian and friendly fire alike. They were at another dead end.

Dan regrouped the team in the small warehouse and conferred with Symon. Riever walked the length of the warehouse and out at the other side. He was in the small outdoor space where the rest of the team had thrown their grenades, between the warehouse, the concrete wall, and what appeared to be a small outhouse. He heard Russian voices on the other side of the wall.

Creeping to the wall, Riever had the same reaction as Ginger and the rest of the team before him. He pulled out an RGO grenade. Listening carefully, he located the Russian position on the other side of the wall.

Riever wanted to wait until the enemy fire started up again. Russian grenades make a small pop as the spoon flips up. It could give enough warning for a canny soldier to get down flat and avoid death.

An explosion boomed. He flipped the spoon and tossed the frag gently over the wall, right where he had heard the shooting. As before, the shooting stopped. He tucked the grenade ring into his pocket and walked back into the warehouse.

They all agreed: they had run out of room. They weren't able, from this side of the block, to get a shot on the target building to disable either the PKM gunner or his weapon. After several hours, they had cleared the rest of the block and plenty of buildings and small sheds, but they could not flank the Russian target building. The only option was to blast a hole through the wall and try to shoot through or climb over it. Either option would be suicide. Flanking all of the way around would force them onto the street, exposing them to friendly fire, a risk that in this environment was not worth taking.

They got on the radio and called back to Prym and Charlie Team. It was a negative on the flank.

The Ukrainians wanted to hold the ground that the Legion teams had taken. The latter were exhausted. Dusk was beginning to settle over the sweltering day.

Alpha returned to the first building they had cleared on this side of the block, the locked-down car wash that was only accessible by the window through which Ginger had belly-flopped. Climbing back in, they took up defensive positions and started to rotate a watch. So close to the Russian positions as they were, they had been spared enemy artillery strikes while they fought. Now the Russians must have pulled back, because the artillery units started up again, smashing rounds into the forward line behind them.

The forward line was about three hundred meters away. At that distance, an artillery round has already begun its descent. The roar as the shells flew over Alpha's stronghold building was tremendous. The ground shook. The men sat, passing around the "combat sucks."

Alpha didn't have enough men or ammo to hold the new positions overnight. Symon and Oleksii went back to the forward line, as Dan put it, to "light a fire under the ass" of the Ukrainian units behind them. They needed men to backfill their position and Charlie's. The rest of Alpha waited.

Dark arrived, producing the disturbing darkness of a modern city at night. The only light came from burning buildings, artillery strikes, and the occasional shot of white phosphorus. Ginger set up his night vision gear and bedded down, waiting for his turn at watch.

His dozing was interrupted by a tremendous boom. It came again, loud, fast, and repetitive. This sound was different from standard Russian shelling. It was more immediate, menacing, and tremendously loud. Ginger's ears ached from the sound and the pressure waves. *Fuck, I'll have a concussion soon*, he thought.

It was a tank. They did not know it, but it was their Ukrainian tank, back for more. The tank commander was aiming at the target building. The rounds were so close that dust shook down from the ceiling.

Dmitri desperately keyed up the radio, trying to reach Symon and Oleksii, who were too far out of range to hear. Charlie and Black came over the radio. "We think it's shooting at the target building, but we can't see it," they said.

The tank fired off its supply and disappeared back into the night. *Like a ghost warrior*, Ginger thought. He settled back in. As the clock turned to his watch, he moved carefully towards Dmitri at the broken window that served as their door.

He could hear murmurs, unexpected voices in the night. Dmitri had the radio, but Ginger could hear no radio squawking. *What the fuck? Who is he talking to?* thought Ginger.

Outside was Symon. "I bring your replacements, *blyat!* Let me in," boomed the pirate, starting to climb.

In came the replacements: eight tired-looking Ukrainian national guardsmen, jumping in through the broken window like some sort of reverse clown car. *I feel sorry for those guys*, thought Greg, watching. *This is not a good spot to be in if you can't see in the dark.*

Alpha was glad to see them, even if their unit had shot at them earlier in the day. Only months before they had been regular civilians, men who wore suits or business casual to work, who took the subway, sat in traffic, worried about taxes and the cost of living and where to send their children to school, and watched TV, played on their iPhones, and argued with their wives like any other member of Western society. Now they were "just dudes with AKs," as George put it, in the hottest part of the biggest war on earth.

They took up their positions, looking down their red lenses in the dark. They had no night vision. *Fuck, man*, thought Ginger. They had seen this position, the brand-new forward line, only in the dark, under Symon's guidance. They expected that the Russian artillery would find them very soon. But there they were, Ukraine's civilians in uniform, holding the line in the darkness.

Ukrainian national guardsmen had backfilled Charlie in the insulation warehouse as well. The teams mounted their night optical devices (NODs) and began the long, slow walk through the forward line, back to their extraction point a few kilometers away.

They were exhausted. It had been over ninety degrees all day, and their GoPros would later show that they had fought for nearly eight hours. They had needed hours more to get to their position, and waited even more to be relieved.

As they left the Georgians' building, walking down the main street, Ginger fell into the deep mortar hole that George had noticed on his way in. One moment he was walking, and the next he was falling straight downward. "Feet met air met ground," as he put it, a Charlie Chaplin-like descent. He landed hard, messing up his ankle and breaking his big toe: their first casualty of the day.

"Where the fuck am I?" he shouted from waist-deep in the hole as the rest of the team laughed.

"This shit ain't funny! I could have fuckin' died!" he sputtered, dragging himself out.

Further back, two Kozaks waited to take them back across the rickety bridge to their not-so-safe safehouse in Lysychansk. Greg was stuffed back into the windowless, handleless back storage compartment. But the vehicle didn't move. *Ah, it decided not to start again*, realized Greg.

They couldn't fit into one vehicle; there were extra Ukrainians with the drivers. Someone worked out a tow. The working Kozak, carrying Charlie Team, was put up front. Slowly, they drove out, over the rattling, Swiss-cheesed structure that Ginger called "Dead Man's Fuckin' Bridge." In the back, Greg was blissfully unaware of just how risky it looked to be slowly dragged over a structure of questionable integrity in the dark, with Russian artillery pounding away beside them.

11

"REGULAR DAN"

Home, thought Ginger, walking into the safehouse. There were Russians five kilometers away in three directions and artillery smashing just about everywhere, but it still had that cozy, if-not-safe-then-comfortable feeling. Michael was there, having set up rattle traps and patrolled the compound all day with the help of the kitten Matador.

Ginger dropped his plate carrier, hit the power button on the hot-water kettle, and started brewing the coffee. *Okay, I survived today, I at least get to eat some food and sleep one more time.* They all told their stories, all the angles of the eight-hour gunfight.

"Never again," declared Michael. "I'm not going to get left behind again. I don't care what it takes, I'll keep up." He watched the footage they came back with. *I can do this*, he told himself. As he patrolled the house he had found a scale and realized that he had lost thirty pounds since his arrival in the country. *I'm capable of doing this.*

As a young Marine in Iraq, he had never hated the insurgents, because he realized that in another life he could have been one of them. But he was so, so angry with the Russians for what they were doing to Ukrainian civilians, especially women and children. *I've never wanted to kill people before*, he thought. *But I want to kill these bastards. I have to put my ass on the line, because anything less than that is not enough.*

Everyone went to bed. Greg and George were sharing an air mattress. Putting two people who were six and a half feet tall on the same bed didn't last long, for they rapidly broke it.

"His fat ass poked it," Greg insisted. "The hole got poked on my side. So it only makes sense that it was him, because when he would plop down on the mattress, it would displace the air into my area and then all that volume hitting my area would pop the hole," the medic explained. "I'm a hundred percent certain it was his fault."

The next morning, Symon and Oleksii went to headquarters for briefings and to get their next mission set. Everyone else stayed in the safehouse. It was as calm as it could be given the circumstances. Black Team came over to use the WiFi, mostly Jordan and Doug, who moved as a pair. Everyone played music. They broke out the hookah and generally relaxed. "It was actually a really nice day," Ginger said.

They were none of them kids, and many of them had collected the complications of a soldier's life over time. One had had a daughter at seventeen, then won full custody to care for her as a single dad while building a career; there were minor brushes with the law, bar fights, failed marriages, the transvestite accidentally brought home from a nightclub, the usual. But Dan seemed like Teflon. The guys called him "Regular Dan."

He wasn't. *There's no reason for me to keep this a secret anymore*, Dan thought, sitting in their basement among the artillery. He'd been in the habit of doing so, but there was no need now. *Why have to pretend or watch myself if I say wife or kids or something? It's better if these guys know.*

So he told them the whole long, tragic story: how he'd been married at eighteen to his high-school sweetheart and had four kids with her. How he'd come back from a deployment only for her to tell him that she didn't love him anymore. Divorce was one thing; sad but common. His own parents divorced when he was a child.

But this was different. He found himself barely able to afford an apartment, unable to see his kids, paying for the civilian lawyer that his wife had chosen but without a divorce attorney of his own, and facing the end of his career in a service for which he had risked his life and that now could not come to his aid. He wasn't going to be, he decided, "a broken-down old man."

So he left. He took his passport and a backpack and simply disappeared. He wasn't proud of it. But he couldn't see his kids anyway. He'd never gotten to tell them his side of the story. He wrote a book for them, hoping that one day at least they could know his version. He mailed a copy to his ex-wife and planned to send more, "so that she at least has to keep throwing them away."[1] He would email his children through his ex-wife, but there was never a response. He wanted them, he said, to know that "I've been trying to reach you this whole time." He also kept a log for his children, in drafts of an email address that he hoped they could one day find. As he prepared to cross the border into Ukraine, he wrote a simple message, one that he realized might be the last: "Well, Kiddos, your papa is headed to war again. I am waiting for a bus to take me to the border. I don't know when I will get my last chance to write. I love you so much. I hope you understand this is who your papa is. I am not a man who rolls over and takes it, and I am not a man who stands by while others fight. If I had stayed, then it would not have been your papa who stayed. It would have been some other shell of a man."

That night Greg drove down to battalion headquarters so that Oleksii could attend a meeting. When they got there, they heard that the rest of the leadership wouldn't be back for an hour and a half.

"We've got some food, though," said the staff officers. Greg and Oleksii went to the kitchen, turned on flashlights, and sat down to eat while they waited. There was salo, the traditional Ukrainian pig fat dish, along with what Greg called "fresh-ish" bread, salted pickles, salted tomatoes, and sausage. Oleksii and Greg chatted, shooting the breeze, indulging in something close to normality. They were joined by a few other Legion staff officers. Then Oleksii went to his meeting and brought back the final details for their next mission.

12

APPROACH MARCH

Ginger thought this new mission looked a lot simpler than the last one. The mission that had turned into the eight-hour gunfight had come with relatively amorphous goals: simply move forward, over a fairly large amount of space, towards a Russian target. There was still plenty of work to do this time—they had been assigned six very large buildings to clear before they hit their target building—but it was much, much more specific. After such a big gunfight in which they took a decent amount of ground and no casualties, everyone was feeling pretty confident.

The mission was set slightly further south than the previous one, not far from the tall building that George had declared two days before that he didn't like the look of. This block was closer to home, still in the industrial section of the city, across the street from a big building that a sizable Belorussian unit was using as a base. They were to bump across into the city, link up with the Belorussians, and then take a team with them to clear a set of half-a-dozen buildings before they hit a Russian target building.

Their assigned buildings ran in two nearly parallel lines. From the satellite images on the maps, they looked like a Stonehenge plinth laid on its side. From the south, Buildings 1, 2, and 3 ran in a northward line, right up to the target building. Beyond them, further east, Buildings 8, 7, and 6 did the same. Buildings 3 and 6, identical to each other, were attached to the Russian target of Buildings 4 and 5 by catwalks. One catwalk ran between Buildings 3 and 6, across a broad alleyway. Another catwalk ran from Building 3 to 4.

Alpha, Charlie, and Black were assigned to clear Buildings 1, 2, and then 3. At the same time, the Belorussians would clear forward from

8, 7, and then to 6. This would land them right up against the Russian target buildings at the same time. From there, they would assault.

Intelligence estimated that the target buildings held approximately ten to fifteen Russian fighters. The teams would have tank support to "prep" the target buildings before their assault; in other words, the tankers would shoot the shit out of the place before they went in. They would have artillery support if they needed it, and the Belorussians were right around the corner.

Greg, with his bright blue, yellow, green, and red "good luck clowns" bandana wrapped around his left wrist, finally got a seat in the interior of one of the vehicles. As they sped along, he saw what the approach actually looked like. *Oh, shit*, he thought.

George sat against the left side this time. Loup was squashed in between the driver and the passenger seat, sitting as far back as possible on the center console so that his legs wouldn't interfere with the pedals. His back was half propped against George's knees. Prym, sharing the passenger seat with Symon, extended his arm across Loup's face in order to brace himself. The Georgian turned his face to the left, his cheek to Prym's forearm, and sat silently.

The Kozak rattled as it bumped over the potholes, mortar holes, and shell holes in what had once been smooth pavement. The smokestacks of Severodonetsk loomed in front of them as the Kozak rolled onto the bridge.

Oh yeah, I'm going back into Hell, thought George. *The bridge is probably even more shit since they've shot at it since last time*, eyeing the destroyed vehicles as they passed by.

"This fuckin' bridge, man," he muttered in English. "I can't believe the Russians haven't taken it out yet."

Inches away, George could see Loup. His handsome, dark-bearded face was a blank, calm and strangely elegant. His deep hazel eyes surveyed the road ahead, peering carefully over Prym's forearm. The B-negative mark on the Georgian's thick watchband was clearly visible. In a fundamentally uncomfortable position, he gave no indication of how he must have felt.

The Kozak rattled harshly as they sped past the burned-out cars and the overturned, empty lorry. The men's bodies rocked, kit and rifles shaking with the vibration. Loup blinked, very slowly.

The Belorussian base was a massive rectangular building, but what was above ground had nothing on what was below. The building continued underground for several stories; how many exactly, they never discovered. Like so many industrial buildings erected during the Soviet era, this one had been designed to withstand a nuclear attack.

What it had been before the war was unclear. Ginger, looking around, thought it had "seriously sketchy, ex-Soviet laboratory vibes," as if it had been used for questionable experiments in days gone by. To Michael, it felt like a former chemical plant or some sort of scientific factory. Dan decided that it looked like something out of the future war scenes from the first two *Terminator* movies.

The Russians, well aware that it was a large base, threw everything they had at it: shells, mortars, airbursts, white phosphorus. Day and night, the base was targeted with the rich variety of the Russian artillery arsenal. In a tribute to Soviet bunker architecture, it did very little. To the Belorussians, it was home. The base housed sixty men.

The International Legion teams entered through a series of long tunnels. They were narrow, perhaps the width of two men's shoulders across, and only about eight feet high. Crumbling and damp, the walls bore a dark green paint that covered the lower six feet and peeled off in large patches, along with chunks of wall, shaken out by the repeated artillery rounds. It was the middle of the day, but the generator did not light the tunnels. They could see only by the white lights mounted on their rifles or the NODs on their helmets.

They waited. Oleksii and Symon conferred with the Belorussians, who were tasked with escorting them to their target block, and who would back them up in case of an emergency.

The teams sat in the basement, in the dark. The men were mostly quiet, smoking e-cigarettes or chatting to pass the time. Michael conferred with Jordan, whom he had met that morning. The minutes turned to hours.

The drone operator ran down the stairs, his cell phone providing illumination. "Everyone gather round, we're going to do a brief," he declared.

He had sent up a drone. Positioned in the alleyway between the crosspiece of the Stonehenge (Buildings 4 and 5) and the "legs" (Buildings 3 and 6), the drone had hovered across from the Russian position. On video, it had captured what appeared to be a guard shift changing over. Ten Russians walked into the building. *Ten ducks in a row*, thought Ginger. Greg identified one as a member of Rosgvardiya, the Russian National Guard. Another had the classic Chechen look. Bald head, scruffy chinstrap beard, an AK-47 on one shoulder and a Dragunov sniper rifle on the other, he had no helmet and no protective gear but did wear a set of dark sunglasses. *Whoa*, thought Ginger, *that's a straight-up, no shit, like I've been killing people since the eighties sort of vibe.*

Taking down the AK, the Chechen shouldered the rifle and took a potshot at the drone. He missed, but the quadcopter's battery died, and it landed in the street.

"Holy shit," said Ginger. "Talk about eyes on."

Everyone got their kit ready to roll out. They moved across the basement, to the bottom of the stairs that would lead them to the front of the building. A second drone saw nothing. They had been briefed that the building held ten to fifteen guys. Now, looking at the footage, they assumed that the ten-man team they had seen were the only residents of the target building.

That's fuckin' too easy, thought Ginger. *We can take ten guys on our own.*

They crossed the street: Alpha, Charlie, and Black, plus a team of ten Belorussians, led by a broad, burly, red-bearded young man called Brest. The entry to the target block was through a blown-out concrete wall, not unlike the ones that had thwarted them on their previous mission. They climbed through the hole, down the rubble pile, and split up.

The Belorussians moved eastward to clear their sector: Buildings 8, 7, and 6. Alpha, Charlie, and Black moved to clear 1, 2, and 3. Building 1 was, Ginger complained, "super uneventful." As they waited to cross to Building 2, George stood just inside the door. Marti paced in front of him; the other men held close outside. Riever came to Marti's left shoulder, shifting on the balls of his feet.

Michael saw it first: a small, white quadcopter. Presumably, it was doing forward observation.

Michael strode back in through the door. "Drone," he said to George.

Everyone came back in. They waited. Riever turned and took up a kneeling position near Ginger, who was standing a few paces away, perpendicular to the door. Everyone was silent.

The drone did not appear to have seen them. It continued on its course and flew away. They moved up.

Charlie found a rathole in the first floor of Building 2, obscured by some sort of barrel. Outside, artillery boomed. Loup found a ladder. He carried it in one hand and the big SAW in the other, moving swiftly. He mounted a white light, installed his ladder, and climbed into the catacombs.

"Loup! Wait for me!" hissed Prym as the Georgian pushed ahead in the dark alone. There were no Russians or booby traps either above or below. They had hoped to find a connection to their target but had no luck.

The rest of Building 2 appeared similarly uneventful. Very large, it was some combination of auto-body shop, storage, and office space. The mostly open first floor was a blown-out, artilleried mess. In the middle of one big hall sat an old, Soviet-era Lada car, rusted to hell, with hood propped open. Random junk was strewn everywhere. A bright yellow barrel lay near the metal door, which looked southwest towards the Belorussian base. Greg sat behind the barrel, curled partly on his back, with rifle propped on his knees, trying to find space for his tall frame as he held security towards the north.

Alpha cleared forward while Charlie moved upstairs.

On the upper floor, a hall bore half-a-dozen doors opening into small rooms. Each was blown out, rubbled, nearly destroyed. The hall may have been in need of repair to begin with. The effect of repeated shelling, however, gave the place a look of a frat house after a really bad kegger. Everything was everywhere: bits of furniture, paper, random assorted items strewn across the floor. Some doorframes were completely missing, except for the big door to an interior room made of thick metal. Someone had been looking for something.

The floor was littered with pieces of concrete. There was no clear surface to walk on; chunks of wall, ceiling, and floor were strewn wherever artillery and gravity had deposited them. There was dust all over everything. The walls had once been painted a shade of robin's-egg blue, but now it peeled away in weird patterns, like dead skin after a bad sunburn. One wall had what looked like a childish elephant outlined on it with silly string; another bore a mark that looked suspiciously like a bloody handprint.

George was tail. Ahead of him were Loup and Marti. As silently as possible, they moved down the hall, checking each room, one man per side.

Loup halted, raising his right fist and closing his hand. Everyone stopped. Loup waited, rocked back on his right leg, with left knee slightly bent, ready to move: his standard holding stance. He pointed back down the hall.

George turned, and they all jogged back to the corner, moving left down the hallway. The interior of the building was now in between them and whatever Loup had seen. Loup stood at the corner junction, watching down the hall.

The sound was like a thousand tiny whistles, rockets coming one after the other, like fireworks, but louder and much, much faster. The pressure and percussion were much stronger than those of fireworks. It was not standard artillery. George took a knee, recognizing the telltale sound of white phosphorus: the Russians had lobbed a few shells of it at the Belorussian base.

From his position holding security on the first-floor door, Michael, sweating bullets but keeping his cool, saw the white phos burst in the air perhaps fifty to one hundred meters away. At night the chandelier shells looked very like much like silver fireworks. Now, during the day, they looked incongruous against the clear, bright blue sky. From somewhere, small birds still chirped. As the shells burst high in the sky, tiny streaks of the burning rain sailed downwards. They looked like flaming metallic strings or Christmas tree tinsel from Hell.

Very weird, thought Michael. *And very cool.*

Ginger was standing inside the building. At the awful, whistling shrieks, he turned towards Michael in the door. *Motherfucker*, he thought. *What the fuck is that?*

"They just white-phos'ed the Belorussians," Michael said. The sound was incredible.

Charlie completed clearing the top of the building. They were ready to move to Building 3. They needed to make sure that the

Belorussians were also ready to move into position in Building 6, directly across from them. Then they would both be right up against the target building.

The Ukrainian officers tried to raise the Belorussians on the radio. No connection. They could not be so far away, yet they could not make contact. Not wanting to give away their position by crossing in view of the Russian target building to confer in person, they tried again on the radio. Nothing.

It was wait or move forward. Clearing the two buildings, while simple, had already taken hours. They decided to move up.

They would infiltrate slowly, hoping to hear from the Belorussians. Alpha moved forward to clear Building 3. Black would pull security for them towards the rear, while Charlie held Building 2. George ended up at Greg's old position near the bright yellow barrel in the west-facing door of Building 2, another very tall man stuck in a very small spot.

Building 3 was empty, but it hadn't been so for long. It was a long, rectangular warehouse, perhaps two hundred feet long and seventy-five feet wide. From the sky, it would look something like a Duracell battery, if the copper-colored part of the battery were just a bit fatter than everything else. The wider part was closest to the target building.

Most of the building was made up of a massive, multi-story hall. There were small office-type rooms at either end, but this building was in even worse shape than Building 2. Rubble was everywhere. The only way to get across the building was by going up the staircase at the south end, closest to Building 2. From there, the teams climbed to the fifth floor. On the way they found rooms full of Russian sleeping bags.

Well, they're either using this and they're not here now, or they were using this building and they abandoned it, thought Ginger.

The landing on the fifth floor led to what had once been a hallway. It must have been hit by an artillery round on the roof above, because it was now full of big chunks of concrete. Moving carefully, they picked their way over the rubble. Turning a corner, they could see the wide-open hall of the fifth floor in front of them: a massive room that took up most of the building.

Alpha halted in the hallway. Rubble was everywhere, and the small, square tiles that covered the walls were chipped and falling to the floor. The Ukrainian officers tried again to contact the Belorussians on the radio and the Ukrainians across the street. The massive open room had enormous windows on both long sides, and they would have to cross within range of a Ukrainian position as they breached the target building. They did not want anyone on their own side to shoot them by mistake.

Riever sat perched on some rubble. Across from him, what looked like a medicine cabinet with a big, dusty glass sliding door hung crooked on the wall, catching him in a muddy reflection. Tired, streaked with sweat and dust from the hot summer day, he was already a mess. Ginger leaned nonchalantly against the jamb of another door, his feet planted crookedly on the piles of rubble that made up the floor, and exhaustedly smoked an e-cig and debated whether to take a shit before they got any closer to the target. Dan took out his impersonal, wiped "mission phone," and took pictures of both of them, just in case.

After twenty minutes or so, they had not been able to contact the Belorussians. They moved across the wide open space, slowly and carefully. The ceiling, which appeared to be made of metal, was held up with two sets of rafters, which met at a series of pillars that bisected the loft. The floor was littered with pallets and what appeared to be the remnants of grain. There was a massive hole, perhaps twenty feet long, from an artillery shell in the ceiling.

This far up, they had a spectacular view of the city. Dan looked out. It was not the eerie glow that he and Ginger had seen from the rooftop a few days before, but it was a sight nonetheless: a big, modern, first-world city, slowly on fire, in a perpetual haze not from the usual pollution but from the dust constantly thrown up by the shells that landed everywhere. Plumes of smoke rose in every direction.

Tex and Michael were ordered to set up in a ground-floor doorway of Building 3. Directly across the street from them was Building 6, now visible as a Nova Posta facility, the Ukrainian equivalent of a USPS sorting center. Their job was to wait for squirters—any Russians who decided to flee towards them down the alley. Tex set up his PKM, along with his belts containing eight hundred rounds of armor-piercing ammunition. Michael readied his Bren and laid out his grenades on the ground beside him. If worst came to worst, a dozen Russians might be coming their way in a relatively confined space.

Lying prone in the west-facing door on the ground floor of Building 3, George looked out to see an old man riding a bike from north to south alongside their buildings. *Where's he going?* the Canadian thought, confused. It was so bizarre that it didn't register properly. The man was unarmed, but he had no business being where he was. There was nothing to the south of them other than Ukrainian positions. "Hey, a guy with a bike just rode past," George called. "Fucking someone go get him."

Greg ran after the cyclist. *There is no rhyme or reason to be riding a bike with artillery and shit going on*, he thought. With his long legs pumping, the medic raced after the man and caught up with him, speaking in Ukrainian. Artillery was exploding everywhere. There were no more true civilians in Severodonetsk: anyone who claimed to be was probably just a Russian sympathizer and spy, like the prisoner the Georgians had caught during their last mission. *He's likely looking for positions.*

Oleksii took another soldier and delivered the cyclist to the Belorussian base, where the men there said that they had seen someone riding a bike just before they were shelled on several of the previous days.

In Building 3, George walked carefully towards the corridor that led to the stairs, as Charlie moved into position. Ahead of him was an auto-body shop in whose western door he had just been lying prone, with a very shiny black Jeep and a silver Land Rover neatly parked in the bays. To his left was the access to the staircase, through a dark, narrow hallway. George looked back towards Building 2. Jordan was holding security, sitting on a black office swivel chair, eyes on the door, with his rifle at ready, propped for firing on a tire set on top of a barrel.

George followed Prym up the stairs, with Marti and Loup right behind him. The heat weighed on him as he trudged up the stairs. Debris was everywhere, the result of more Russian looting. On the landing between the second and third floors, George passed some of Alpha's gear, including Riever's jerry-rigged bag and rocket carrier. As he turned to go up the next half-flight, he heard Prym clucking, trying to scoot a large, chestnut-colored dog out of the way. It had a splotch of white on its upper right shoulder and a dent in the thick fur around his neck, as if a collar had once been there. The dog moved slowly but amiably out of the way, climbing down the stairs past George, its hips and haunches looking thin. The rest of the men ignored him.

The debris worsened the higher they climbed, the apparent result of both shelling and junk storage. On the fifth floor, Prym turned right off the landing. The same pale-blue paint peeled from the walls. The floor was covered in pieces of rubble the size of large bricks. Prym picked his way carefully, tottering from side to side, overbalancing to compensate for the Matador slung across his back.

"*Shh,*" Prym held his finger to his lips as he came to the corner, where Riever had waited across from the barely hanging medicine cabinet. Squeezing the radio, he called, "Alpha from Charlie, Alpha from Charlie. We come from behind. Repeat, we come from behind. How you copy?"

After confirmation, they pressed ahead. Marti and Loup moved forward, the Georgian covering the big window to their right. They crept carefully across the big, open grain loft. George walked behind and to the right of Loup, who carried his big SAW like a simple rifle, a double-action 9 mm pistol strapped to his right thigh in a drop-leg, fast-draw holster. As they entered the hall at the northernmost end, closest to the Russian position, Loup carefully pulled his electronic ear protection back over his ears. Dan stood at the corner, quietly confirming the passage of Charlie Team. Ahead of them in the hall was the entrance to the staircase down which they would descend and make their assault.

Waiting for the Ukrainian officers to finish their assault planning, Riever and Ginger sat quietly on the top floor, overlooking the target building. They were seven meters from it. They could see the boxes of MRE stores, and see and hear the Russian generator outside. They were practically on top of the enemy. Riever could look through the row of smashed windows into the wrecked apartments. He scanned, imagining what a Russian head would look like if one was dumb enough to be so high up in the building. There was a huge Ukrainian flag in one room hanging on the wall. It had a yellow trident in the middle, and one corner had come unfastened and drooped.

"Ginger," said Riever, "what do we do if our generator goes out?"

"We send Tex's dumb ass out there to fix it," replied Ginger.

"Yes, exactly. We should wait for an explosion and hit that generator with a rifle. They won't realize it was us, so they'll send one of their privates out to check it. We fucking whack him with a couple of suppressed rifles and wait for the next one. Then they'll send someone looking for him, and we'll shoot that guy."

"Dude, that's some movie shit!" scoffed Ginger, and they both laughed.

"Goddammit, what the fuck is Yuri doing out there; go check it out, Ivan," Ginger said, imitating a pissed-off Russian NCO. They laughed. It was a situation they lived through many times a day. The generator went down and the Starlink went down and everyone yelled for someone (usually the amiable Tex) to get off their ass and restart the bitch.

"We could probably get at least a couple of them, maybe even the whole squad," said Riever.

"Dude, that makes sense. Let's do that." They started debating the specifics. Neither thought Symon would go for it, but the absurdity of it made it an attractive minor tactic.

On the ground floor, Michael and Tex learned that they were being reassigned as a support-by-fire element to Mykola, in the northern stairwell of Building 3, right up against the Russian target building. They packed up their gear, squeezed through the dark antechamber, and started to climb the stairs.

In Building 3, everyone was crammed into a tiny hallway, made even smaller by the thick pile of concrete debris and slabs of what looked like slate that took up all but a foot of passable space. Dmitri took a knee in the fifth-floor stairwell, holding security towards the window, which looked directly out onto the Russian target building.

Now they were very, very close. When Michael and Tex came in from their position holding the alleyway door, Michael was surprised to be shushed. "They're right there," everyone mouthed, pointing. *Oh*, thought Michael. *Okay. This is happening.* The Russian generator was still running in the background.

Leaving his big medical bag for safekeeping as directed, Greg switched places with Dmitri, leaning his long frame forward in order to take a video of the alleyway with his phone. Coming back into the stairwell, he held it out for the officers, who debated in Ukrainian.

George watched the proceedings from his spot on the wall, in front of Loup. "We're making a new entry?" asked Loup quietly in French, as George shed his backpack and rocket with Prym's permission.

"Yes, I asked Prym and he said yes," whispered George.

The Georgian's face was impassive. George's thoughts whirled in his head. Of all the things that soldiers can do, an urban assault on a fortified position is one of the most complex, arguably even the worst, of assignments. The angles of fire are challenging, intelligence can be poor, visibility can be awful, resupply and casualty evacuation are limited, and the possibility of getting trapped in a bad position is high. The enemy can be right next to you without you even knowing it, as they had proven with the Russians just now. It was not the sort of thing you generally did with fewer than two dozen men, no matter how highly trained they were.

We're doing this? For real? Actually? This is retarded, George thought, suddenly realizing how surreal the situation was. Would he really be coming back for the backpack he'd just left on the floor? But there was no other option if they wanted to accomplish anything. A few feet away, Prym, Symon, and Greg hissed quietly in Ukrainian. Artem, grinning at Marti, caught George's eye as he turned back, and stopped smiling. *I guess we're doing this.*

13

MAKING AN ENTRANCE

There turned out to be two versions of the plan. In French, it was explained to Charlie Team that they would descend the staircase first, fire two Matador rockets at the door, and make a full-on assault, with Alpha following behind and Black Team after them. Prym, Marti, and George would go down the stairs. Loup, with his SAW, was directed to find a good position on a higher floor, from which he could provide covering fire. "Mykola," whispered Prym, "you stay here." From the base of the stairwell, Mykola and his PKM would provide cover.

Meanwhile, Symon, speaking quietly, huddled with Dan over a cell phone bearing a map of their target building. Dan heard a slightly different plan. He expected Alpha to mount their night optical devices (NODs), despite the daylight: they would be creeping into the open door to the target building's basement, from which they would infiltrate for an assault while Charlie waited for word to enter the first floor.

Dan came up the stairs to find Riever and Ginger.

"Mount your NODs, guys, we're going in."

"Mount our NODs?" demanded Ginger, looking out of the window at the bright blue sky.

"We're going to infil the basement and clear it while Charlie and Black cover the top floors," said Dan.

"Alright, whatever, dude," said Ginger, giving up on the generator idea and getting his NODs ready.

Tank support arrived. The tankers would fire into their target building from the northern side. This would mean that while they were shooting at the Russians, they were also technically shooting at the teams, who were holed up on the far side of the target building.

Dan wasn't worried about the possibility of friendly fire. These were very large buildings, with a lot of concrete. The target building, Greg had noted, was marked as a Cold War-era atomic bomb shelter. The tank wasn't going to take the Russians out and do their job for them, but it would certainly rattle the enemy and keep their heads down while the teams set up for their assault.

While everyone stacked up in Building 3, the Ukrainian tank rolled up outside the target building. A drone captured the impact of the rounds from afar. The tank drove along the backside of the target, the rounds producing massive yellow muzzle flash as they burst from the barrel. The impacts created huge puffs of dust, miniature mushroom clouds turned on their side. The pressure wave was easily visible on the watching drone's camera, where it made the entire screen ripple, as though it had momentarily turned liquid. The backside of their block turned a shade of mixed taupe and grey, forming its own localized sandstorm of vaporized concrete.

Though the target building was still standing, it had definitely been rattled. Intercepted chatter on the radio was passed down: the Russians had one wounded that they might try to evacuate. One down, nine to go, the teams thought.

On the fifth floor everyone was sweating in their kit, making final plans. Oleksii stepped forward to adjust the straps on Dmitri's plate carrier. Marti shook out his limbs, the boxer staying limber. Symon gave his big pirate's sigh, finally looking as young as he actually was. Loup double-checked his instructions, his face still smooth and brow unfurrowed, and went to take up his position in the stairwell, covering what would be their position in the alley through the big window.

Dan, Riever, and Ginger climbed down the stairs and took up their positions in the stack. *Like fish in a barrel*, grumbled Ginger to himself as he crammed in. *What a tiny-ass fuckin' entrance to this stairwell*. It was still over ninety degrees.

Then they moved into the stairwell itself. Prym was first, George just behind him. Prym moved quickly but carefully, his rifle holding on the big windows that illuminated each floor as he went. On the first floor, he turned on the white light on his rifle to strobe in order to clear a long, messy closet off the hall. Then he followed the jigged hallway as it turned away from the stairwell facing the target building and led to a door onto the alleyway between Buildings 3 and 6, just under the big catwalk. Behind him, everyone filed slowly and carefully down the stairs.

The approach to the door was completely dark, except for small shafts of light from bullet and shrapnel holes in the metal door. From inside, the door glowed like a much taller and uglier version of a colonial tin lantern.

"*Shhhh! Kurwa*," whispered Prym to the men behind him as he crept up to the door. It was actually two doors, almost like fancy French doors in basic design, except they were entirely metal. Inches away, Prym bent down, trying to use the crack in the middle of the two doors to see. He put his left hand forward, checking for the handle. He found it, an L-shaped metal rod that slid from the left-side door across to a catch on the right. He worked it back and forth, sliding it away from the locking position. The rod came free.

Prym exhaled sharply, and slowly removed both hands from the door. Then he gently took the left door's handle in between the thumb and forefinger of his gloved left hand, and slowly pushed it open.

The sunlight illuminated the doors, revealing them to be bubbling, flaking, and barely holding together, their metal nearly incinerated by what must have been a huge explosion. The completely burned-out car just outside the door and what had once been a Sprinter van parked just beyond it looked little better.

The door thunked and creaked, scraping along the rubble at its base. It would not swing all the way out. Prym got it about eighty degrees open, looking through the crack at the hinges towards the target building, now to his left. He stepped out, turned his rifle left, and crept across the alley under the catwalk, taking cover behind the Sprinter van, whose tires had melted off the wheels.

Behind him came Marti and Dan, tucking behind the van. As George crossed, he stepped awkwardly on a piece of debris and sprained his ankle. Adrenaline dulled the pain as he took a spot behind Riever and in front of Dmitri, across the alley, where they used the bump-out on the side of Building 6 as cover. From there they could lean out for shots. Ginger was behind Prym, Greg just beside him, heading towards the men on the projecting corner of Building 6. Black Team stacked up in the doorway, ready to go, with Doug on point.

Prym held security to the left of the van, which sat facing the target building. Dan stood to his right, Marti kneeling at the right side of the van, and Alpha moving towards Building 6. They waited.

What the actual fuck is going on? thought Greg. *Why are we all bunched up?*

"Marti, Marti," whispered Prym hoarsely. "Towards that door there! That door there, in front, in front," he said, in French, as Dan stood by next to him.

Marti swung his Matador off his back, kneeling on the ground as he prepped the rocket. Then he shouldered it quickly and stepped into the middle of the alley. Ginger stood behind Prym, facing away, expecting that the Matadors would not be fired until Alpha had infiltrated the target building's basement.

"Watch out for the backblast. He's gonna fire," Greg said to Ginger, quietly but urgently. Ginger turned and saw Marti with the Matador on his shoulder. He started running out of the way of the backblast, diving towards the bump-out corner of Building 3, across the alley from the rest of his team. Doug ducked back into the stairwell of Building 3.

"*Attention!*" hissed Prym. Dan looked sharply to his left. *Oh, shit*, he thought.

"*Direct, direct!*" ordered Prym, motioning Marti towards the target building. Marti took a knee.

"*Attention*," said Prym. From the opposite side of the target building, they could hear the Ukrainian tank sending rounds into the Russians.

Boom! went the Matador, striking the target building's door. Somewhere, a window broke, and the sound of shattering glass filled the air.

Dust flew everywhere. For a moment the target building was completely obscured in a vaporized concrete haze. *Slapslapslapslapslapslap!* An enemy rifle opened up, firing rapidly on semi-auto, sending rounds flying down into the cross-alley in front of the target building. The confusion as to whether Alpha or Charlie was supposed to go first may have saved them all: the enemy was shooting right where Alpha had expected to infil into the enemy basement. The Russian fire increased: there were more than ten men in that building.

Dan, tucked against the right side of the van, fired several shots towards the enemy positions. But he could see that the enemy were on the upper floors of the tall target building. *Well, gig's up*, he thought. The low ground would not help them now; they needed to get back up their original staircase in order to duke it out with the Russian gunners firing from the upper floors.

"*Kurwa*," said Prym. In Building 3, Loup and the other machine-gunners fired back. The sound was tremendous.

"Shoot that way," Prym shouted in French towards the stairwell, gesturing towards the Russians. "Enemy, enemy!" Marti swapped places with Dan, who was already headed towards the stairwell, trying to gain the higher ground. Prym swung his own Matador off his back. Ducking behind a narrow metal pillar that held up the catwalk, he prepped the rocket while everyone else fired towards the target building. He braced, and fired, hitting the wall next to the door. *Boom!*

Marti fired from behind the van, Prym joining him. Tucked behind his bump-out corner, Riever fired carefully placed single shots in each window. George took a knee behind him. Everyone looked for shots. Bullets flew everywhere. Prym threw a grenade, one of the French ones that George had found on their last mission. Marti dashed towards Ginger, while Prym ran to the opposite side, next to Greg and Dmitri.

"I see muzzle flashes," shouted Dmitri, gesturing up towards the catwalk. He tucked behind a bump-out south of Riever's. "Riever, behind you!" he shouted, firing rapidly from behind the other soldier.

From his position along Building 3's projecting corner, Ginger could see three or four rounds hit the stairwell door, not ten feet from him. Then they adjusted, three or four more walking along the ground closer and closer to him. He took cover and put just his barrel and suppressor around the corner, following the bullets' trajectory through his optic. On the first floor of the target building, in the doorframe one room deep into the building just to the right of the door, was a Russian soldier aiming right at him.

Smart, thought Ginger. It didn't matter so much when the buildings were made of such stout concrete, but fighting from deep within a building was the right way to do it. You had much better cover that way and you stayed in shadow, so it was harder for the opposition to see you. These guys weren't conscripts; they knew what they were doing.

He saw the Russian peeking out. He fired once. The Russian stuttered, having been hit in the arm. Ginger fired twice more. The Russian went down hard. *Well, he dropped like a sack of shit*, thought Ginger, *I must have got him in the chest.*

He took a knee and looked up. Someone was skipping rounds off the ground at him. Ginger saw the gunner, a Russian on the second floor this time. Ginger shot, and saw the other soldier duck behind a window. The angle was hard. Ginger watched as one of his rounds pinged off the catwalk above him. *Too high.* But the Russian soldier never reappeared. *No way I fuckin' hit him*, Ginger thought, looking at the angle. *Hopefully someone else killed him, or he just fucked off.*

Dan moved up the original staircase of Building 3 with his big SAW. In the alleyway, he had been able to see PKM machine-gun rounds chopping down from an upper window, but he needed to climb higher in order to get an angle on the enemy gunner. As he made his way up the stairs, a window broke behind him as he was about to turn the switchback and head up to the next floor. He sucked into the tight corner, right up against the wall, barely missing the rounds flying past him. *I'm glad I'm as skinny as I am*, he thought, surprised at himself. *This guy's sending concrete into my face.* The rounds were disintegrating the concrete next to his head.

Shit, thought Dan. *I was trying to go up to get an angle to kill this PKM gunner and there's another guy waiting to ambush* me.

He waited. It felt like an eternity, though the SEAL knew that in fact it was probably not even a full minute. Then the firing stopped. The enemy gunner needed to reload. Dan ran across the window opening and continued up the stairs. He moved up, carefully and alone, firing at muzzle flashes as he went. It was dark on the other side; all he could see were muzzle flashes a room or two deep. At the top was Loup, with his SAW. Dan called to Loup, and the impassive Georgian covered the rest of his moves up the stairwell.

On the top floor, there were several rooms, lined with windows. Dan moved between them, taking shots when he could see Russian targets.

Michael moved up the stairs in Building 3, trying to find a good angle. There were no shots from the level where the rest of the team had left him. He came across a series of bathrooms just to the east of the stairwell, with windows. From there he could see shots into the enemy building as the firing lit up.

But he was also keenly aware that the enemy building was taller than his, and that there were windows above him. He couldn't see anything in them, because the Russians had duct-taped black garbage bags across them as cover. As the bullets flew back and forth, the bags got shredded, turning into eerie dark plastic streamers or screens that still gave cover to the enemy within. *I'm going to get shot out of one of those windows*, Michael thought. He moved from bathroom to bathroom, hoping to make himself a harder target. He looked for smoke and muzzle flashes, trying to find the enemy gunners.

"Prym, this doesn't make sense. Let's clear this building to the right," shouted Greg, waving and gesturing above the noise in the alley towards Building 6. The Belorussians had never moved up to clear it, and they had no idea what was inside or if it could help them flank the Russians.

They ran together halfway down the building, past what seemed like several garage doors, jumping up onto a foot-high platform that rested outside a row of doors. "*Attendez!*" shouted Prym, a call in French that Greg would not have understood even if he'd heard it. Prym called to Symon on the radio, warning him of their progress.

Greg found a standard door, for people rather than vehicles. It was locked. He backed up and aimed a kick at the handle. It didn't budge. They kept running, looking for another one.

Near the far end of the building, past a grey, shot-up Sprinter van whose tires had been looted, was an outdoor metal staircase. It looked almost like a fire escape and led to a door on the exterior of the second floor. They raced towards it.

"Fuck!" shouted Greg.

Prym reached the door first. Leaning against it was a piece of debris that had probably been part of the roof at one point. It looked like an enormous slab of puffed rice cake. He shoved it to the side, muttering *suka* as he went. Finally, he jerked the door open. It opened outwards, towards him. He stepped back and Greg jumped inside, rifle up. George was just a few steps down, heading towards the door.

Feet inside the door, Greg nearly tripped over debris from shelling in the hall. "Fuck!" he declared.

The medic started clearing the first room on the left. Suddenly, rifle fire burst down the hall, from the direction of the door he'd just come through. It was Prym.

Alarmed, Greg stuck his head back out into the hall. "Did you see somebody?"

"Oh, no, just in case," replied Prym. He was breathing heavily as he loaded a new magazine.

Um, that makes sense, thought Greg dryly. *Reasons.*

Marti jumped in, taking the spot in front of Prym and Greg as he led the way down the hall.

Stacked up at the base of the stairwell, Black Team waited their turn to cross. Artem fired covering shots out of the door towards the target building. As he pulled back in, someone yelled, "Contact! It was close," in French.

Artem could see his team standing in a row: Doug ready at the door, Jordan just behind him, followed by Big Max, Samuel, and Pedro. Oleksii gestured towards the target building, Artem just behind his right shoulder.

Oleksii jumped out into the alley, using the door for cover as far as he could. He shot towards the target building, providing covering fire. Doug sprinted out of the door, tapping Oleksii on his left shoulder as he went. Right behind him came Jordan, followed by Artem and the rest of the team. Doug dashed to the bump-out corner of Building 3, past Riever and Dmitri. Jordan was almost literally on his heels, the young Brit practically flying, with his rifle in his right hand. Black Team made it to the side of Building 3 and worked their way down, following Charlie Team as they entered Building 3 from the outdoor metal staircase.

"Move, move, move!" came the order. "Get in!"

"Yeah, come on in," called George from just inside the door.

"Come on," said Prym.

They cleared forward into Building 6. The ceiling was falling in, cheap panels busted open above them, detritus of insulation hanging down into the hall. At the end, they came upon a T-junction. Left would take them back towards the target building, giving them the ability to flank. They turned, finding another short, office-like hall with small rooms off it. Beyond it was a huge bay, almost exactly like the long grain silo of Building 6.

"Wait, wait, before you run!" said Greg as Prym was about to step out. "Belorussians." They were holed up in Building 7, beside and behind them. A few bullets flew across the open area. From their position the Belorussians could see through the huge open windows of this bay. The chances of friendly fire were high.

"We need to get contact with Belorussians! They are in that building," Greg gestured, "so they don't shoot at us!"

Prym worked the radio in Russian while everyone stacked up in the hall: George in the corner closest to Prym, Jordan next to him, then the rest of Black Team, and Marti across from them.

"Watch that fuckin' window, it has a hole through it," George pointed out. "Yes, come here," Marti gestured, pulling Doug across the hall and away from the window angle.

Prym bellowed on the radio, announcing their position in the Nova Posta building. He was so loud, echoing across the big room, that it seemed the Belorussians next door might hear him without the electronics.

He got confirmation. "Go, go," said Prym, in a smattering of French, English, and Ukrainian. They moved out, in a cautious but fast dance down the broad, windowed bay.

Ginger cracked in over the radio. "Black Team, this is Alpha, what's going on?" After a few moments with no response, he tried again. "Black Team, this is Alpha, what's going on in there?" They weren't getting through. The radio waves were too full.

Finally, Dan managed to break in. Symon had told him of Prym's flanking maneuver. "Okay, boys, we want to keep 'em tied up on this side while Prym flanks. Keep your fire controlled." As Charlie and Black approached the north end of their building, the enemy fire got louder and louder. Outside, the artillery boomed.

Greg made it across the big room first, passing through a small dark corridor that led onto a stairwell.

"Two people, clear right," said the medic, gesturing towards a room while he investigated the stairs.

Prym pushed forward into the small, dark space, with his white light on strobe as he swept the gun up and down, checking walls and ceilings in the style of the French Foreign Legion's urban warfare specialists. Marti was soon behind him. The tiny spaces were tiled everywhere, perhaps former bathrooms. Now debris littered the floor, but they were otherwise empty.

On the landing, Greg was taking charge.

"Black Team! Up," he said, pointing towards the upper floors. "Go up, right here."

"We're going downstairs?" asked Jordan as he arrived, his compact young body moving easily into the space without hesitation.

"You guys are going up. We're going down," said Greg. "Up, up!" He gestured to the rest of Black Team. "We're gonna try to open a door so we can communicate with our guys. You guys go up. We're going down," Greg repeated, heading down the stairs in the lead.

Above him, Black Team moved carefully, leaning around the angles of the switchback staircase, checking how visible they were to the target building across the street. The staircase was a near mirror of its sister in Building 3 across the alley: huge windows opened onto the street on almost every floor. If any Russians were watching, they would easily be able to see anyone moving up or down the stairs.

Prym followed just behind Greg, Marti behind him, with George as tail. Greg looked down the stairs, framed against the window that led towards the first floor. There was no angle for covering fire. He dashed down as quickly as possible, with Charlie Team following close behind. "Friendlies, friendlies!" Greg shouted as he went, yelling for the rest of Alpha still fighting it out in the alleyway outside. From above, Big Max's voice drifted down in a shout: "Bogey to our right! Give me two, give me two!"

"Marti, you covering this side?" Greg asked as he approached the next section of the switchback. Prym fired out of the window, his unsuppressed Bren 2 booming in the stairwell, to clear the way for Marti and George to descend. Greg had made it to the bottom; Black was still heading up.

"I need somebody with me!" shouted Greg as Charlie Team started to move.

"I'm here, I'm here, I need help!" Greg shouted as he began to clear a small antechamber between the stairs and the rest of the ground floor.

"Hey! We're here!" Greg shouted from a window to Ginger and Riever in the alleyway. "Yeah, we're upstairs, this is all ours!"

At the same time Prym was trying to open a creaking metal door out into the alleyway, but it was locked.

Marti broke down a grated metal door that led to the rest of the ground floor. It was the Nova Posta sorting center: pallets, packages, cardboard boxes, and bright red metal shelves and racks littered the floor. Mail still waiting to be sent sat in cubbyholes at Marti's left shoulder. On the same wall as the stairwell, facing the target building, were a series of small offices, also looted and trashed. The rest consisted of two open rooms with large garage doors, presumably used for loading the mail trucks.

They cleared the small rooms and the large one. Prym tried to raise Symon on the radio: what was going on, and where was everyone? The volume of fire was still high; a few shots seemed to come from the east, where the Belorussians were meant to be.

Inside Building 6, Greg heard Dmitri shout, "I'm on my last mag," as he reloaded. Within ten minutes the Green Beret had gone through seven magazines.

Holy shit, thought Greg, *this is World War III here.*

"*Blyat*," said Prym.

Black Team had moved up the stairwell. It was a mirror image of the one in its sister building across the alley. The staircase crisscrossed back and forth in front of enormous windows that looked directly into the target building, the one from which the astonishingly heavy volume of Russian fire was coming. It took traversing two sets of steps, nine apiece—one directly against the window, the other running next to it—to move between each floor. A narrow landing marked each floor and half-floor, where the stairs turned.

What they had was only a staircase. The landings led to nowhere except on the fourth floor; beyond them was probably the giant lofted areas of the lower floors that had once served as a postal depot. They reached the roof, connected to their mirror-image sister building by a skyway. They ran across to the next staircase, cleared it, and started to move back.

Bullets began whizzing past their heads. They ducked back into the far staircase, looking for a moment to cross back to their original passage up. They took it one at a time, covering for each other. Doug took a knee facing the target building. Muzzle flashes and smoke blew out of a window opposite them. Doug, exposed but cool, fired back, covering.

The enemy now knew exactly where they were. There was only one way down.

14

STAIRWELLS AND A TANK

Tucked in his shallow corner in the alley, Riever was still facing the target building. His right shoulder was to the wall. In order to see the enemy, he had to lean out left in order to get a clear shot. He was limited in his angles by the rifle resting in his right shoulder.

Riever was right-handed and, like most people, shot that way too. But all special operations soldiers are trained to shoot from the left side as well, for a situation just like this. *I'm not gonna shoot lefty*, he thought. *That's just some gamer shit.*

The bullets flew past. The roar of the dueling machine guns increased. *That's so dumb. If I was ever going to do it, now would be the time.* He switched hands and kept firing.

Across the alley, just forward of him and next to the burned-out door, Oleksii was still firing. He took a grenade from his kit, grinned his television star grin beneath his dark sunglasses, and gestured to Riever.

"Fuck yeah!" Riever replied, grabbing one from his kit. He ducked back into cover, behind his little corner bump-out wall. He grabbed the frag from the right side of his kit and pulled the pin. Quickly, he stepped to the left and threw the grenade overhand. It was one of his favorite Russian impact grenades, heavy and tricky to use but very effective. He threw, and the grenade exploded on impact just short of the target building's door. He looked back towards the door to the stairwell. Oleksii had disappeared.

The burned-out door provided some cover for Oleksii, but it was a bad spot. Partly obscured by its position under the big catwalk, the door was still a magnet for the enemy gunners. All sorts of ammunition and pieces of shrapnel were flying into the alley and into the first few feet under the catwalk, very close to the door, pinging everywhere. Still, they were so close to their target.

Oleksii pulled the pin on the grenade. He stepped to the right, in between the door, which was stuck almost perpendicular to the wall on its screaming hinges, and the burned-out car next to it. He pulled his right arm back to throw the grenade.

Just as his arm went past the vertical, he felt something hit him. "*Pizdets!*" he muttered. He finished the throw, the grenade exploding in the street in front of the target building. Turning, he stepped and tripped back into the base of the stairwell.

There was a gaping hole in his throat. A bullet had cut open something big as it descended downwards into his chest. He needed a medic, immediately.

A few minutes later Riever saw Brest, the Belorussian leader, suddenly pop out of the door, shouting. Dmitri yelled back in Russian, then took off towards the door and the back of the building.

In Building 6, Greg heard a calm and quiet voice in English break over the shouting on the radio. "Get your aid bag. Get your aid bag, first floor." Somewhere, someone was down.

In Building 6, Greg and Prym worked to open one of the big, garage-style doors that gave access to the alley. They were not electrified. Large, chrome-colored chains, wrapped around anchor points, served as levers to raise the door.

It was locked. Prym unhooked the chains. As he worked, hand over hand, a boom and a flash lit the air in front of him as Greg shot the lock off. Prym hauled on the chains, and the door rose. In front of them was the alley, filled with gunfire.

"Holy fuck," exclaimed Greg. To his left he saw Dmitri running towards the entrance to the stairwell.

"Dmitri!" shouted Greg. "Dmitri! Third floor, Dmitri!" He pointed up, to where he had been told to leave the bag. *Well, I guess he's got that building*, thought Greg as Dmitri ran past, *and I've got this one*.

In Building 3, Dan's radio was useless: there was yelling in Russian and Ukrainian, but he couldn't get a connection or a word in. As ground commander of Alpha, the SEAL needed to be able to communicate. That meant going back down the stairs.

He made it without getting more concrete thrown in his face by enemy gunners. On the first floor was a body lying in a pool of blood, with Dmitri working over him. *Is that Doug?* Dan thought, seeing the dark beard around the chin. But it was too dark to tell, and there was no time anyway. Dmitri needed Greg's aid bag, the one that Dan knew Greg had been told to leave at the top of the stairs on the third floor. *Priorities have changed*, thought the SEAL grimly, running back up the stairs for the med bag, timing his runs to avoid the enemy gunners who were watching for him as he went.

Collecting the aid bag, Dan started to move back down the stairs. Below him he could see someone heading up, not realizing that Dan had already gotten the bag. "Stop there!" Dan shouted. "Don't cross the window! They've got this thing keyed in." He threw the bag down, across the window. He turned and began to move back up the stairs to continue firing his SAW from the upper floors. He still didn't know who had been hit. He also had no idea where Ginger or Riever were, and he couldn't raise either man on the radio.

Soon he was pinned in the stairwell again. He shouted up to Tex two floors above him, who had a PKM. Dan tried to walk Tex in on the enemy gunner as the Texan hammered armor-piercing rounds across the street. Michael joined in on another machine-gunner, working with the SEAL.

A Russian F1 pineapple grenade came sailing back at Dan. He watched it land fifteen feet from him, just outside his window but one floor beneath him on the ground. Then it exploded, practically in his face. He felt just a bit of wind and pressure—like George two days before, he was either very lucky or Russian grenades were, as he put it later, "not quality stuff."

At the corner of one Building 3 landing was the skyway to the Russian target building. The corner formed a pillar, the anchor beam of the skyway. Immediately to its left was the huge window that looked into the staircase and across to the Russians shooting at them. To the right of the pillar was the skyway.

Mykola ordered Michael to hold the skyway at all costs. Michael tucked as tight as possible behind the pillar, trying to take as much cover as he could from the small piece of concrete.

At one point, he fired a few rounds down the skyway when the whole staircase was ordered to give covering fire. He saw tracers fly back at him in response from the hallway in the Russian building. Just a few feet away, in the darkness, someone was doing the same thing as he was.

At the corner of a set of stairs there was a concrete beam lying horizontal and in front of the corner, allowing Michael to prone out. He could see and shoot down at the bottom three floors while under cover. Though he couldn't shoot directly across, an enemy machine-gunner was shooting directly at him. Michael could see the dust and bits of gravel thrown up from the enemy PKM rounds hitting just on the other side of his position.

Mykola popped out from above and to the left of Michael, up the steps. He let off a huge Rambo burst with his PKM, shouting "Welcome to Ukraine, *sukas!*" in English. *Well, that's a highlight*, thought Michael as he looked up just in time to see Dan, further up the staircase, say in frustration, "That's not tactical. You don't need to yell."

On the ground floor Oleksii was struggling to talk or breathe. There was no visible exit wound. Presumably shot from a high angle, the bullet had entered Oleksii's neck and driven downwards into his chest.

Anything that goes into the neck will likely damage something critical to survival. A bullet traveling at high speed or an irregular piece of shrapnel will cause not just holes but tears, and will likely damage multiple things—vessels, tissue, etc.—on the way.

Oleksii was bleeding heavily. Whether the bullet had severed the trachea, the esophagus, or both, Dmitri did not and could not know. The amount of blood indicated that a major vessel, probably an artery, had been hit, and the bullet was still inside. External bleeding can be stopped, with sufficient tools and effort. Internal bleeding is another matter, and it will kill you. Internal bleeding that pools in the lungs will kill you, by drowning, very quickly.

Dmitri managed to get the external bleeding stopped. But Oleksii was choking on his own blood. Dmitri made the decision to perform a cricothyrotomy, also known as a cric: he would cut straight into

Oleksii's neck, insert a tube to the lungs, and essentially create an alternative airway, free of blood. If Oleksii was bleeding into his esophagus, and he was simply choking on the blood that was getting stuck in his throat, then the cric would save him.

If the bullet had torn through his trachea and he was bleeding into his lungs, there was no hope. It takes very little blood in the lungs to kill a person. In that case even a full surgical team in a level-one trauma center would have been unlikely to be able to put Oleksii back together. They had no evac available to get Oleksii to any hospital at all, because the Russians were shelling the bridge. Dmitri did not know whether the trachea was compromised or not, but the cric was his best and, even with the big aid bag, his only option.

A cric requires very specific tools. In layman's terms, you need to find a very specific set of cartilage that sits on the front side of the throat, slice into it, and shove a special, flexible tube down the incision, down alongside the trachea, and into the lungs. This leaves a small piece of plastic tube sticking out of the throat. With luck, the patient will breathe on his own. If not, you can attach an empty bottle to the end tube and pump it in order to press air into the lungs. Dmitri tore Greg's aid bag apart, found what he needed, and started working on the cric.

In Ukrainian, over the radio, Greg heard Artem calling for help: he was trying to reach the men in Building 3, across the alley. "We're pinned down! We're pinned down!" Greg heard Artem yelling. Black Team was stuck in the stairwell, exposed to Russian fire. There appeared to be no other way down.

Greg turned to Prym: Black Team needed help. Prym tried again to raise the officers on the radio, looking for permission, and to stop what appeared to be Belorussian friendly fire from the east.

The noise increased again, a tremendous repetition of automatic fire from the alleyway and the direction of the target building. Greg was still moving: Black kept shouting on the radio that they were stuck. "Don't leave us!" Artem called again in Ukrainian. But there was little other information on where exactly they were or what they needed, and the radio was garbled to begin with. Only the Ukrainian speakers could understand the parts that were coming through.

173

"Okay," said Marti to Prym. "That side is the Belorussians. The enemy is found where …" Gesturing towards the target building, he reconfirmed their position. "You're good?" the Hungarian asked Prym with a grin, playfully punching his bicep. "*Oui*," sighed Prym.

Greg pushed past. He needed to open a door. With Prym following, he ducked into the next section of the building, under the small, red conveyor-belt ramps that must have once put packages on the Nova Posta trucks.

Riever was still in his corner in the alley, carefully scanning each window with his scope to try to catch a muzzle flash. It was frustrating. The volume of fire was incredible, but he couldn't see anyone. He was too low. While Dan and Loup and Tex several stories up were all able to fire down into the rooms, Riever found that he couldn't see anything. Eventually the frustration built. He snapped his Bren to full auto and let off the whole magazine in one burst through a first-floor window by the wrecked door. Before each mission the Ranger would take belts of SAW ammo and remove it from its links to load his mags. They were green tips, with a steel core inside the bullet. *Fuck it*, he thought, *maybe it will punch through a wall and get someone by luck*. As he reloaded, he looked up to see Ginger across the alley. Ginger was rolling his eyes and shaking his head. Riever could see what he was thinking: *rookie move, bro, not very professional*. Riever laughed and shrugged his shoulders at Ginger and went back to fruitlessly scanning the windows.

In Building 6, Greg again shouted to Prym that Black needed help: other than Prym, he was the only one in the building who could understand their calls. They were still stuck in the staircase and couldn't find another way out. Prym and Greg went back and forth in Ukrainian, the pressure weighing on the younger man. "Fuck," said Greg, walking towards George, who was holding a position at the midpoint of the building.

Over the radio, a fragment came in English. "This is Black," said a voice whose stress level was evident. *They're losing it*, thought Greg. *Explain what's happening! We don't know what's happening*. More conversation went back and forth in Ukrainian.

Greg was looking for another way down. Could the stairwell really have no access to floors other than the one they'd come across? It must connect somewhere else in the building. They just needed to find where.

Prym, crouching at the open garage door and shooting down the alleyway towards the Russians, shouted to Artem on the radio, telling them that Charlie was on the ground floor.

From the alleyway came another voice. "Prym, I'm coming in," said Riever. He had grown tired of waiting for a Russian to expose himself at a first-floor window where he could see. If Prym was going to flank the building, he wanted to try to make that happen.

"Yes, come on, Riever, fast, fast!" shouted Prym, all rapid movements.

Riever walked in, slowly and carefully. "Are you trying to get back?" he asked, unsure exactly what Prym was trying to do.

"No, we try to get closer, *blyat*," said Prym. "Trying to get closer?" asked Riever. "Yes, we try to get ... from the right side," said Prym, gesturing. "Yes, let's look now, we will check, come on," he continued.

Together they moved into the Nova Posta building, past George and Marti in the center doorway, towards the stairwell that Charlie had descended and where Black was now stuck.

Prym switched out his magazine. Over the radio, came Artem's distressed voice, garbled, in Ukrainian.

Riever moved smoothly towards the shooting, examining the office next to the stairwell, looking for an angle on the Russians. As he took a knee behind a tall bookcase—the office had been looted and a Dell computer tower thrown along the floor beside papers and other office supplies—Prym shouted back at Artem in Ukrainian. Riever had no idea what they were talking about, and no idea that Black Team was stuck.

"*Attention*, Riever," said Prym as the Ranger moved closer to the window. "What's up?" the American replied, turning back. In the background, Greg was on the radio to Artem, still in Ukrainian.

"They try to ... go downstairs, Akula, shark, shark," said Prym, referencing Artem's call sign.

"Where are they?" asked Riever.

"They upstairs. And each time when they start to move, they shoot it, from there. So steps are over there," Prym said, gesturing.

The safest way to move through a hostile environment is with covering fire. For Black Team, the stairwell did not provide very good options, especially now that they were all at one end of it. They tried to target the Russians shooting at them through the big windows. Big Max and Doug each dropped a guy. But soon the volume of fire pinned them in the stairwell.

Jordan and Big Max raced to the next floor. With Big Max holding his kit to brace him from behind, Jordan tucked himself hard up against the wall, his right shoulder crushed up against the concrete. The rest of the team stacked up on the landing just above him and Big Max.

Jordan fired, sending a series of bursts through the window. Samuel came down, then Pedro took his chance. As he descended the steps, there was a resounding *slap ... slapslapslapslap*. The bullets whizzed just behind his head, crashing into the sister leg of the staircase. Each impact was individually, painfully visible, the rounds turning chunks of the concrete of the stairs to sandy-colored dust that hung in the air.

"Fuck you!" screamed the heavily bearded Portuguese, in English. Pedro swapped in to provide cover fire. Then down came Doug, dashing and ducking his head in just the right place as the rounds nearly hit him.

The Russians had them zeroed. Artem was still stuck on the upper landing.

Holding security towards the east on the ground floor, George heard a huge burst of fire. "Where's the shooting coming from?" he demanded, not realizing that it was Black Team trying to descend the stairs. Greg approached.

"What's up, Greg?" asked George.

"They're on sixth floor, they can't come down, they're being shot at," said the medic. "We're going to go down to the end, find a staircase, locate them, and get them out," he continued, the last words drowned out by another huge round of fire.

Prym took Riever's place in the office as rifle fire boomed through the building, and slid towards the window on his hands and knees.

"Shark, uh, Black is on the sixth floor, but they can't come down because all the windows are being shot at," said Greg to Riever, combining Artem's call sign with the team's name. But as with Greg and Artem, Riever needed more information. Everyone was being shot at. Riever still was not sure who was actually where, and who needed what.

Over the radio came Ginger's voice. "Hey, Riever, I'm still outside, can you tell me what the fuck's goin' on?" But Riever couldn't get through, and the answer wasn't clear to him either.

The repeated fire came again. Black was trying to move, but no one downstairs, at least none of the non-Ukrainian speakers, knew it.

Artem again came on the radio in Ukrainian. Greg and Prym responded in kind.

Greg pushed into the office to find Prym. "We need to help them out. They're on the sixth floor, they can't come down," Greg said, in English.

"Yes, I know," sighed Prym, still on the floor of the office. Greg continued in Ukrainian, pressing for Prym to help him get Black down. But Prym wanted them to wait; he was still trying to reach the Ukrainian officers for permission.

"Any call signs," came Artem over the radio, this time in English. "This is Black. We're on the sixth floor, on the stairwell. We can't go down, every time we go down we get shot in the stairwell. How about you, copy?" But the radios were jamming with too much traffic. Neither Ginger nor Riever, the two people most able to help Black, heard that one call in English.

In the stairwell, Jordan had jumped down a half-flight to the next mid-floor landing. Big Max held Doug so as to brace him while the Royal Marine put more covering fire out of the window. He said he hit someone. Big Max called to Jordan, "Hey, I'm gonna jump it, I'm coming down."

"No, stop," said the young Brit from below, "there's nowhere for you to land. Don't do it. Let me move first." Communications weren't working; he wanted to get to the ground floor to bring up the men from Charlie to help them evacuate down the stairs.

"Alright," said Big Max. The noise from the shooting everywhere was enormous; it was so hard to hear.

"Give me some cover fire," said Jordan, "and I'll jump down."

"Let me know when you're ready to move," called Big Max, "or when you're on the next floor." The shooting from the next building was still loud. Jordan fired on his own from his corner to give cover.

"Give me some cover fire, sir!" shouted Jordan, but he didn't know that no one could hear him. Then he jumped.

The sound of a single shot—louder, heavier, menacingly different from the firing that had gone before—rent the air.

The men on the stairs above heard no response from Jordan's rifle covering them from below. "Jordan, you good?" yelled Big Max. They opened up towards the Russian building.

"Jordan!" Black Team shouted down the stairs.

"*Jordan!*"

George heard the huge single shot all the way back at his position midway down the length of the ground floor. "You good, Greg?" he shouted to the medic, now near the entrance to the stairwell.

Greg explained their task to the others on the ground floor, then tapped George's shoulder and took off running towards the far end of the building.

"Slow your ass down, I've got a hurt leg!" George called to Greg. He had sprained his ankle crossing the alley in the first moments of the firefight. He still relied on nature's best painkiller: adrenaline.

The tall medic never broke stride. "There must be a staircase here somewhere," he muttered.

When George caught up, he said, "I sprained my ankle, just FYI. I'm running on adrenaline."

"Shit, I know it. I think everybody is. This is shit," said Greg.

"Yeah, fuckin' friendlies everywhere and they don't know we're here!" replied George.

"There's no way up there," sighed Greg in frustration, checking the only other door on the far end of the building. "I'm gonna go get them. Let's go back." He took off again, running back to the original staircase, then slowing down to talk to Artem in Ukrainian on the radio. He would come to get them down.

Greg returned with George in tow. He pushed towards Prym, moving towards the doorway of the antechamber outside the stairwell where Black Team was pinned down. Symon's voice crackled over the radio. "I warned you, I warned you, to stop shooting a lot. We need quiet, we need quiet to bring the wounded people out. When you shooting, they shooting back."

Behind, Riever and Marti joked to break the tension. "Don't shoot?" chuckled Riever. "That's not why we're here."

Prym was on the radio, trying to obtain permission from Symon to go up the stairs. Greg pushed past, done with waiting. Prym got no response; he tried to call Oleksii instead. "I'm going up," Greg declared, after several exchanges back and forth. "They need help. They don't know where one of their guys is." Prym finally backed down. "Okay, I'll cover you," he agreed.

Greg entered the stairwell. He dashed up the first half-flight, taking cover in the corner of the switchback. Below him Prym grabbed a stack of building materials in the opposite corner, throwing it around the base of the stairs, trying to provide additional cover to shoot from.

"Guys! I'm coming up! Don't shoot!" Greg shouted as he continued up the stairs.

From above a voice shouted back in English. "Okay, one of our guys is down on the fifth floor!"

"Okay, I'm coming up," Greg called back.

Prym, having moved the collection of insulation and small wooden planks, rushed up to join Greg. They leapfrogged, now speaking between themselves in Ukrainian and with Artem, who had switched back to Ukrainian. Together they passed the entrance to the enormous room that spanned the fourth floor, from where they had crossed the building initially. Pausing on the small half-landing in between the fourth and fifth floors—a safer space given the lack of window on the floor beneath them—Greg looked up.

"*Pizdets*," he muttered.

On the fifth-floor landing, Jordan lay still, his feet on the stairs, his head towards the corner, his rifle pointed in the same direction, his face towards Greg, and his right arm slumped across his chest as he lay on his left side. A perfect head shot from the sniper's bullet had entered just above his left cheekbone and just beneath the helmet that still covered his skull. Head shots usually disfigure grotesquely. The face either implodes or looks swollen. But Jordan still looked perfectly like Jordan: young, elfin, but now covered in his own blood, still bright red, which created a pool that stretched from his elbow to a foot above his head.

Greg got on his knees and stretched his body up the remaining half-flight of stairs, so that he was almost lying on his belly. He kept his head low, poking just around the switchback of the staircase, looking for the sniper's angle and the rest of Black Team. He checked for a pulse, even though he knew it was useless. Jordan was gone.

Prym tried to raise Oleksii on the radio, still unaware that the officer was down. Above them, Black Team traded shots with the Russians in the target building. Someone shouted down to Greg: what happened with Jordan?

"I'm sorry, guys, he's dead," Greg shouted back. "Is there another way down?" But the only way out was the staircase.

Greg and Prym conferred in Ukrainian. Then Greg tipped his head to call up the stairs in English. "Hey, guys! Can you hear me?" Prym shouted to Symon on the radio, and was finally silenced by Greg, who was trying to communicate up the stairs. Artem yelled that they were taking fire, but Greg needed more detail. *Fuck, there's a big-ass building*, he thought. *I don't know where you're getting shot at from.* Above, shots boomed in the stairwell. "Oh, I heard that fucker," Riever said to Marti on the ground floor as the shooting stopped with a telltale click. Someone was reloading an AK. More shots boomed. The Ranger tried to raise Dan on the radio but couldn't get through.

"Guys, we're gonna get you down," Greg called. "What we're gonna do, we're gonna get our guys, and they're going to fire everything they have while you guys have to run down."

Voices traded disagreements above. "Shush!" came Doug's calm baritone. "What's that, mate?"

"Guys, look, what we're gonna do. We're gonna get all our guys online. And they're gonna start firing. And you guys have to run down, there's no other way."

"Run down to the first floor?" called Big Max.

"We're on the fourth floor!" called Greg.

Prym gestured for Greg to take Jordan down the stairs, to clear the way. Below, Riever shouted up, "What's going on up there?"

Prym took Jordan's rifle while Greg pulled his body down the half-flight. Prym removed Jordan's magazines from his webbing.

1. Riever at the base of the stairwell as the evac begins in Building 6, Severodonetsk.

2. Ginger shooting a Javelin towards Russian positions in Blahodativka.

3. Ginger in Bakhmut.

4. The evac across the top of Building 6, Severodonetsk.

5. Riever's team on return from the overwatch mission across from Andrivka.

6. The team in the Lysychansk safehouse, between missions in Severodonetsk.

7. Before the road trip to the end of the world.

8. Dan and Riever training for a maritime mission.

They might need them. Someone was still firing at Black Team above. The staircase was full of noise. "Are you firing at this bastard?" Doug called down. "No! We don't have windows!" Greg called back. "We're working on it, guys, wait a second!"

Prym and Greg conferred in Ukrainian. Prym gave the medic the belated news from Symon: *Oleksii three hundred*, a reference to the old Soviet codes from the Afghan war that marked the cargo loads of airplanes. *Oleksii wounded.*

Riever tried again. "Hey! Can somebody up there tell me what's going on and how we can help?"

Marti shouted from below. "Hey, Prym," he called, switching over to French, "what's up?"

"Guys! Coming, one sec," called Greg, heading down a flight. "Guys, can you hear us? Can you hear us?" The rifle fire boomed; it was hard to hear anything else. "We have one killed. And they're stuck on the sixth floor. They're firing from the top floors. We need our guys to start firing at the top floors."

"One second! What?" called Riever. All they could hear on the ground floor was rifle fire. "Alright—hold up. Say that again."

"For fuck's sake," exclaimed the frustrated medic, "they got one KIA [killed in action]. We need to fire at the top floors, everybody, so they can come down because they're pinned."

"Okay," called Riever. "Is there any way out from the sixth floor? Can they go out to the roof?"

"No!" yelled Greg. "There's just this fucking staircase."

"Okay," Riever called back. "Then get a count, and we'll fire at the top window."

"But from who, where?" asked Marti. "I can't see anything," he muttered, pushing around the construction debris that Prym had left on the floor. "There is one KIA, he said? From Black Team, no?"

"Fuck," said George to himself quietly, as he held security to the rear.

"I think so," said Riever to Marti.

"No good," said the Hungarian.

Prym pulled Jordan down the stairs to the fourth floor while Greg had moved down a flight to shout to the men on the ground floor. Greg dashed back up to meet Prym. Greg picked up Jordan's rifle; Prym found other magazines that had fallen onto the floor. Together, they pulled Jordan into the antechamber that separated the stairs from the big room they had run across initially. It was now their only way out.

Dan broke in over the radio. "Anyone have eyes on Riever, Ginger, or Greg?"

Ginger responded: "This is Ginger, I'm still out in the middle of the fuckin' alleyway."

Greg and Prym put Jordan down. Greg turned and looked out of the windows on the east side of the big room. He could see smoke and hear a motor. *What is that?* Then he saw it, two hundred meters away: a tank headed straight for them. "Prym! There's a tank!" Greg said. "*Pizdets!*" exclaimed Prym.

Above them, Black Team heard everything go silent. *This is not awesome*, thought Big Max. *What's up with that? Did we get 'em all?* Then they heard it: tracks approaching. *Hey! That sounds like a tank. I think our tank's back!*

"Guys," called Greg up the stairs. "They got a fucking tank coming."

"Friendly?" called Big Max from upstairs.

The men on the ground floor heard Greg as well. "What?" said Marti, dumbfounded.

"No! It's not friendly. It's coming from the right," Greg called up to Black Team. "You guys have to get the fuck down."

Motherfucker, thought Big Max.

Prym shouted on the radio. Rifle fire splattered across the street.

The men on Black Team looked at one another: this was it. "Well, it was good knowing all you guys," said Big Max.

"Don't go!" Artem shouted from the floor above.

"We're not leaving you, fuck," replied Greg angrily.

"Hey," called Riever, his voice calm, "we're not leaving you, we're trying to figure out how to get out of here."

"We're aware, we're aware," called Big Max from above.

Rifle fire exploded, louder than before. Prym was on the radio; voices went back and forth in Ukrainian. Now fire exploded from Building 3, covering the attempted egress. "Akula, *davai!*" screamed Prym to Artem. Greg's voice shouted down the stairs at full volume: "Start firing at them from the bottom, guys! At the top floor, start firing!" Riever and Marti lay across the debris on the ground floor, firing up at the top floor of the target building across the way.

"Let's go, let's go, let's go!" shouted Greg to Black Team.

Greg ran up to the landing between floors four and five, shouting to Black. Prym screamed down for Marti, who couldn't hear him.

Doug came first, leaping onto the half-landing while debris flew near his feet. Somewhere, more glass shattered. Big Max covered for Artem as he came down, and dropped another Russian. *Oh my God*, he thought. *I did it! I got the guy who got Jordan!* He made his own run. *Slapslapslap!* came the bullets crashing right behind his head. *Nope, that's not the guy.*

A new, rumbling boom shook the building: the tank was shooting at them. "That was behind us, that's not friendly!" warned George on the ground floor. Above, Greg shouted again: "There's a fucking tank coming!"

Across the way in Building 3, Michael felt as if he had belly-flopped off a high dive into hot air, with a nasty smack of concussion: the heat round of the tank. *What the hell was that?* thought Dan, further up the same staircase in Building 3, just above the wave of high temperature.

In Building 6, the rest of Black Team came running down the stairs. Prym shouted again for Marti on the radio, in French: a call still inaudible on the ground floor. Greg ran down from above.

"Marti, Riever, get the fuck up here!" screamed Greg. They could hear the tank's engine revving outside.

"Alright, we're coming up," called Riever. "Marti, I'll shoot, you run. Then you shoot, I'll run."

"I'm right behind you," called George.

Prym moved into the antechamber, where Black Team had assembled. Doug was just behind Jordan's body on the floor.

"Okay, guys," said Prym. "Take the body of your friend and start moving over there. Move, fast!" Doug took Jordan's right shoulder, Big Max his left, with Pedro picking up just behind them. Prym turned back as Black Team began their run.

On the radio, Dan's voice crackled, "Start moving up the stairs!" Across the alley, in Building 3, the rest of the teams were egressing as well.

Despite all the shooting, the sound behind Ginger in the alley was unmistakable—boots walking on broken glass.

Fuck, dude, we're surrounded, thought the infantryman. The last he'd heard from the Belorussians, they'd taken contact from the east. Maybe that same enemy force had pushed this way.

He got on the radio. "I can hear guys to my rear." No response.

He was alone. *Alright, I'm gonna go check this shit out*, he thought. Ginger turned to face the sound. Slowly he skirted the wall, trying to stay out of sight of both the windows opposite him and the other buildings. He wanted access to quick cover if he needed it.

Ahead of him, from behind and to the east of Building 6, came a man dressed in dark green fatigues, with no bands on his arms. He looked exactly like a Russian soldier.

Ginger put him in his sights. As he looked down the optic, he saw a giant, dark green "Iron Man" pack holding linked ammo for a machine gun on the other guy's back. He'd seen one of the Belorussians wearing the same thing hours before. He paused. Was that guy one of theirs? Was he about to shoot someone like that Ukrainian who had very nearly killed him just days before?

The pack was the only reason he didn't take the shot. Instead, he waved.

The other guy ducked behind the building. *Oh my God*, thought Ginger. *Maybe that wasn't him.* Rifle holding on the corner, he put one leg over the side of a broken bay window; then the other leg. He crouched behind the wall.

At the north end of Building 3, everyone was exfiling up the stairs they had initially come down. Dan got on the radio and called to Ginger. "Ginger, can you make it to the stairs?"

"Negative, they're out moving, I can't really move. They're not responding to me," Ginger replied. But Dan had never heard his first transmission about the men circling from their rear.

"I copy none of your last," said Dan, the radio fuzzing out.

"In the rear of the parking lot, a bunch of dudes showed up. Can't confirm if they're friendly or enemy," Ginger replied. Dan's voice came garbled over the radio.

In Building 3, men started moving up the stairs towards Michael: they had a casualty with them. The tanker moved even closer to the pillar at the skyway corner so that they could carry the casualty past. He looked down and saw a large body with a bloodied face, but he didn't recognize the man. He heard Dan's call: it was time to go.

Dan needed to make sure that they weren't leaving anyone behind in the chaos. Tex was now a floor below him. "Tex," called Dan. "Go to the bottom floor, make sure nobody's there, and then come up as last man and we're gonna pull back."

"Got it," responded Tex, easily hefting his PKM.

Above, Dan stopped suddenly. Tex was a natural fighter but still technically had no military training. *He's gonna do whatever I tell him without question*, Dan realized, horrified. The younger man would have to cross all of those keyed-up windows. "Tex, wait!" the SEAL shouted. "Are you good to do this?"

Below, Tex looked up. "Yeah, man," he responded. "I got it."

Tex took off while Dan and Loup covered him from above. "There's nobody down here. I'm last man!" Tex called.

The SAW gunners opened up for Tex's last run up the stairs. And for the first time in the whole firefight, Dan's gun jammed. Belt-fed guns were prone to jamming, but he still felt like an asshole. Tex made it anyway. They helped Loup break down his SAW, then began to move out across the big, open grain silo with the huge hole from the artillery round in the ceiling.

Riever, Marti, and George prepared to make their run up the stairs to escape the tank that they could clearly hear outside.

"Ready, set, go," said Riever, laying covering fire out of the window as the Hungarian sprinted up the stairs.

"Go," called George.

"Cover me!" said Riever, beginning his run. Then, suddenly, he went down, flat onto his stomach. *Did he just get shot?* George thought as he put down covering fire.

The Ranger scrambled up and ran up the half-flight, turning to provide cover. "George!" Riever called. *Well, I guess he's fine*, thought the Canadian. Riever had tripped on the debris at the base of the stairs.

"Alright, I'm coming up!" George shouted over the din. There was rifle fire everywhere. The tank rumbled.

George and Riever regrouped on the first half-landing. Marti was already gone above them. Riever peered out of the window, trying to find the angle of fire. It was so loud that they still had no idea what was going on upstairs, or what Greg needed them to do. George loaded and charged a new magazine. The tank's engine roared.

"Hey!" Riever shouted.

"For fuck's sake, guys!" came Greg's voice, stressed.

"Do you want us to come up?" asked Riever, each word clear and slow.

"We want you guys come here, we're evacing out of here!" yelled the medic.

"Coming up!" shouted Riever. He and George ran up the next half-flight, mostly obscured from the window by the switchback of the next set of steps.

"We're coming up a floor. Cover us?" called Riever.

"It's safe, it's safe!" yelled Greg, but they still had to pass one more window.

"Go. I'll cover you," said George. Riever raced past the window at his right side as George fired, breaking the window. Stopping at the next half-landing, Riever turned.

"Alright. George, I'm gonna fire two shots. I'm gonna drop them, run past 'em, okay?" Down on one knee, he shouldered the rifle, in a movement so smooth it looked slow.

George didn't have time to think about running directly into fire from a man he had only really gotten to know a few days ago. "Okay."

"Ready, set ... go!" In front of George's eyes the first bullet left the muzzle, the flash laser-sharp and yellow-gold. He ran, the next shot firing as he passed the first two steps.

"Let's go, let's go, let's go!" called Greg as George hit the half-flight landing. "There's a fucking enemy tank out here!"

"Yeah, I hear it!" called George, his voice tired but calm, as he and Riever moved up the final, covered half-flight of stairs.

"Fuck," muttered Prym on the fourth-floor landing. "We have one man, one man down."

"Okay," said Marti, pushing into the big room. "Now, we should run fast!"

"Okay guys, *c'est bon*, we will moving, come on, start," said Prym.

They spread out. Greg was first, along the west wall. To his side was Prym, and behind him Riever. Marti ran behind Prym, with George last. "George!" Prym shouted suddenly, turning his head to check behind him. They headed for the small hallway and exterior staircase through which Charlie and Black had entered before. Gunfire and huge booms echoed in the street. Greg turned around.

"Come on, come on, let's go, let's go, let's go," the medic called in encouragement to George and his still-sprained ankle. "Careful of those windows! Careful of those windows!" Greg shouted, gesturing east, as they entered the hallway.

Greg heard the tank fire a second shot. *He's going to take us apart*, he thought, racing across the open room towards the exit. But then the tank stopped firing.

A Belorussian had saved them by sneaking up on the tank with a Matador: possibly George's, which had been left in the south staircase of Building 3. Though the Belorussian only clipped the tank with the rocket, that was enough. Tanks have notoriously bad visibility, Soviet-designed tanks most of all (they are, even more so than most tanks, not designed for crew comfort). There are only two small slits for viewing out of a standard Soviet T-72. That tank crew likely had no idea what hit it or where from: a Ukrainian tank, a rocket, it didn't matter. The tank was operating alone—a dangerous thing for a tank to do. It ran. "I don't know who that Belorussian is," Greg said later, "but I owe him a *lot* of beer."

In the alleyway, the most intense firefight Ginger had ever seen was still going on at the intersection of the target building and the stairwells of Buildings 3 and 6. Bullets were screaming everywhere.

There was another sound, the unmistakable rumble of a tank. *No*, he thought. *There's no fuckin' way*. It was coming from the east to the west: unlike the Iron Man pack-wearing Belorussian, it was undeniably the enemy. *No fuckin' way, man. This is not real.*

Eeeeeeeeh went the barrel of the tank's main gun, cranking upwards. *Ba-boom!* A chunk of the roof of Building 6 flew off into the middle of the alleyway.

Fuck, dude, they're all dead, Ginger thought. *All those guys are dead. Fuck. What the fuck!*

He got back on his radio. "Was that a goddamn tank?" The radio was bonkers. There was screaming in Ukrainian, Russian, but nothing that he could understand.

They're dead. What do I do? Where is everybody? thought Ginger, still alone.

A new sound wafted across the alleyway: of running, from the top floor of Building 6. *Oh, thank God.*

15

EXFIL FROM HELL

George entered the hallway behind Marti and Prym, breathing hard. "Ah, cunt," he spat, moving to the end and taking a knee. He looked down at the floor: grey but covered in a fine silt from all of the artillery, it was a mosaic of boot prints.

Jordan's body was laid out on the floor on the left side, with Doug standing at his head, Artem opposite Doug against the right wall, and the rest of Black Team stacked down the hall. "*Fuck*," muttered Prym, also breathing hard. "*Fuck.*"

"Okay," declared Greg. "This is the staircase we came up. So, we need to make sure it's safe, and we need to get to the back of here, and reach those fucking buildings that we cleared earlier."

"No, wait, wait," said Prym, "I will call the Belarus ... Beloruss ... ah," sighed Prym.

Dan broke in over the radio. "Anyone have eyes on Riever?"

Doug, still next to Jordan, looked around and suddenly stepped forward, his left arm outstretched. "Cameras off, cameras off!" he gestured to each man with a GoPro on his chest. "They're off, they're off," came several responses.

"Hey, Dan, this is Riever, how copy?" the Ranger called over the radio. The American voices were an island of calm professionalism in the chaos of yelling on the net that rarely stopped.

"Copy. Good to hear you. Start making your way to the staircase. Do you know what Ginger's situation is?" Dan replied. The SEAL had heard none of Ginger's transmissions about the men to their rear.

Now Prym was on his radio, trying to raise Symon. Everyone was trying to evacuate—including, probably, the Russians, using their tank as cover.

"We're trying to push back to Building 3," Riever called over the radio. Dan confirmed.

189

Riever turned the hallway's corner, the one that headed towards the only exit and the alleyway. "Show me this stairway," he said to Greg. Of the group, he was the only one who hadn't come up it.

"It's shitty. It's an outdoor stairway," the medic replied.

"Outdoors? Fuck that. Is there anything else?" Riever asked.

"Riever!" Prym called from down the hall. "Did you have some connection with your guys? Because I call ..."

Riever came back. "Yeah, yeah, yeah, turn it down, turn it down," he replied, as Prym's radio squawked on full volume. "Turn your shit down. We have to figure out how to get out of here, then I will call them and get what we need from them. So is there a staircase that goes to the downstairs?"

As Riever was speaking, Black Team came around the corner, moving Jordan's body towards the staircase door.

In the alley, four agonizing minutes after Ginger had first heard the footsteps on broken glass, the Belorussian team's commander came around the corner. Ginger recognized him, and the Belorussian did likewise. They waved. *Oh, thank God*, he thought. He got on the radio. In Charlie's hallway, Riever heard Ginger's voice come crackling through. "The guys to our rear are the Belorussians. We're good."

The outdoor staircase was the only way out for the men in the hall. Everyone lined up. Across from Prym, Doug—again next to Jordan—lit a cigarette and held it to his lips with his left hand. His right held his rifle, the A-pos patch clearly visible on his right shoulder. Above the burning embers of the cigarette, his eyes looked very different from the way they had that morning.

Greg and Riever investigated the staircase. Returning, Riever said to the group, "Okay. There's an outdoor stairway here. There's a bus to give us cover, and then we can make a run back to Building 3. You guys okay with that?" Nods went down the hall. "Alright, give me some security shooters. Who wants to shoot?" It was clever phrasing by the salty sergeant: "who wants to shoot?" sounds a lot better than "who wants to go out and get shot at?"

While Prym was still trying to raise Symon, Riever, Greg, and Samuel moved towards the door. "Anyone got a stretcher?" asked Doug in the hall. Nobody had one.

Prym finally got confirmation. "Okay, guys. Start moving to the building where we were before."

"We'll take some shooters down, we'll set up security, and hold 'em while the rest get across," Riever said.

"Yes," said Prym. "Does anybody have something anti-tank?" "No, *suka*," came the responses.

"Goddammit," said Riever. "Give me a mag." He leaned forward, rustling among Prym's webbing. *How does he have so many?* Riever thought. From the end of the hall, someone said, "I have one smoke." Prym responded, "I have also one smoke!"

As Riever tucked the extra mag into his kit, Prym turned. "Take this one," Prym said, handing Riever a different mag; the Ranger didn't realize it had been Jordan's. "Give me this one."

"Okay," said Riever. "I'm gonna take Samuel, Greg, we're gonna get to the bottom of the stairs, get prone, and see if anybody pops up. All of you need to move down, get behind that bus, and go straight across to the alley. It's gonna be to your front, slightly left." At the door, Greg pointed out the other teams moving across the big open floor of Building 3. He shouted, waving, trying to get their attention to deconflict.

Riever stepped out first onto the metal staircase, his body tensed and all of the nerves in his skin on alert. It was a high and exposed position; he expected to be greeted by a hail of bullet fire. But none came. In the hall, Prym stuffed more of Jordan's magazines into Marti's kit. Prym turned to Doug, standing next to him, still at Jordan's head. "I take those," Prym explained. "His magazines. He don't need anyway."

"Yeah, it's fine," said Doug, looking down at Jordan.

Riever popped back in. "They've got eyes on a tank," he said, referring to the Belorussians. But then Greg heard the all-clear, and shooters raced down the stairs, taking up covering positions at the little Sprinter van.

Marti turned to Black Team, handing Big Max his rifle. "I offer you something," said the big Hungarian. "Put him to my back. I'm not gonna run with him," said Marti, but he would be able to carry Jordan down the stairs.

Prym pushed out of the door, calling for George. At the base of the stairs, Riever had a standing position to shoot through the van. Samuel lay on his belly, angled around the rear tires. It was suddenly, eerily, quieter: now they were the only things making noise.

Above, everyone rushed down the staircase. Marti carried Jordan with the dead man's arms draped over his shoulders, like a child doing a piggyback.

Ginger watched as he charged towards the back of the buildings. Riever, Samuel, and Doug ran down the stairs to provide security for everyone else, taking up positions behind another Sprinter van less damaged than its cousin under the catwalk. Prym crossed to his side of the alley. Ginger looked up to the staircase just in time to see Marti reach the lower half of the stairs and lose his fight with grav-ity. Greg had tried to help rebalance Jordan on his shoulders as Marti passed the staircase landing. Now Jordan's body, weighed down by all his kit, his feet catching on the railings, slipped from the Hungarian's broad but exhausted shoulders.

Fuck, man, who the fuck is that? thought Ginger. *I thought the casu-alty was in my building! Somebody died?*

Marti and Artem grabbed Jordan. "Pick up his head, pick up his head!" someone shouted. They sped across the alley, Marti pulling both arms while Artem pulled both legs, sliding the rifleman's body on his kit across the sandy, dusty ground, heading for Building 2. Jordan's phone fell out of his pocket; Big Max picked it up, and kept on running.

George was now behind the big industrial trash dumpsters, eye-ing a lone, apparently unarmed man standing in the catwalk between Buildings 3 and 6: the first potential enemy he'd clearly seen the whole day. *Fuck,* thought George, *do I shoot this guy? He's not shooting at us.* Doug, now climbing into the van to provide cover, saw him too. The Brit wanted to fire a warning shot.

Riever ordered him to hold. The man had no gun and looked more mystified than anything: he had to be one of the Belorussians who had congregated in Building 3. "I fuckin' hope he was," George said later, "because if it was a Russian and I didn't kill him, I'd be upset."

The rest of Black Team crossed the street. Prym shouted to Samuel. "C'mon, Ginger, c'mon!" Ginger heard Prym call as he made it to the end of the block and past the other man.

"George, run," said Riever. "Moving!" responded the Canadian. "Doug, run. Samuel, run." Finally, Riever crossed, passing Prym on the far corner as he ran. "Prym, you're last man."

As they made it to the short alley between Buildings 2 and 3, the Russian artillery started to boom again.

Black Team carried Jordan into Building 2, one man at each limb; they still had no stretcher. "Let's get inside, and then we can call 'em," said Riever, referring to the rest of Alpha. "Eagle, eagle, eagle," called the Ranger as they entered, the traditional sign for American friendlies. Riever got on the radio, calling Symon. "Black Team, Charlie, and myself have moved back to Building 2 with the KIA." He didn't hear Dan.

"Dan, this is Riever," said the Ranger on the radio.

"Say again your last," returned the SEAL as the radio crackled. "We are pulling back on the top floor of the original building."

"We are in Building 2 with Charlie Team and Black Team and the KIA," replied the Ranger.

"I'm not hearing any of that," Dan came back over the poor radio connection. "We're moving."

"Copy."

In Building 3 Michael was helping to carry Oleksii across the rubble-strewn floor with Dan. From his position near Oleksii's feet, Michael could see Oleksii's face as he carried him towards the exit of Building 3. He looked different: bloodied but also bruised, puffed, as if a different face. Michael kept looking at Oleksii's eyes. He looked at his injury. The cric was good and correct but grotesque: plastic where flesh should be. The men hadn't been terribly close, but they had spent many hours together working on intelligence and mission planning. Michael considered Oleksii a friend. Now his death was literally in Michael's face as he struggled with his body. The suddenness of the transition from living to dead, from a person to a physical burden, shook the Marine. *Like meat. Like an object*, thought Michael as he carried the Ukrainian. *This is really horrible*.

Exhausted, he handed off Oleksii at the door. Instead he picked up the officer's plates and heavy gear, which had been stripped from his body in order to make him easier to carry, along with an anti-tank rocket.

"Greg, stop," said Prym, standing in the door to Building 2. "George!" he shouted. "Come here, please. Help Greg."

"What's Greg doing?" asked George, approaching the door. "Greg! What are you doing? You crossing?" No one told him anything. *Why do they need another medic? The casualty is already here*, George thought. George followed Greg as he ran across the small street, to the entrance of Building 3.

"Friendlies! Friendlies!" Greg shouted as they moved up the stairs. Outside, gunfire boomed again. The artillery picked up.

On the ground, with Dmitri still hovering over him, was Oleksii. Someone said that he was wounded. Greg tried to find a pulse: there was nothing. George looked down and saw the blue cric tube in Oleksii's neck. The Ukrainian officer was stripped to the waist. Exhausted and full of adrenaline, George didn't recognize their commander. Oleksii's face looked different: his beard red with blood instead of dark brown; his face puffed, bruised, starting to turn blue. *Wounded? He's dead. He's fucking dead*, George thought.

The men loaded Oleksii onto a soft stretcher. They pulled him towards the back of the building and down the debris-strewn staircase. They started the wrong way, feet first. "Man, we should turn around," said George, seeing Oleksii's feet hanging off the stretcher and catching on things, "we're going to break his legs." His long legs were hanging off the stretcher at the knees, catching and bending at weird angles on the steps. *I really don't want to snap a leg and have to put it back on the stretcher*, George thought.

"Yeah, no, he's dead, he's not wounded," said Greg at the other end of the stretcher. *I know he's dead, but maybe it's easier if we carry him the other way*, George thought.

From his position at the door of Building 2, Riever saw Prym exit Building 3 with an AT-4. The Ukrainian hurried towards the main alley. "Where you going?" asked Riever. "I will shoot!" said Prym. Riever went after him as he saw Prym start to prep the rocket.

"Prym! Save that, in case we run into a tank," said the Ranger. "You're right," said Prym, taking the AT-4 off his shoulder and returning to the rear door of Building 3.

They carried Oleksii down through the dark antechamber at the base of the rear of Building 3, between the stairs and where Prym was holding security at the door. Prym turned and saw Oleksii, clearly dead rather than wounded as he had been told. Out came a slew of Ukrainian, ending in *blyat*, the last word breathed out in a sigh, in a voice that sounded dismayed.

"Three hundred," insisted Dmitri in English as he walked in: the old Soviet air cargo code for wounded.

"He's two hundred, guys," another voice responded gruffly, using the code number for dead. "Double-check."

In the rear door of Building 3 a few moments later, Prym held up two fingers to the men in Building 2. Then he moved his hand across his neck in a cutthroat sign: *two dead*. On the second floor of Building 2, pulling security out of the window, Ginger was confused. *Two? I thought the Brit* was *the casualty*. Riever saw him as well but interpreted it differently. *There are two dead in there? Did we lose Michael or Tex too?*

Artillery boomed, and somehow small birds sang, as a group of men exited Building 3, carrying a body on a soft stretcher. *That motherfucker's dead. He's limper than fuck*, thought Ginger.

Dmitri and someone Ginger didn't recognize were driving the train. The other man was Belorussian, one of a group who had come up from the Belorussian base at some point during the firefight, but who had mostly stayed in the south end of Building 3.

"Damn, dude, who the fuck is that?" Ginger said to Riever, now standing beside him.

"I don't know," replied Riever.

They watched as the other men struggled closer. They moved down to the door as the body was brought in.

"Dude, that's Oleksii!" Ginger said.

"Yeah," said Riever slowly. "I think it is."

"Fuck!" exclaimed Ginger. "That sucks."

One of the young Belorussians went to sling his rifle on his back. The Belorussian government was Putin's ally, but these Belorussians objected to both their own dictator and Russia's. But they were dissidents, not necessarily former soldiers—brave but frequently only lightly trained.

Suddenly, a boom rang out in the front hall of Building 2. A single, unsuppressed shot ripped right past the head of the young Belorussian commander and into the wall. Voices screamed in Russian. For one second Riever's heart rate spiked as both he and Ginger thought they were getting shot at from close range by advancing enemy forces. They instinctively took up position on the door before they realized what had happened.

"AD, AD, AD!" shouted Riever, warning of the accidental discharge, while the Belorussian commander started beating the young soldier in response.

Dan was counting up Alpha Team. He couldn't find Greg. At the door, Riever stopped Prym. "Prym! Did Greg go across with you? Greg ran across with you?"

"Yeah, yeah," said Prym, breathing hard.

"He didn't come back," said Riever. "Where is he?"

"No way," breathed Prym. "Greg inside, normally."

"Can you find him?" asked the Ranger.

"Yes, yes," replied Prym. "Greg!" he shouted down the hall. "Where is Greg? Find me Greg!"

"Greg!" shouted George, further down the hall. "Where the fuck are you?"

"In here!" came a call from the big open room.

"All is good!" shouted Prym. "We are all here!"

"Okay, Alpha's up!" called Dan, walking further into the building. "Alpha's up."

They regrouped, counting up and confirming that everyone was present. The Ukrainian officers conferred in the big room on the west side of the building, the one with the decrepit Lada where they had stashed extra ammo cans, and where Greg and George had taken turns to hold security on the door, near the bright yellow barrel. They needed to run back to the Belorussian base.

Prym walked into the hallway, where the teams were stacked up. "Alpha! Alpha! Charlie! Everybody! Black! Come on," he shouted. "Take the bodies also."

They formed up at their egress door, Loup holding security to the north with his SAW along with Mykola and his PKM. They ran in groups, heading towards a hole in the tall wall that separated this block from the Belorussian base's. It was bad terrain: there were shell holes and debris everywhere, rubble from buildings, walls, anything that had been hit by artillery, plus scrub bushes and stacks of industrial detritus.

Prym went first, followed by Black Team, running and carrying Jordan feet-first: Artem in between his feet, one hand on each pant leg, Doug at his left hip, Marti at his right, a Belorussian supporting his arms. Others followed: Tex with Riever's extra gear from the Building 3 staircase, Michael with the body armor that had been stripped from Oleksii's body to make him lighter to carry. Big Max was loaded down with Jordan's rifle and those of several of the men carrying him. Then came Oleksii's body on a soft stretcher with his knees bound together, carried by George, Greg, Dmitri, and two Belorussians.

George rolled his ankle for the second time, taking a misstep on the rubble. They put Oleksii down to regroup and shift gear. Greg had his own rifle, plus two of Black Team's, someone else's backpack, and a rocket slung effortlessly over his big frame as he worked. The rest of Alpha and the remaining Belorussians, seemingly multiplying, came up behind them. Prym ran to help carry Oleksii.

At Oleksii's head, Prym and Greg moved towards the small passage between a stack of concrete slabs and the wall, partly blocked by rubble, that they would need to climb over in order to reach the hole.

As they approached the small passage, they placed Oleksii on the ground for a break. The rest of Alpha caught up. An artillery round screamed just overhead: the Russians were targeting the egress. They knew there was only one place the assault team could have come from, and only one place they could retreat to. They already had the Belorussian base bracketed. Now they added the ground outside Building 2 and the road towards the Belorussians. The fire was extremely accurate. The only way home now was through an artillery barrage.

One shell passed so close that to George it felt like a giant holding a knife had cut the air open over their heads as they carried Oleksii. The sound was incredible; the ground shook. *Fuck me, that was close*, thought George, realizing again that he was standing next to Riever during a we-just-nearly-died moment.

"*Suka*," said Prym. They reorganized: Riever moved to Oleksii's left shoulder while George took the Ranger's rifle. Dan appeared and took the spot at Oleksii's right shoulder, with Dmitri behind him along with Ginger and a host of Belorussians. They carried Oleksii over a slab of concrete positioned like a precarious balance beam in the ground, then over several feet of additional rubble, until they got to the hole in the wall.

The wall was made of reinforced concrete, the hole now littered with wires that stuck out at odd angles. In the narrow, rubble-strewn passage Dmitri fell, wrenching his leg and tearing something in his ankle. As they approached the hole in the wall, they had to move over the rubble that had once formed the wall. It was higher on Dan's side; on the other side of Oleksii, Riever struggled to keep the body level as Oleksii started to slide. Riever tried to grab his commander and put him back. Oleksii was bloody; his hair was slick. The Ranger couldn't move him. Riever stood up and put his entire body weight into the effort, intentionally falling forward to move the litter a few more feet.

At the hole they needed to lift Oleksii higher in order to make it through the space. Riever slipped on rubble and pitched forward again, his face just next to Oleksii's. The dead man partially slid off the stretcher. The artillery boomed.

"Wait, wait, wait, wait, wait! *Suka!*" Prym shouted, turning back to help.

"It doesn't matter!" said Dan, already hauling Oleksii through the hole. "Just get him over."

Prym lifted Oleksii's head—bloody, blue, and bruised—above the wires that had caught the handles of the soft stretcher, tugging the fabric back into place as the other men pulled the body through. "Let's go!" called Dan. "Alright, *move!*"

They shuffled towards the base, carrying Oleksii in the heat. "Come on, guys," called Dan, his voice even, "let's get a buddy shuffle in before another mortar hits."

They passed a small lorry, stripped of its wheels and tires, then moved around a tree that had been downed by shelling. The terrain was still bad, with small bricks of concrete and rubble everywhere. Climbing over another mound of rubble, they headed around the corner of the building; the front entrance was blocked. Behind Dan, at Oleksii's right elbow, was an enormous Belorussian. He looked like he could move mountains, but he had hit his limit. He was dragging, slowing everyone down in the field of artillery fire.

They put Oleksii down again. Dan was exasperated. *All that training that armies did with buddy drags was for* this *moment*, he thought. *You* have *to be able to do it.*

"Come on! We have to move! Fucking dig, motherfucker! Fuckin' *dig!*" The SEAL was still at the front, driving the train, carrying more than his portion of Oleksii, plus his SAW and its remaining ammo.

They switched out the Belorussian, still moving towards the base. They rounded the side of the building, and came into a two-story car park.

Marti was still with Black, on the far side of the building. Prym walked towards them. Marti approached, with helmet off, exhausted and looming. He looked at Prym, breathing hard, and sighed. They said nothing. Marti just nodded, eyes turning to Jordan, who was laid out on the floor, now on a hard stretcher, his armored plates stripped off. At Jordan's left shoulder, Doug sat on an ammo crate, with elbows resting on knees, still tucked next to the body of his friend.

Belorussian voices shouted in the background. "It's here?" asked Marti, in English. He stepped over Jordan's body, standing next to Doug. The Englishman bent down, hand next to Jordan's shoulder, preparing to carry him one last time. Beside him, Marti leaned over too. Along with a few Belorussians and Artem, they lifted Jordan up and carried him towards the Kozak that had just zoomed into the car park.

"Take off his helmet! Take off his helmet, *blyat!*" shouted Prym as they loaded Jordan into the back of the Kozak.

The team carrying Oleksii arrived a few minutes later. Riever jumped into the Kozak to help lift the body. Jordan was already inside, neatly laid out at an angle in the square, windowless back of the armored vehicle. His head was in the far corner, his feet tucked on top of one of the benches that ran from front to back along the sides. As Riever looked down, he saw the young Brit's golden hair slicked down with blood. He could see through the bullet hole into the hollow of his skull. It was just dark where his brain was supposed to be.

He turned to grab Oleksii as everyone else handed the Ukrainian up. The only way he would fit was right on top of Jordan, also angled longways across the compartment. They each lay face-up. The older man was much taller; Riever had to jam his feet into the upper, opposite corner in order to get his legs to fit at a nearly forty-five-degree angle. *They're dead*, he thought suddenly. *It's like they're a bag of something*. It wasn't the first time he had seen it, but it was jarring to stack both men up like that.

The Kozak drove off. As the men began their descent back into the base's tunnels, they passed a Ukrainian fighting position with sandbags. Everyone at the base had heard the enormous noise of the fight for the last hour and a half. At the entrance Dan saw a sentry. He stood holding a salute as they passed solemnly by.

Everyone sat down, drinking water, trying to rehydrate. What Dan called "the crash" settled in as the adrenaline wore off. Ginger walked around, checking on everyone, unable to stay still, suddenly anxious. "Yeah, dude, that was horrible," said Michael. "I am definitely done."

"Yeah, it's alright, dude," said Ginger.

"Ginger," said Riever when the younger man came to him, "I did not like that."

Tex had been the closest to Oleksii. *Tex is all fucked up*, Ginger thought. Ginger sat down next to Tex, smoking his "combat suck." Symon sat on the Texan's other side.

"Ginger," said the pirate, "give me this shit."

"This?" asked Ginger, holding up his e-cigarette.

"Yes, this shit," replied Symon.

"I thought these were for pussies," said Ginger. The Ukrainian had teased him mercilessly since his shift to e-cigarettes earlier in the week.

"Yes," sighed Symon. "And I am one for today."

Okay, holy shit, thought Ginger.

Dmitri was rattled. Oleksii was his first man to die while the medic tried to save him. Dmitri's ankle didn't help; Riever saw it and thought he had never seen skin with such a hideous shade of purple blue. Greg dosed Dmitri with ketamine, relieving the physical pain and getting him high as a kite. The tall medic then checked the rest of the teams for bullet holes, keeping minds occupied. He talked the Belorussians into getting them something to eat, which turned out to be cookies.

Riever walked out to the twenty-foot-wide set of steps that went back up to ground level, under a small alcove. Doug was sitting there, smoking a cigarette. The Brit's eyes were a brilliant blue-green, but they bore the same look that Riever had noticed in the hallway of Building 6, just before they carried Jordan down the stairs. Jordan had been like a little brother to Doug. *That's not Doug*, Riever thought. The Royal Marine smiled at the Ranger, giving a small nod of acknowledgment.

Artem was crying, bawling his eyes out on the stairs. Big Max was quiet. Riever looked over at Loup. The Georgian was exactly as he always was: same expression, same calm silence, same impassivity. The only thing bothering him was a bit of dirt in his beard, which he eliminated with ruthless, methodical pawing. *Untouched*, thought Riever, watching. *Completely untouched*.

They smoked, Riever borrowing a real cigarette from Doug. The Belorussians looked at them. They knew what the feeling was. They left them alone.

Symon reported that he had ordered the launch of two Switchblade 300 missiles just as they'd gotten back to the base. The story went that they had been delivered by President Zelensky on one of his ballsy, unannounced visits to the front. One Switchblade went into a window, targeting the men inside. The other hit a group of men exfiling from the building, adding to the team's overall toll on the Russians. It was "one more fuck you," as Greg put it.

Vadym, their former commander and now head of the Legion, arrived with the head of military intelligence for the area. Vadym debriefed the Legion teams. He wanted to orchestrate a counterattack by another unit. "You guys are going home," he said.

"No," said Ginger. "I'll bomb up my mags and we'll go back out."

"No," the senior officers said. "You're going home. Get your shit, get in the Kozak, and go back to your safehouse."

They went back, helping Dmitri with his bad ankle into the Kozak, and rattled their way over the bridge.

16

DREAD

They walked into the safehouse like the warriors they were, stooping from the weight of their kit and dripping sweat. The ammo and grenade pouches were flat and empty, with the flaps open. They had no rockets left. Several men were smeared with Oleksii's or Jordan's blood. Dmitri was limping badly, and everyone was glad to be alive. There were hugs and backslaps and the joy of living. Marti stripped off his kit and threw it on the bed. The big Hungarian walked up to Riever. They hadn't been close; a small dispute over differences in urban battle tactics in the early days had caused a chill. Marti opened his arms, and the two embraced. "We survived," said the Hungarian, "and today you are my brother." *That meant a lot to me*, the Ranger realized as he stepped back.

They sat up all night until Vadym and Symon came back from headquarters. There was work to do: Black Team needed help to contact Jordan's family, and to get his body evacuated to the UK. Both bodies would be evacuated to Kyiv. They sat and quietly compared their experiences.

Tex told the story about Oleksii refusing to take the money for his watch. He'd thought about it every day since then, even before Oleksii died.

"Wow," said Ginger.

"Yeah, dude, he knew it was going to happen out here," said Tex.

"Yeah, no shit he did," replied Ginger.

Tex had brought eight hundred rounds to the firefight. Most of it was armor-piercing and incendiary. He fired everything but half a belt. He had seen someone duck behind cover; he filled the wall the Russian ducked behind with holes. Having seen the power of armor-piercing rounds on concrete days before, Ginger thought the Texan must have killed at least a dozen people on his own. He had seen Tex's tracers go straight through the catwalk. Ginger knew that he had killed at least one, the guy on the first floor. Doug killed two from the staircase; Big Max three; Artem one more on the third floor. Dan and Loup, the SAW gunners, had held the best positions. They had fired the most rounds and had likely hit more. The twenty rockets fired by others had probably taken out others. Not including the Belorussians, they had shot more than three and a half thousand rounds of ammunition.

They had inflicted more damage than they received, but after losing Oleksii and Jordan it didn't feel like it. "But we killed fuckin' twenty of them and they killed two of us," Ginger said. "I'll take that any day."

Before the mission, Black Team had been planning to leave Severodonetsk for other missions in a few days. Michael, whose visa expiration was fast approaching, had planned to go with them. That evening, Black Team told the Marine that they were leaving at 6:30 the next morning, to take Jordan's body back to Kyiv. He had to go: they were his only ride out.

Michael talked to Prym and Symon, who went to headquarters and cleared his paperwork for him. He handed in his rifle and his green book. He sorted his gear, leaving anything useful or issued on his rack so that others could take it. Everyone was upset, tired, and a bit wrung out. Michael talked to Greg, then went to say goodbye to the rest of Alpha in the next room. They were already asleep. He didn't want to wake them.

Michael woke up early the next morning and started organizing his stuff. The night before he'd talked to Greg about the idea of evacuating Matador, the kitten, with him. He was frantic, grabbing and packing kit. He had about three minutes. *Fuck it*, he thought. *I'm taking Matador. I can do this; I can take care of him and get him to a better home. I can't save all of these cats, but I can take this cat.* The tiny kitten went into an MRE box lined with a towel.

Nearby, George woke up, still confused and partly asleep. "Did that just fucking happen?" asked George. *What is happening? Is that a kitten in a box?*

"Yeah!" said Michael, rolling out with Black Team and the tiny kitten.

Later in the day Greg drove Symon back to headquarters. More intel had come down. Radio traffic indicated that the Russians had been building up forces in their target building in order to assault the Belorussians' base. Their drone footage showed perhaps fifty to seventy Russians in the target building. It had an underground bunker, much like the Belorussians' base. They confirmed at least thirteen dead, with more wounded.

"And we scared the shit out of them," Greg reported. "As soon as we stopped shooting, they grabbed their wounded and went out the back to their next position because they thought they were being attacked by a battalion." A battalion usually holds about a thousand men. Only twenty had attacked the Russians.

They started planning new missions, crammed into the basement: Riever at the table, Dan on his bed, Greg perched on Tex's, Ginger stalking around.

Greg offered to load their massive stash of C4 explosives into a satchel charge, infiltrate the Russian target building, and blow up the enemy. The tall medic was also a wizard with explosives. Both Riever, who had been certified a "master breacher" by the U.S. Army's demolition course, and Dan, who had some of the most extensive training the U.S. could offer, were repeatedly impressed with the extent of Greg's knowledge and skills.

"Greg, you'll die doing that shit," Riever replied. The SEAL agreed.

The medic was adamant. "We're all going to die!" he snapped.

They were told to stand by. Symon went to Kyiv for Oleksii's funeral, and was supposed to be back in two days. Prym went back and forth to headquarters to meet with Vadym. They assumed that Symon would come back and they could go back out and fight the Russians. They got new grenade launchers, some kind of copy of the

South African Milkor. They had six chambers, like a huge revolver, and shot the NATO standard 40 mm rather than the more common ex-Soviet 30 mm. Marti instantly adopted one as his own. Tex took another. *We're getting fed*, thought Ginger, *we're going to go back out and scrap.* They planned a mission for the next night.

The next morning, the Russians blew the bridge. "I think it's because of us," Dan said later. The Russians could have destroyed that bridge at any time. They wanted the Ukrainians to have a way out, and they wanted to save it for themselves. "But after a couple of days of us going out and duking it out every single time, they were like, *yeah, this shit has to end* ... some Russian commander was like, *we're not going to do this every day.*"

This made future operations much more difficult. They would have to infil with all of their gear and a lot of rockets and ammo, only on foot. The distance each day had already been a kilometer; walking five or six kilometers, plus crossing the river in little boats, in order to get to their previous drop-off zone would likely find them with much-reduced combat effectiveness. The other problem was casevacs: as they bitterly knew, moving casualties out was extremely difficult. A wounded person would stand little chance of surviving, and they might have to leave bodies behind. *Can we even do anything at this point?* George wondered. *Is there any point in the Ukrainians holding this town at all? They can barely resupply the guys on the other side.* The entire pocket was getting smaller and smaller. The Russians were closing in.

They patched up their minor injuries while they waited. Dmitri's ankle was serious: still a tremendous shade of purple and Prussian blue, it was, in Riever's technical terminology, "fucked." The Green Beret went back to Kyiv; eventually they heard that he had an MCL tear. The overall rate of lower-limb injury from the two big firefights was high. Ginger had messed up his ankle walking into a mortar hole on the egress from the long day. George had rolled his ankle in the first minutes of the most recent firefight and had run on adrenaline, even carrying Oleksii, for the rest of it, and then rolled the same ankle again in the rubble. Days later, Riever's left thigh still ached. Finally, smoking his watermelon e-cig, he noticed that the melon-pink tube, which had been sitting in his front-left pocket during the second firefight, had a burned-out chip in it. Probably the result of hot shrapnel whacking into it at high speed, it had pushed hard into his leg, causing the latent pain. The burned e-cig case had prevented any penetration. "Smoking saves lives!" the Ranger cracked.

Riever liked his own space. Early on he had gone to the house's little root cellar and cleared a place to sleep on a shelf. He found insulation with shiny backing and put down a few layers. He found a pillow and used his sleeping bag. All of his kit was stacked nearby, with his gear and weapons on the two shelves above him as he slept. He would listen to Denys Davydov's "Updates from Ukraine" on YouTube and other positive, very pro-Ukraine channels, hoping that he would not hear that Severodonetsk had been cut off. He would calculate his chances with the artillery in the little root cellar: there was the one layer of concrete that formed the ceiling, and another laid unusually in the attic, as though the owners had expected to get bombed. If the round landed in the alcove door, he would be safe from one angle, but if a round landed in a different part of the alcove, he would be less safe. He would go through the math over and over, and figured that he was *pretty* safe. But you can never really persuade yourself that you're safe when you're being surrounded. Being taken prisoner wasn't an option.

Riever and Ginger would sit under the alcove entrance to the cellar, smoking their e-cigarettes with just enough cover. At first Ginger would tease the older man about his encirclement fears. Then, eventually, when it started to get really bad, he stopped. *Not because he's scared*, Riever realized, *but because he knows that I'm scared and he's not going to make it any worse. Which is very nuanced of him*, he thought of the soldier they were starting to call the "oldest twenty-five-year-old in the world."

They killed time anxiously. They fiddled with their gear, cleaned everything, worked out. Riever read Lord Byron's "The Destruction of Sennacherib" aloud for Tex and Ginger.

> For the Angel of Death spread his wings on the blast,
> And breathed in the face of the foe as he passed;

And the eyes of the sleepers waxed deadly and chill,
And their hearts but once heaved, and for ever grew still!

They played old songs like "Roland the Thompson Gunner" and the mercenary song. Tex had an amazing collection of war songs, Rhodesian stuff and songs from the Russians' war in Afghanistan. Outside, the artillery kept booming. On Liveuamap they could see the bulge that gave the only way out of the pocket as it got smaller and smaller and smaller. Symon was still gone; they had no connection to headquarters, where they weren't allowed to be present without a Ukrainian commander. Some joked that they wouldn't even know whether they'd been abandoned or overrun or not. But it was mostly joking—they could hear their favorite neighborhood mortar crew moving around, still drawing counter-battery fire. There was a plan that someone, probably Ginger, proposed to separate their house from the rest of the world. "When the Russians come we will make a deal, don't fuck with us and we won't fuck with you. We can just live here with the dogs," he said. Humor was running short. The situation just wasn't that funny.

As they waited for news, Loup managed to fix the shower. He found the cistern, figured out all the plumbing, and indicated in his silent way that he could get the shower working. They plugged it into the generator, which was out at the back next to the outdoor toilet, itself merely a few boards over a hole. It worked for a few times before the system shut back down again.

Riever was not a cat person and would always tell any feline, even the otherwise universally adored kitten Matador, to go away, a grumpiness that earned him the nickname "Grandpa Riever." (Dan, meanwhile, became "Daddy Dan.") One day, Riever petted one of the cats. "Oh man," everyone else teased, noticing it, "you think it's that bad, huh? You finally broke down and you're being nice to the cat!"

After five days, Symon came back with news: the Russians had crossed the river and now were on the Lysychansk side. "The entire Legion is being pulled from Severodonetsk. We're about to get surrounded. They can't risk more Westerners getting surrounded like in Mariupol." They all knew that being taken prisoner wasn't an option. Two Westerners had recently been captured by the Russians.

Under obvious torture, they had started singing like canaries, their "confessions" broadcast all over television and the internet.

They started to pack. "We're leaving tomorrow morning," the pirate said.

A few hours went by. Symon went to headquarters again, then returned. "Okay, you guys," he sighed. "You know how in Ukraine everything is always changing. Well, for this second, we are staying." The Legion would pull out, but they were going to stay to extract the Ukrainians from the other side of the bridge. Vadym, who had visited a few days before, was trying to sort out the possible collapse of the northern flank and thought he might need a team of shooters. Symon went to take a phone call.

This isn't a war, it's a comic opera with a lot of death, Riever thought, adapting a quote from the audiobook of George Orwell's *Homage to Catalonia* that ran in his head on repeat. *It's a bloody pantomime.*

Forty-five minutes later, Symon came back in. "*Pizdets, blyat.* Pack your shit. We leave now."

"What?"

"Now," said the pirate. "It is *pizdets*. We are leaving."

Fucking what? thought Ginger. They packed frantically, the entire armory, Black Team's gear, everything. They were ordered to pull back to Bakhmut.

They were not all happy to be leaving. Some, like Riever, were worried about getting surrounded. Others, like George, took the view that with the bridge down, a unit like theirs could do little to help and should get out of the way. But Ginger was pissed. *This is the most disheartening thing*, he thought.

He was riding with Riever and Dan. They drove past a destroyed excavator. There were artillery craters in the roads. "This is chickenshit!" Ginger insisted. "We should've stayed and fought. We lost two guys and we left. We didn't get any sort of vengeance."

"Yeah, I get it, dude," Dan said. "I would've preferred staying too."

"Fuck that!" declared Riever. "I'm glad to be getting out of here." He did not want to participate in Mariupol 2.0.

As they drove out, convoys of BTRs and MLRS rocket systems with 777 howitzers in tow were going in. *What the fuck?* thought Riever. *There's no way they'd lose a 777. We must not have been as close to getting surrounded as we thought. If we'd known this was the situation, we'd have been fine staying. But no one told us anything!*

"I've got half a mind to hop out of this truck with my rifle and my ammo and hop on that one and go back," Ginger said.

He was angry. They learned later that the heavy stuff going in was going to cover an orderly retreat. The Ukrainians pulled their men out of Severodonetsk properly: there would be no other encirclements as in Mariupol, for the Legion or anyone else.

They finally arrived in Bakhmut, where they had kitted up on their way in weeks before, listening to "Pink Skies" on Tex's playlist. They were out: out of the pocket, just beyond the reach of the guns. *Cool*, thought George. *Made it to Bakhmut. Not going to die today*. Riever thought he had never felt such relief in his life. They all knew that if they had been surrounded, they must die. They could not be captured. Getting out of the encirclement was like starting a new life. Still dressed in full kit, covered in sweat, they paused at the famous Dzoker's street food shop. They stripped off their kit, peeled off sweaty combat shirts, and bought shawarma and hot dogs at the tiny market. They ate and smoked and loaded back in the vehicles.

The civilians just stared at them, wide-eyed. They all looked like shit. "Yup," Ginger said, staring back. "Alright, bye!" They drove on to Kramatorsk, which would be their next operational area, changing two flat tires on the way. They all stood on top of one another to repair the thing, arguing over which jack to use and borrowing bricks from someone's lawn to set it up. It was a minor annoyance, but everyone was so happy to have a minor annoyance. It was almost fun.

17

KRAMATORSK

Ginger looked around as they arrived at their new posting. It wasn't a school but probably some sort of orphanage. They stacked all their gear in a root cellar and another basement, alongside pallets of a Pepsi energy drink. In the main building there were big, open-bay barrack-type rooms with beds, plus a playground at the back and a cafeteria. The bathrooms were for the children, with tiny, toddler-sized toilets. For the first few days, no one realized that there were adult-sized options in the separate cafeteria building; eventually Riever found them. It was a plumbing disaster. They had arrived in the middle of the night. *There's no flushing a man turd down that thing*, Ginger thought upon entering. *Ridiculous.*

Their own space was a big, long room, like something straight out of the musical *Annie*. The room was lined with child-length bunk beds. The men stacked the miniature bunks together, clearing spaces to sleep on the floor in between. Everyone crammed in. Riever texted his girlfriend the all-clear. "I'm safe and tucked in," he wrote. "Exhausting day. Relieved tho."

Kramatorsk was beautiful—green with thick forests and mountains, it was a great fighting area. The woods were dense and the towns were small. They men were told that it would be a temporary position for Alpha and Charlie. They would help out in the operational area while they waited for their turn to rotate back to Kyiv. A small river separated them from a Russian-held town. They settled in to get the lay of the land and prepare for new missions.

Soon Symon called Tex, Ginger, and Riever over. "Hey," he said, "you guys are going to get medals. Right now, the plan is that

211

Zelensky is going to give them to you when we get back to Kyiv, and there's a possibility that Biden will be there." It was clear to everyone that they wanted three presentable people, three American faces, for publicity and morale. Dan bowed out; with his backstory and his ex-wife, he didn't need the scrutiny. Tex already had three medals for valor. Greg saw them once as they were packing. "Wow," said the tall medic, looking over, "you've got *that* one?"

In the orphanage one day, the group chat pinged. Riever saw a video, something that looked like a clip from one of the *Pirates of the Caribbean* movies. It was from Greg. *What the fuck is this?*

Made with a Ukrainian app called Reface, it was a dead-on impression of Prym's most common Prymisms, laid over a scene from one of the later *Pirates of the Caribbean* movies, where a bewigged officer steps regally down the ship's deck stairs while everything around him is blown to smithereens. "You don't understand, mate," said Greg's Prym impression. "I have an order, *blyat*. It's okay. It's normal. This is Ukraine, okay? This is our artillery. *Giiiin-ger!* Get the N L-*ow*."

Riever started giggling. Suddenly, there was a wave of laughter as everyone else started to check their phones. Throughout the day peals of laughter echoed through the building at odd intervals. George chuckled for three days straight.

"And that's what happens when you get really bored," the medic admitted later. He usually kept himself busy by organizing his medical gear. He was running his own network, raising funds to import supplies from the West and distribute it to other medics. He was always out in the hall, in his cargo pants and bandana, sorting his gear and repackaging stuff for others. *He's a hub*, Riever realized, watching. *He has all these deals going on.*

Also in the orphanage were six new guys for Alpha Team. It added a strange feeling to the mix. There's always a tension with "replacements." *Band of Brothers* had a whole episode dedicated to the term. The original Alpha Team didn't initially want them there. Lots of them still wanted to be back in Severo; everyone, obviously, wanted their dead teammates still to be with them. *It's that petty "new guy in the unit while you're on deployment" grudge*, thought Ginger.

Black Team had a new influx of men as well. Among them were two Brits. The one was a lean, quiet professional with close-cropped, light-brown hair, called Rory. The other was an effusive former fighter with a missing tooth and an accent so thick you could cut it with a knife. Like so many Scottish soldiers throughout history, he was nicknamed Jock.

Along with Black Team's new men had come British George, back for more. He joined Artem's team. As Riever was driving out of the orphanage one day to do errands with a few others, British George poked out of one of the upper windows. With perfect aim, he threw a bright, three-foot-tall Barbie down into the bed of the moving truck. No one else had any idea, and they drove around the combat zone for the rest of the day with a giant Barbie in the back.

The new guys had brought in replacement gear, with plenty of stuff from DRMO, the U.S. military's secondhand store. Everyone patched up their kit. Riever carefully upgraded his system to the model that Dan had taught him, placing his magazines one deep all around his body, rather than stacking them two deep on his chest. If you have to go two deep, the SEAL had advised; do it on the sides, to balance the weight better.

In Kramatorsk the Ukrainian Army was feeding them and the Belorussians together. Every day, someone would arrive with a giant old Soviet container backpack. It was a huge metal soup tub with straps, just like something out of Stalingrad in World War II, where the German snipers had shot at the men crawling forward to feed the frontline troops, covering them in hot liquid in freezing temperatures if they didn't kill them outright first. This time the backpacks were full of borscht and other local classics, like salo, plus bread and cheese. The MREs were stored under the stairs.

Riever and Ginger would go through the MREs to find the coffee and hot chocolate, and would brew them to pass the time. Dan still had an electric kettle, though his original had been left in Lysychansk. It was one of the few times, aside from his screaming at the big Belorussian slacking on Oleksii's litter, that anyone saw the SEAL unruffled. "Where the fuck is the electric kettle? Who loaded the electric kettle?" he had snapped upon noticing its disappearance. Someone produced a replacement: a two-liter black version.

They went down to the range to prep the new guys and to align the sights of every weapon, including some new sniper rifles. Riever got a British .338 sniper rifle. Alpha's new sniper, a former Marine named Kyle, got Loup's personal bolt action. Loup brought along his battlefield acquisition, the .50 cal Barrett.

The Ranger finished zeroing with his third shot. Looking up, he realized that Loup had sighted in with a single shot at a 900-meter target. The Georgian was hiking up a hill towards a crane in order to get a longer shot, which he made in two. *Crazy*, thought Riever. *He's so fucking good at that shit. Stupid good.*

When everyone was done, Symon brought out bread and meat and a strange, savory beer that reminded Riever of Marmite. They sat on the dusty range and had a picnic.

Two sniper teams went out on missions for long-range, three-day overlooks. Prym had Loup, George, and Marti, while Dan took Riever, Greg, and Kyle. They drove past massive factories in the middle of nowhere and finally found the local HQ, where they were warned to keep the sniper rifles under cover and away from prying drone cameras. *Professional*, thought Riever.

The Americans set up on a long power line cut, on a hill overlooking Russian positions on the other side of a river, waiting for movement and a good shot, right at a bend in the road where someone walking out of the position would be coming straight towards them, thus eliminating the need to lead a moving target. The two teams shared a SOPHIE thermal imager between them. It was quiet, a rarity in an area usually full of drones and artillery.

They started digging, one hole for the sniper and one each for the rest of the men. Riever, in his hole, looked over and saw Dan working. *He has a nice hole dug*, thought the Ranger. Greg's was, admittedly, "a less nice hole," but no foxhole was ever going to hold the giant medic anyway. Riever cut down a small tree and collected brush, providing overhead cover and camouflage.

They would swap off time on the gun, carefully looking down the gap. Over in Prym's position, the view was terrible, and Loup started getting steamed.

At Dan's spot it was quiet and, aside from the sleeping-in-a-hole bit, fairly fun. Greg was happy; he liked getting to talk with Riever and

Dan though he liked attempting to sleep in his hole less. His tall frame fit poorly. Someone took a photo of his best attempt: grey socks peeking out between his fully laced boots and camo pants, cargo pocket stuffed near to bursting, with a blue-grey jacket pulled up around his ears, and his good luck clowns bandana sweeping his golden hair off his forehead. He was snuggled up to his own hands and the side of the hole as a pillow, in the same position in which so many parents have found their children sleeping at night during one final check before turning in.

Riever picked Dan's brain on the state of the U.S. special operations community. The SEAL had briefly gotten out of the service in order to become a police officer, and had a good perspective on his experiences before and after the break, since he had done the entire process twice. Greg told them stories about Hostomel and the beginning of the war.

One day Riever gave Kyle a wink and said something about Thai women. Dan was off, talking for ages about his theories about their differences from American women and his experiences over several years in the country. Kyle, on the gun, with his hat folded back like a sailor, finally looked up. Newly arrived, he knew nothing of Dan's tragic backstory. "Man," said the Marine, "you haven't said a thing for two days. Apparently Thai women is what you like to talk about!"

Greg regaled the group with his tales of being in Right Sector, the coalition of Ukrainian nationalist organizations, when he was younger, and the relationship between politics and soccer hooligans in Ukraine. It was a thing, the medic explained. You have a club, they have a club, and you call each other up and set up the rules (no crowbars etc.) and then you rumble in the park.

"Uh, is it *friendly?*" asked Riever.

"Well, some," said Greg. "You go and you fight and you all drink afterwards. But if you fight the anarchists or the communists, it's serious. You're trying to hurt them." The medic had only fond memories.

This is fucking weird, man, thought Riever. *Strange.* But the hooligans weren't for show; they had been integral to the protests in Kyiv's Maidan, or Independence Square, in 2014. Greg had been one of the first men through the door when the protesters stormed a government building, fighting with the riot police. Eventually they'd caught him and beaten him quite badly with more than just their fists. He'd taken a few months to recover before starting the insurgent training that had introduced him to the old German medic who had gotten him into medicine in the first place.

When the sniper teams arrived back from their mission, another small team needed a Gus (pronounced "goose") gunner—someone who could shoot the Carl Gustaf, a multi-purpose anti-tank and support rocket named for its original Swedish designer. Riever, who had zeroed their Gus in Lysychansk already, went to help hit a Russian Nona auto mortar. The new team drove out and crept up to a location near the river. On the other side, they could see the smoke from the chunking mortar rising into the air, but the shooting position was poor. Tex and Ginger stayed to keep watch while Riever, Artem, and Kyle scouted for a better position. They picked up a Ukrainian guide, armed only with a notebook, and searched around in lower ground, an experience that started with climbing into an empty house through a window and ended with Riever and Artem clearing an overgrown backyard orchard together after the Black Team commander heard nearby voices in Russian saying, "This is where the apples are."

Despite their efforts they never found a better spot. Finally, the next day they settled on an unorthodox tactic: lasing the smoke cloud, setting a time-delay airburst on the rocket, and then lobbing it in. Riever and Ginger started to work on the mechanics.

They were interrupted by a new request from Artem, who had been co-opted into planning for a raid. They moved down to a small basement that had been previously used by a Ukrainian Stinger team. The approach was hairy: driving ten miles through open fields whose skies were thick with Russian helicopters to a woodline full of dug-in Ukrainian positions, from which you walked up and dropped down into the town on the river. Riever was carrying the Gus, a juicy target, as a drone flew up and hovered right over them. *Holy fuck*, thought the Ranger, *we're going to die*. But the drone flew on.

They arrived at Artem's basement position: it was crumbling from artillery hits. There were dead birds littered about; Riever found Stinger end-caps from a previous mission on the floor. The Ranger chose a firing spot for the Gus, near where the Stinger had been fired, to support the raid. Riever conferred with one of the Belorussians who had joined them about the details. With a few hours to go, he bedded down to catch a bit of sleep before the raid. When the Ranger woke up the next morning, the raid was cancelled. The Ukrainians had a conflicting plan. The Americans made the hair-raising drive back to Kramatorsk and the orphanage.

They planned more sniper missions, operating from a precipitous hill overlooking a huge monastery and church, rotating teams to provide overwatch. Stone steps led up to a high position overlooking the river and the Russian-held town on the northern side. The hill was covered in forest, and high up, almost at the top, was a small concrete parking lot. There was also a small service shack, probably for a groundskeeper. An elegant, neatly paved terrace led to a huge staircase that wound down the side of the hill. It overlooked the gorgeous Orthodox church, with its beautiful, almost teal-green cupolas and gold onion domes and spires on the top. The river lay beyond.

Alpha set up sniper teams at the top of the staircase. The team leader, Riever, working from the .338, didn't like the position. *It's perfect*, he thought. *Too perfect. They have to know that someone will use this.* The whole area was sprinkled with debris from the artillery smashing into the trees.

Riever watched a whole file of Russians moving from the northern woods down into the town itself, but they were too far away for a shot. The Russians were smart: they kept the Luhansk and Donetsk People's Republic (LPR/DNR) men in the town but stayed in the safer spaces in the woods themselves. The Ranger also saw a group of military-aged males wandering around and hanging out near one particular house, bullshitting. He tried to look closer: were those white Russian armbands or just someone's shirt? He couldn't tell, so he and the sniper Kyle didn't take the shot.

Their small team reported to Symon after the rotation. The pirate was less than impressed. Every military-aged male on the other side of the river was an enemy combatant, he explained. "Just fucking shoot them," said the commander.

Riever mentioned to a Belorussian commander that he could identify the house that the military-aged males had been using. If they could find a good spot, they could hit it with the Gus. "Well, let's go right now!" the other man declared.

"Alright," said the Ranger. "Let me get some sleep, and then we'll go."

When he woke up, the Belorussian he had been talking to was gone. The Belorussian team had taken a new mission out closer to Severodonetsk: the Russians were making an armored push, and they wanted to try to kill a few tanks.

Later that day they heard that the Belorussians had been wiped out. They were all dead and captured, including their leader Brest, who had fought with them on the day Oleksii and Jordan were killed. Symon went back to headquarters at Lysychansk to see if Alpha could help with a body recovery, but there was nothing to be done.

Ginger went back to operate out of the dead-bird basement for a few days. Chad, one of the men from the team's earlier days, who had left after the bad peninsula mission and missed the fighting in Severodonetsk, had come back with the new guys and was antsy. He declared an intention to cross the river with eight men, break into a building, capture a DNR man, and interrogate him.

"What?" said Ginger. "How are you going to get him across the river?"

"We're not!" said Chad. "We're gonna interrogate him and let him go."

Ginger looked at him. "Okay." His head was aching. The dead birds were still on the floor and he was pretty certain asbestos was everywhere.

There had been multiple versions of a cross-river raid plan. Riever had identified the house base of the military-aged males, the one he and the Belorussian had been planning to hit with the Gus before the Belorussians were wiped out on a different raid. There was the option to just hit the house base with the Gus. Another idea was to go across and get a Stinger shot from the other side of the river, taking down a helicopter. They collected rope, inflatable boats, and other gear. Dan was doubtful; the conditions didn't look great.

Chad left with Artem. Ginger sat down, smoking an e-cig. He turned to Noah, whom he'd met less than a week ago. Noah was one of their new guys. A former U.S. Army paratrooper, he was lean, heavily tattooed, and squared away. Greg was dozing in the next room. "Hey, dude," Ginger said. "Can I ask you a question? Like honestly?"

"What?"

"So, Chad wants to take eight guys across the river tonight. None of us have slept, we have no idea what's happening on the other side of the river. No one's crossed the river. We don't have any sort of support, no drone support, no artillery, no nothin'. He wants to sneak through two kilometers of this city without being spotted, without being heard, break into a house that could very well be an OP [observation post] with armed guards that are up at night, there could be armed guards on the street. We don't know 'cause we just got here. He wants to take new dudes across there, break into a house, interrogate somebody in their house, and then just leave like it never happened."

"Yeah, dude, it's a hard pass for me," said Noah.

"I just don't understand," said Ginger. They only had six sets of NODs anyway. Greg's had been lost in Severo, when Dmitri ripped apart his aid bag trying to save Oleksii. They had no idea about mines or the river approach. *They just want to do it because they're bored. Because Chad just showed up and he missed Severo.* "Am I just trippin' or is this actually retarded?"

"No, this is actually retarded," said Noah.

"Okay, good, 'cause I don't feel comfortable doing this, at all," said Ginger.

Greg's voice piped up from the other room. "Dude, thank you, I was thinking the same thing this whole time! This is fucked!"

Oh, thank you, Jesus, thought Ginger. *This is Mr. I-want-to-die-in-this-war-for-my-country-because-I'm-an-animal-of-a-man-and-I-am-just-insane. If Greg thinks it's fuckin' stupid, it's stupid.*

Symon's orders were clear: shoot any military-aged males you see on the other side of the river. The teams started rotating in and out of the overlook position, staffing it 24/7. The new plan was to observe and confirm, then hit the house base with the Gus.

Riever led another team back to the monastery overlook: Ginger, Tex, and Kyle. They brought the sniper rifles and Stingers, hoping to hit either Russians on the other side of the river, or helicopters, or both. Riever thought it was a numbers game. They could absolutely see the enemy. If they waited long enough, they would eventually get a good shot. They just needed to keep that place manned.

As they were getting ready to go, Doug and British George asked to join them. "Fuck yeah, you can come," replied Riever, who was ground force commander of the op. *Those guys are fun*. He gave Doug his .338 sniper rifle for the mission.

For a few hours before dawn, they were on the stairs, watching with the SOPHIE imager. On the thermal, Ginger saw the MLRS rocket system, picking it out among other vehicles. They had no Javelin, and their comms weren't working. But the MLRS was too good a target to pass up, so Riever ran back through the town, down the entire woodline, and back to Artem's temporary base. They drove down the hair-raising road in the dark—a dangerous proposition aside from the Russians, since everyone was forced to drive without lights and near crashes were not uncommon. Together they found the local headquarters and armory but could locate no Javelins or anything else. The Ukrainians promised to send a Stugna, another anti-tank missile, so Riever and Artem went back to their overlook position. The MLRS had gone.

They were on the gun line when they heard the salvo of artillery heading for their hill. It sounded almost perfectly in line with the stairs, as if it was just ten feet over their heads. They leaped into holes; in Riever's case it was an actual gutter. Later they would realize that there must have been something about the shape of the hill that affected the sound. For one long second the whistle extended, sounding exactly as if it was about to hit them. Then it flew over, striking on the farther side of the hill.

Riever pulled everyone back, not knowing if they had been the target or if it had been a lucky shot. A helicopter showed up, but it was too far off for the Stingers. Riever tucked into an alternative sniper hide site further up the hill.

Soon Doug and British George approached Riever, overlooking from the upper hide site, looking out with the sniper rifle. "Why'd we leave?" they demanded.

"Because we don't know if they have us zeroed or not. They may just be shooting at us and just hitting long, so we should try to stay under cover."

"But why don't we go back down there?" the pair demanded.

Riever let them go; there was no holding them anyway. Doug took the .338 and they inched down the hill, to where Ginger had taken a lower overlook position with the SOPHIE.

Days before, they had been briefed about two Orthodox priests who were informing the Russians about Ukrainian Army activity on their side of the river. The Ukrainians had decided that they were protected, an episode that Ginger called "religious ridiculousness." The priests would walk around, taking photos, and send them straight to the Russians.

The Brits weren't having it either. Doug had cooked up an idea, soon expanded on by British George. "Well, mate," said British George to Ginger as they huddled on the overwatch position on the staircase, a stone's throw from the church. "Mate! What do you think would happen if I just threw a fuckin' grenade through that window, mate?"

"George!" hissed Ginger. "Shut the fuck up, dude! There's Russians thirty-five meters in front of us. Shut up."

Doug wiggled down towards them. "George! Did you tell Ginger our idea, mate?"

"Doug! We're not throwing a fuckin' grenade through the window!"

"But, mate!" protested the Royal Marine. "You said you wanted to kill him too!"

"I said *if* the opportunity presents itself! We're not going to throw a grenade through the window of a church," said the American.

"But, mate! It would be too easy. We could just say it was artillery."

"Dude, it's a fuckin' frag grenade! You had better throw a thousand of them in there."

"Well, I ain't got a thousand of 'em, mate," grinned Doug, "but I got two. You think it'll work?"

Ginger started laughing. "Oh, my God, dude, no fuckin' way."

British George started getting antsy. "What the fuck, mate? There's nothing to do out here. Let's go get them fuckin' priests!"

"You know what, dude, fuck it, let's go," said Ginger. Doug's eyes lit up as if he'd just smashed a line of coke. Ping! *Oh my God, no, I shouldn't have said that*, thought Ginger.

"Mate, let's go get the 66," said Doug, using the British term for an M72 LAW anti-tank weapon, "and we'll put it through the window. Come on, mate! We've got two of 'em. I'll even let you shoot one!"

"Of course you're going to let me shoot one! It was my fuckin' idea."

"Oh, okay, mate, come on, let's go!"

The plan ran straight into Riever and Artem: "You guys cannot fucking shoot a church with a rocket launcher."

Ginger and Tex were still egging the Brits on. "Ginger!" said Riever. "Shut the fuck up! You guys are just instigating." *Yes, Riever, that is* exactly *what we're doing*, thought Ginger.

Soon the Brits were back at Riever's location. "We've got somebody!" they declared. "We're gonna kill him! It's legit, he's got armbands and shit!" Riever sighed. They were completely brave, completely willing to die, hysterical to have around, and absolutely impossible. *Fire and gasoline*, the Ranger thought. *Just walking manifestations of chaos.* He later learned that Artem wouldn't allow the pair to go on missions together because they were so difficult to handle.

Riever was doubtful of the target, but Kyle, wearing Jordan's ghillie suit which he had been borrowing since his arrival, agreed to go down to check it out. Doug still had Riever's .388. The Ranger took up a separate position, watching across the river on a scope.

It was a 1,100-meter shot across the river. Out of the corner of his eye, Riever saw the Raufoss round from Kyle's rifle explode in a bright flash. It was a dead calm day: cool, no wind, the perfect atmosphere for shooting.

Tex called it up: "You hit him. He's down."

Through his scope, Riever couldn't see the body, but he could see the opposite side of the street. A fat old man in a wifebeater was standing with his arms straight out, like Jesus, completely stunned. The Ranger wasn't sure if it was him he heard, but somehow over the river wafted the shouted words "*pizdets, blyat!*" The old man looked like he'd seen a thunderbolt strike right in front of him.

The team got off the hill, avoiding counterbattery, and went to headquarters to report the kill.

After a lull, Riever took sniper and Stinger teams back up to the overlook position. Ahead of him at the edge of the hill, Rory lay on his belly, peering out between the several spires of the big church.

Above them, on the concrete pad, they set up an observation post with a Stinger crew of Ginger and Tex. They were hoping to spot Russian attack helicopters and take them out.

All day, strange things had been going on. The mortars had been increasing. The usual whistle of the incoming, indirect round made a strange echo off the big hill; every one sounded as if it was just about to hit you. They thought they had heard Russians in the woods. Everyone was on edge.

Whoa, thought Dan when he arrived. He had been at their base, trying to work out a plan to swim the river that would have better chances than Chad's pitch. The SEAL had offered to recce the river crossing on his own for the team's new additions, who would be staying for a week while those who had fought in Severodonetsk rotated back to Kyiv. *Any time there's water involved, he wants to do something*, thought Ginger. Dan had returned with bad news: the Russians had places pinned, and there was only one possible spot for a river crossing. It was a dead mission. Vadym, the Legion commander, agreed: it was off.

Dan came out to brief the men on the overwatch spot. He could tell that no one felt good about the position. *Maybe we just need to pull these guys off*, he thought. A Russian helicopter arrived and lofted rockets at them, but it stayed out of Stinger range. Ginger and Tex watched in frustration. The Russians suspected they were there; they were trying to draw fire in order to find the position. The boom of the rocket sent everyone scrambling into foxholes.

The sniper and Stinger teams had been meant to remain for the night to swap out with a new team in the morning, but scrapping the cross-river raid meant their presence was less crucial now. Dan added up the evidence from the day. *The Russians are fixing to light this place up*, the SEAL thought. *I don't want my guys staying here all night just to get bombed.* He ordered the teams off the hill. They headed back to Kyiv the next day.

18

MOS EISLEY

They were told that they had a just a week's leave: be ready to go when it's over. Most settled into hotels for a decent week's sleep, rather than go back to what Michael had always called "Sascha's Hell Hotel," the simultaneously melancholy and tremendously loud former girls' dormitory, where they each shared rooms with up to three other men. Dan moved right back into the dorms, into his original room: it was practical, cheap, and efficient. He lucked out and got his old room to himself. He found a gym and settled into a rhythm while he waited to go back out.

He fired up Tinder and found a match with a woman who turned out to be a Russian sympathizer. She started going on about how Zelensky was trying to create a new Israel because he was a Jew, and other standard antisemitic tropes. *Jesus, you are crazy*, he thought. *Dodged a bullet before I made a date with you!* Dan sent a screenshot of it to the group chat for fun. *Took one for the team.* When the war broke out there had been all sorts of talk about neo-Nazis and right-wing extremists in Ukraine. There are nut jobs everywhere, and wars certainly attract a few, but most of the hubbub was just Russian propaganda. Dan, who had been following the conflict for years before the full-on war broke out, had once been exasperated by a Western documentary. The journalist featured in it was sent to meet different units. Watching, Dan thought, *They're trying to talk about the war and the fighting, and all he wants to do is find Nazis.* Despite all the Russian propaganda, this Tinder match was the only antisemitic thing he'd seen in the country. He found a better woman.

"Stay close!" the three medalists were warned when they arrived. Someone suggested that they keep shaven and presentable. A text came through the group chat from Symon: "I don't care if they're presentable. They're warriors. They can have a bottle of whisky in their hand if they want."

What a special place, thought Riever.

Someone managed to get in contact with Oleksii's widow. His funeral had been a few weeks before, but most of the men on his team, stuck in Severodonetsk, hadn't been able to attend. His wife, a slender, pretty brunette, met them at a restaurant in a park in Kyiv. Their daughter, five years old, stayed behind with a babysitter, but Oleksii's wife brought their son. Dressed in a blue onesie with elephants, giraffes, and hippos drawn on it in white outline, and blue-striped socks with stars on them, he was about four months old.

She spoke no English, so Symon and Oleksii's young unofficial aide, a man named Borys, translated. The men broke the tension the best way they knew how, with soldiers' jokes.

The man they called Baby Scott, who served as what Dan called one of their "logistics or smuggler dudes," picked up the actual baby and posed for a photo, just as Tex loomed into the frame and pretended to kiss Baby Scott on the cheek: an imitation gay–interracial couple holding a Ukrainian infant in the middle of a beautiful park in Kyiv. Everyone was laughing. In the photo, Baby Scott's eyes are crinkled with laughter, while the confused infant gazes into the distance. Scott's right arm supports the baby's bottom, his left—the black metal memorial band for Oleksii visible on his wrist—crosses the child's chest just below his chin and holds him steady.

They tried to tell their stories, to give Oleksii's wife some sense of the version of the man they had known, the man whose body they had willingly carried into an artillery barrage to evacuate. But as they left, Riever kept thinking about the young widow and her baby. *We kept trying to tell stories*, he thought bitterly. *But now that's all she has left.*

Despite the formative years in Canada, Kyiv was Greg's home, and he wanted to make sure that everyone had a good time, war or no war. He pinged the group chat. "Hey, guys!" chirped the tall medic. "Check out this sexperience!" He attached two flyers. "Pet Play!" declared the first. "A gentle cat that snuggles up to its master or a naughty dog or even a horse/mare. Do you want to play the role of your favorite animal? Purr or bark, sit, milk, or bring a ball to be caressed or be punished. The choice is yours. Performance hall 1,300 hryvnia/minute. VIP room, 1,900 hryvnia/15 minutes." The other was called Baby Born. "If you once dreamed of returning to childhood, trying a pacifier with alcohol, or putting on a diaper, or sitting in a children's chair and being capricious, this is for you. Performance hall 1,300 hryvnia/minute. VIP room, 1,900 hryvnia/15 minutes." The flyers were in English.

Oh, Greg, thought Riever of the man George called "the best medic I've ever seen," and whom the Ranger was always pushing to go to officer school because his combat and leadership instincts were so good. *Our handsome weirdo.*

For his part, George was pretty done. He had spent all that time with the Norman Brigade before joining Charlie Team, and he had a mortgage to pay on his condo back in Canada. They were paid as Ukrainian privates, and money was tight, especially with the exchange rate.

"But I'm staying for another month," Riever said, deadpan, "and I don't feel safe if you're not here, because every time I almost die you're right there." They had counted: in Severodonetsk they had nearly died three times, and each time they had been standing right next to each other. The dance up the stairs as the tank ripped into them had laid a lasting foundation.

There was still the issue of the mortgage. Riever made George a trade: he'd find the money, and George could come over to Alpha Team with him. Riever gave the Canadian a few hundred dollars of his own dwindling funds and found a donor through a friend in Poland to pay the rest.

Prym was upset. "Why you not on the team?" he asked George.

"Well, Riever paid," George said. "I can't take his money and not be on his team."

Prym went to Riever. "Riever," he cried, "why you take George?"

"But, Prym," protested the Ranger, "I paid for him!" This basic principle no former French Foreign Legionnaire could deny, and the distinction did not matter so much: the teams often swapped members between them.

For everyone but Dan, one of the main attractions during leave was the drinking hole in their favorite hotel, which they called the "Star

Wars bar," after the Mos Eisley cantina made famous in the original film. It was a place where you could go after curfew and get a margherita pizza (and margherita only) and a double screwdriver (pressed upon the bartender's memory by Riever), since you couldn't go anywhere else.

There were well-dressed Western journalists who drove the nicest cars in town and only ever talked to each other; as well as Westerners posing as badasses who weren't just "there for the 'gram [Instagram]" and wanting to be seen; people purporting to hire for security contracts; foreigners from countries that didn't even exist, watching and listening for the latest on modern warfare. There were few Ukrainians, and no women.

One night Riever was approached at the urinals by a secretive, wealthy-looking young man who claimed to work for a group of Jewish oligarchs. Riever thought he was a sketchy rich kid playing games but turned him over to one of the team's networkers, who was soon attending synagogue with the young man, looking for introductions, just in case. *Everyone claims to be Mossad, or CIA, or whatever*, Riever thought, watching the bar, *and no one is. Everyone is just chickenshit.* He sat back down next to the commander of a sister team that worked out in Kharkiv, a fighter who was also a dashing, handsome, and effortlessly charming former British officer whose skills were rivaled only by those of Peter Fleming, one of his younger brother Ian's models for James Bond. They called him "Princess" and borrowed his advice on logistics and team management.

People watching around the hotel had other compensations. Journalists would come out of the building, smoking cigarettes and hanging out, holding their microphones. Then the cameraman would come out. They would cross the street to the median strip, which still had concrete barriers and sandbags, the roughest-looking place they could find next to the hotel. They would stand there and record their "live from Kyiv" segments, and then go back to the hotel. *Fucking goofy, man*, thought Riever, watching. *They're living in the nicest hotel in Kyiv and walking out to the median strip just so it could say "live from Kyiv."* It wasn't the first time he had seen it. On his very first day in Kyiv, as he waited for his turn to go to Legion headquarters, sign his papers, and draw his weapon, three Western women walked into the lobby of a different hotel he was then staying in. They were journalists.

"We should go get a massage," one said. *What?* he thought. Kyiv was shut down, in the middle of a war. The three went back and forth on the proposal. "That's kind of messed up," said one. "No, no," said the other, "we're putting money into the economy, so it's good." *Holy fuck, man*, thought the Ranger, *you guys are just pieces of shit. Go find something to report, for fuck's sake.*

The NGOs were little better. When he had crossed the border at night, he found that the Ukrainian side was lined with tents belonging to one international NGO after the other, with big signs announcing their names, rows and rows of them. None of them were manned, despite the refugees flowing past him in the opposite direction. They were just like the journalists standing in the median: as safe as they could be, but positioned for war-zone face time, this time for donor dollars.

Their period of leave dragged on. As Dan regularly complained, leaving never seemed to happen on time. Cash started to run short. They were mostly feeding and, in plenty of cases, housing themselves. The Ukrainian armed forces did their best, but it was a system under severe strain, and the logistics and support structure simply was what it was. Biden didn't come, and the medalists forgot about the awards. They started to get antsy, then finally received new orders to move south.

19

BEGINNING THE KHERSON OFFENSIVE

They road-tripped back down to Mykolaiv. Everyone was pretty depressed to return; the place hadn't been good operational territory for them before. They had heard about the Kherson offensive on the news, but when they arrived, they couldn't see many signs of it. They'd just lost a bunch of ground out east and two of their own men. *A low point*, Dan thought.

Despite the promises, they were sent back to what Dan still called "the roach motel." This time Mykolaiv was a bigger target for Russian fire, so missiles hit the city every night. They could only drive in the dark. It was a bum deal, or, as Ginger put it, "we were all pretty butthurt about it." Everyone complained.

In the meantime they took to teasing one another. Tex had an affection for women with generous behinds and liked to run his prospects by Greg. "No," the medic would insist, "that is *too* big a bottom." Likewise, everyone teased Greg, who one day came in with a picture of a young woman on a motorcycle who looked extremely tempting. She had a connection to another unit working locally. They were squared away, said the medic, and the team should consider working with them.

"You have our interest," everyone replied, eyeing the woman on the motorcycle. "Which unit?"

"Well, they're Azov," replied Greg.

"*No*, Greg!" Riever sputtered in protest. "We can't be doing that!" For his part, Greg's approach to the ideological units was pragmatic: they weren't the best fighters, but the ones who believed in something tended to outperform their training. One militia unit working in Moschun early in the war had been told to hold a World

War II bunker for a week. It cost them eighty percent casualties, but they did it. This unit had its own artillery and its own logistics train. And she *was* hot.

Noah didn't escape the ribbing either. In a fit of youth years earlier, the paratrooper had had DNR, for "Do not resuscitate," tattooed on his chest. In Ukraine, DNR also served as the Western initials of the Donbas breakaways, the Russian patsies.

Like Dan, Noah rarely wore a shirt. "So," the guys would tease him when they saw his bare chest, "do you really want us not to resuscitate?"

"No, no!" Noah would hasten to respond. "Please do resuscitate me! I insist!"

"Don't go out of your way for me!" Ginger would crack from the sidelines.

"No, no, I insist!" Noah would respond.

"You could just add in a few letters," Greg suggested one day, "and it would be doner kebab!"

They took the teams to the local impromptu range for practice. It was a field with a hill behind, with foot-high plants and scrub covering everything. It was late July, warm and dry. Alpha tried out the new guys while Loup effortlessly whacked everything. *Like it's nothing*, Riever thought, watching the Georgian with envy. The sniper hit a steel target at 550 meters with a Raufoss round, the same Mk 211 Norwegian-made explosive, incendiary, and armor-piercing bullet that Kyle had used for his 1,100-meter kill in Kramatorsk. Loup liked to use them to shoot through the view slits on tanks. The generous sparks from the well-endowed round hitting the steel target landed in parched grasses. The range went up in flames.

Fires on ranges are common, but this one started to spread. Soon lines of flame were creeping everywhere and climbing up the scraggly trees downrange. The fire flowed through a ravine where the shooting position was located, and turned dangerous. The flames grew to a height of five feet when the fire torched the small trees in the ravine. It was not going to burn itself out.

Riever, who had worked briefly as a wildland firefighter when he got out of the army, started a backburn to starve the fire of fuel. Shirtless, with his t-shirt tied around his mouth and nose and a pistol belted on his hip, he walked his line. He carried a heavy stick wrapped in a burning plastic bag, whose drips of molten plastic fell into the dry grass and lit the backburn. The rest of the team spread out along a dirt road to make sure the fire would not send sparks across and start another fire on the other side.

"Dan!" Riever shouted to the SEAL, standing on the other side of the range, "let's just hold here on this road," gesturing to the dirt track behind him. "We'll hold this road, you hold that one so that it doesn't wrap back to the Mazda." *I should take a video to send my old firefighting crew boss*, Riever thought to himself as he worked. His mind rebelled at the ridiculousness of such a conversation: *"Hey, how's it going, I graduated from this fancy college and I am in Ukraine fighting the Russians and a fire we started with a sniper rifle. How's your day going?" Surreal, just fucking surreal.*

It took hours, but they put it out. While everyone else pulled back to the road to wait for the fire to reach the backburn, Loup stayed in the field, silently fighting the fire on his own. When they finally got back to the roach motel, Riever looked in the mirror. He was covered in soot, his beard and hair standing on end, like a charred character in an old slapstick cartoon.

But they still pressed Symon for a better operational area and to leave the roach motel. "Hey, guys," said Symon. "I know it sucks. But we've got a pretty good mission packet, we're going to move and find places to stay." They were given work a bit further north, on the front line closer to the town of Andrivka.

They rented a single room to share in three different houses, which were immediately christened, in a soldier's take on Goldilocks, the Lux House, the Middle House, and the Shitty House, based on size. With more men they had to expand. Dan remained ground force commander, and Ginger and Riever were the team leaders.

Even in the Lux House, they were stacked up, Riever, Dan, Ginger, and Tex all in one room, very nearly on top of one another. The Lux House, which was not lux but was a bit larger than the others, came with a collection of outbuildings, including a wood-shed. Riever split and stacked a huge pile of wood. There was also a shop with a vehicle pit and a cellar that they used for sheltering from artillery, plus a stall that still smelled like cows. They kept losing water, so they dug slit trenches in the back to serve as latrines.

233

A few days after they moved to Bereznehuvate, which they referred to as B-town, an armored column of the Ukrainian Army came rolling through. Greg was out on an errand with one of the pickup trucks. Dan was on his morning run, a group of guys were at the corner store, and everyone else was getting ready to do some mine training later that morning with a squared-away local Ukrainian unit.

The town started getting smashed. The Russians must have gotten good intel or had a drone on the road, because the barrel artillery landed accurately on the pavement, destroying chunks of it. The explosions were seven or eight hundred meters from the Lux House. Ginger watched as the place rattled and stuff fell off shelves. *Whatever that is, is big as shit*, he thought. Everyone regrouped and started to look for Dan, who was still out running. They were pretty sure they heard a cluster munition hit nearby.

Dan walked back in. "Boys!" he exclaimed, "d'you hear that?"

"Yeah, we fuckin' heard that, dude!" Ginger replied, staring. "This fuckin' town is only thirty meters wide! Yeah, we heard it!"

"Dude, that shit was close," said the SEAL. "I was running and that shit landed in front of me! I turned right around and went home."

Oh, my goodness, thought Ginger. *Dude, what the hell*. The group chat pinged. It was Greg. He'd taken a video of five huge plumes of smoke rising from their town through his windshield. "Well, guys," he said in the recording, "this is slightly shit, but I'll try to get to you guys in time. Fuck."

Their objective was a part of the Kherson front line: an M-shaped trench line on rare high ground, called McDonald's, next to the town of Andrivka and another nearby village called Blahodativka. Both were across the small Inhulets River. The week before, the Ukrainians had taken Andrivka, but the Russians were still right next to it. On their side of the river, they could operate from an abandoned town called Ternivka. They were all so close together that Ginger joked that you could throw rocks between them.

Dan, Greg, Noah, and a new former Marine sniper named Ben went down to recce Andrivka with some local Ukrainians, who wanted to see if they could cut a Russian supply line near the town. The

Ukrainian Army had taken it only a week before. With them was a member of the Ukrainian special forces, who wanted to take recce videos for his own team. They drove a pickup down to the river and parked in a low ravine, which gave the vehicle cover from the Russians' high ground at McDonald's across the river. The bank on the Andrivka side was steep, probably fifteen meters high. The mud covering the banks was slick, dusted with early morning fog. The crossing itself was, as Greg termed it, "a river, a rope, and a rubber boat." Dan called it a dinghy, insisting that it "barely qualified as a boat. Almost an inner tube." The ropes were used to pull the vessel, or whatever you wanted to call it, across the water, one person at a time. Noah eyed the inflatable, which looked like something purchased at Walmart. *Fuck, alright, I just need to not eat shit on this bank and I'll be happy*, thought the paratrooper as he approached alongside Dan. Immediately he went down hard, covered in mud and water just before he climbed into the dinghy.

They moved across one by one and found the Ukrainian Army guys in a badly bombed-out trench on the Andrivka side of the river. The whole town was located in a bowl, surrounded by Russians on three sides. They were dug in, but it was still low ground and hard to defend. Dan recognized it as a shitty position, but it was what the Ukrainians held on that side of the river.

Treelines extended out from the position, but the rest of the terrain was dominated by the usual open fields of Kherson's "fruit basket." The team investigated a few positions in town as Russian artillery streaked in; Noah looked up in time to see Greg do a full dive through an already broken cottage window.

Treelines ran from the town towards the Russian front line. Dan left Greg, Noah, and Ben with the local Ukrainian unit and took the Ukrainian special forces guy with him.

Noah tucked up against a wall with bushes and vines growing next to and over it, which would provide overhead concealment from the artillery-spotting drones that kept flying over the town. He was in the middle; Ben and Greg took up positions a few meters away on either side of him.

The temperature rose as the sun came up in the sky. It was fairly quiet, with little talking, but the drones and artillery punctured the silence. Artillery would walk closer, then further away, from their position.

In the midst of it Noah suddenly heard a different noise: tiny, high-pitched mewling sounds. He looked towards Greg and saw the delighted tall medic playing with a pair of kittens who had found him in the bushes. They were climbing all over Greg. *Like he's the best thing in the whole town*, thought Noah. *Meowing their little heads off at him. Surreal.*

Meanwhile, Dan and the Ukrainian special forces man crept up the treelines, taking videos and trying to get a sense of the operational space and what was going on. The terrain was mostly flat, but the small treelines and even slight undulations in the terrain could reduce the line of sight and provide dangerous cover for the enemy.

The first few treelines went easily. The Ukrainian was a professional. For the last few treelines, they decided to join up with two local recce men who knew the area better. They followed their young escorts towards the remaining treelines.

Dan and the special forces operator moved through the big treeline, close to the Russian positions, got eyes on a small hill that the Russians held, then returned to their guides. The last move involved the recce men taking them back, towards a friendly treeline, and then to a further treeline that would bring them closer to the Russians again.

The walk took them down a dusty track, one that they could use in the open because they were in friendly territory. It was narrow but beaten by vehicles: grass and other greenery grew in between the tracks made by trucks' wheels. On either side grew green and almost golden plants, perhaps a foot high. Birds chirped: late summer in the fruit basket.

Suddenly, the local recce guy stopped. He pointed. Dan looked: it was a mine. The special forces guy got down and carefully traced the wires. On either side of the little road was a telltale disc, plus one cleverly hidden in the vegetation that grew between the truck tracks. In his gloved hand he carefully held and traced the trip wire, which was no thicker than a standard twist-tie and looked no more substantial. *Really well hidden*, Dan thought.

They started to look around more closely. The discs were anti-personnel mines, designed to take out a person. But what they were starting to see around them were much larger anti-tank mines: they had walked right into a minefield. They had just finished their mine training with a Ukrainian unit days before, at which they had been taught the latest tactics in trip wires. The Russians had been attaching thin trip wires to grenades, with the pin replaced by a needle. These were traditional mines. Standard procedure was to retrace one's steps and move out. They turned around.

Dan looked up as one of the local recce men veered off course and started cutting into the treeline they had been following. The SEAL turned to his new special forces buddy. "Hey! What's he doing? We're in a minefield!"

"There's a road on the other side he wants to—" *BOOM*.

The young recce soldier disappeared in a cloud of dust, twenty feet from them; then they saw him flying through the air. Dan never figured out if he had seen the mine too late and jumped, or if the explosion had thrown his body. As his figure arced through the air towards the road, Dan could clearly see that he was already missing a foot from the ankle down.

The special forces soldier surged forward out of instinct; Dan grabbed him instantly. You can't walk into a minefield. They called to the younger man. Tough and "stringy," as Dan put it, he started to crawl on his elbows towards safety. The special forces soldier put a good, high tourniquet on his leg quickly to stop the bleeding. They stood him up. His recce partner from the local unit took one side and Dan the other, with the injured man's arms draped across their shoulders as he hopped. It was slow-going. He needed a medic; they didn't have time.

Dan stopped. He took off his gun and handed it to the other recce soldier. He picked up the wounded man, put him across his shoulders, and ran the four hundred meters back to Andrivka and Greg.

Actually very impressive, Greg decided, seeing Dan carry the recce guy in. He went to work. In addition to the missing foot there was shrapnel in the same leg and both arms, and a few missing fingers. *Not terrible, actually*, Greg thought. The Ukrainian was a model patient. He never screamed as Greg worked, and didn't even ask for pain meds. Greg got an intravenous bag in him and gave him

TXA to help manage the bleeding, as well as some calcium. Greg adjusted the tourniquet lower—he noticed that it was a nice job—and they loaded the wounded man into a litter. The local Ukrainians picked him up and started to carry the litter to the river crossing.

They stopped briefly, and Greg did a bit more work on the patient. *Why are we stopping?* Dan wondered, but he didn't want to rush the medic. *We really need to get this guy out of here.* The wounded man had turned down Greg's pain meds, but he asked for a cigarette and some water. *Even if you're missing a foot, the dude wants to stop and smoke!* Dan thought. Eventually Greg administered morphine. The man admitted that he was finally starting to feel it.

As they ran down the road with the wounded man to the river, four big Grad missiles landed in a field next to them. Mushroom clouds of earth and dust bloomed in the field. *Okay, that's way off,* thought Dan. *They must be shooting at our guys on the other side.* They kept moving. Then another row of Grad came in, landing closer to them; then another, even closer now. They were heading in the direction of the Grad as the Russians walked it in on them.

Greg assumed they'd been spotted by a drone, but everyone was using unencrypted radios, and the Russians might well have been listening in. There were only so many ways to get to the river, and the Russians knew where the crossing was.

Dan looked at Noah next to him. "I wonder how long the reload is on a Grad missile," he said. Noah started a timer. As they took cover while the stretcher crew moved towards the river, another set of Grad landed nearly on top of them: one in front and one behind. They had moved into a lucky gap.

Noah looked at Dan. "Three minutes."

"Okay, we've got three minutes to reach better cover," said the SEAL, as they sprinted flat out towards the river and the crossing. They slipped into a concrete house just as the Russians converted from Grad to pre-sighted mortars. They were very, very close—the most accurate mortar fire Dan had ever been exposed to—and they continued for a solid forty minutes. These put shrapnel into the arms of the Ukrainian special forces soldier and two of the local Ukrainian Army men as they towed the litter across the river. Greg started to patch them up while they waited, but everyone else had to go one at a time.

Noah, one of the last to go, looked at one of the wounded men as they waited for the crossing. The Ukrainian seemed miserable. "Hey, *dobre?*" the American asked, checking to see if the man was okay. The look he received back said, *You're a fucking idiot.* "No, *ni dobre!*" snapped the wounded man. *Yeah, that's fair, dude*, thought Noah. *You just got some shrapnel in the arm and you don't look like you're loving life too much at the moment.*

Once everyone was across, they bundled into the truck with the other Ukrainians. Dan and four other men got in front; Greg was in the back with a few others. The driver took off like a bat out of hell. *Holy shit*, thought Greg. *Slow the fuck down. Dude!* Greg realized that they were egressing on a different route from the one they'd taken in. They'd come in through a treeline, but now they were out in the open, on a little hill, climbing up out of the riverbed. The driver was absolutely ripping down it. Greg was convinced that they would die in a car crash right there. He was fuming, planning his jump out on arrival and just how to give the driver a piece of his mind.

The Ukrainian beside him said something. The tiny, meek voice uttered one word: "Rocket." *What the fuck?* Greg turned around.

A wire-guided Kornet missile was flying straight at them from behind. *What the fuck?* They all banged on the roof, trying to encourage the driver to go faster. The missile ran out of range, suddenly diving and blowing up fifty meters behind them. *Okay, buddy!* Greg thought of the racing driver. *Good job, buddy, good job!*

Three days later, the Russians hit another Ukrainian Army vehicle on the same road and killed two men, then promptly posted a video of it on the internet.

The recce was supposed to have been a quiet little sneak-and-peek. When he got back, Dan sat down and thought, *That was supposed to be something quick and easy, and it turned out to be quite the ordeal.*

The Ukrainian special forces soldier was impressed with their performance. He talked them up to Symon, who in turn praised Dan. "I'm so proud of you guys!" said the pirate. "He was so happy working with you!" *I thought that was a messy day*, thought the SEAL, confused. *The dude got wounded! But everyone seems to be happy.*

While Greg, Dan, and Noah went to Andrivka, Ginger, Riever, Marti, Loup, Tex, and Prym went to Ternivka, just north and to the west. It was supposed to be a twenty-four-hour operation, designed to hit a machine-gun nest across the river. There were civilians nearby, so the Ukrainian Army was unwilling to take it out with artillery, for fear of collateral damage. Javelin, sniper rifle, the Ukrainians didn't care about the small arms method: they wanted that nest taken out.

It was a bad space; the route was poor and out in the open, forcing them to take vehicles in order to move fast. They had to drive through agricultural fields, then up over a small field to a hardball tarmac road. Once you hit the road, you were in perfect line of sight—and range—of Russian artillery and direct fire from tanks. They would be visible from the entire avenue of approach. *A really sketchy situation*, thought Ginger.

They arrived early in the morning, but it was already daylight. The only way into the tiny town of barely more than a dozen houses was the open, hardball road. As they approached, they could see Russian-held Blahodativka and the trenches at McDonald's. *A real bad approach*, grumbled Ginger. The hardball ended and the ground turned bad as they drove over the countryside: slick, black mud, the perfectly tillable loam that was the famous "black earth" of Ukraine, breadbasket of Europe and the world. Riever took over the driving from Ginger but soon got them stuck in a massive puddle. Riever tried to rock the truck back and forth but managed only a quarter of an inch. Everyone worried they would have to abort and escape on foot. Finally he leapt out, shoveled out from under the tires, rocked it a bit, and then gunned the truck out of the ditch.

"Hell yeah!" Tex shouted from the back. "You're good at this shit!"

"Dude!" protested Riever, "I got us stuck in the first place! Shut the fuck up!"

Prym, who had left five minutes before them in the Black Mazda, found a position and radioed up: Get your asses down here. They needed to disperse.

Ginger, Riever, and Tex ripped down the road in their truck, an old Land Cruiser. They parked and unloaded the Javelins, making their way towards the house Prym had found with a solid basement.

They moved in, putting all nonessential equipment in the basement and leaving one man as guard. Ginger knelt to take half a minute to fix the tangled straps on his Javelin. They formed up to do a recon, and stepped out of the basement.

The tree behind which their vehicle was parked exploded, smashed by an anti-armor round from a tank. The giant round narrowly missed Marti, barely fifteen feet away; the few seconds that they had taken to fix the straps on the Javelin had saved them. A high-explosive round in the same spot would have killed him instantly and wounded the nearby Tex and Ginger, who were at most thirty meters away.

"Fucking hell!" exclaimed Ginger. They peeled back fifteen feet, and another round hit fifteen meters to the right of the initial round. *Boom.* No hiss, no fire: definitely direct rather than artillery. *The fucker's aiming right at us.*

They pulled back into the basement, holding security on the door. Three more rounds landed, one in the yard, one in the street, and another on top of an already destroyed building, about one hundred meters away. The Russians definitely knew where they were.

Loup held security on the door while everyone else regrouped in the basement. They knew the first round was direct fire, but they didn't know where it was coming from; the rest may have been artillery rounds. They radioed back to headquarters but got nothing. They decided to wait. If the fire kept up, they'd have to get out of there. That would mean the Russians had a spotter with eyes on, and a tank in range. The Russians had taken to using tanks as direct fire mortar positions. They could keep them more than three thousand meters away. That distance wasn't great for shooting at another tank, but it was nearly twice the effective range of a Javelin and perfectly good for doing exactly what the Russians were doing to them now. The team didn't have many options.

They sat for an hour, getting smashed. Marti kept up a stream of worry about the Black Mazda parked outside. Loup looked up, face impassive, and shook his head. "*C'est fini*," he said, with a rare, wolfish grin.

The Americans wanted to kick out recons, see what they could see, and try to get a shot on the village. "It's too dangerous," Prym and Marti protested.

"It's always going to be dangerous!" Ginger snapped. "There's always going to be artillery, we're always going to get shot at. We came out all this way, we put our lives in danger, we might as well accomplish something."

They went back and forth for fifteen minutes. Ginger and Riever made the call: they were going. They took Tex and left the other men in the basement. They handed over a contingency plan, checked their radio comms, and left a frustrated Loup at the house with Prym and Marti.

They moved down the road, clearing the rest of the village at their end. They found a promising spot that would give them eyes on the target building with the machine-gun nest. Riever holed up in a blown-out building, using their SOPHIE thermal imager to observe the town and the treeline behind it, looking for the tank. He couldn't find it, and they never got shot at by the tank again.

Meanwhile, Tex and Ginger cleared a few more bombed-out buildings, climbing on top of a few of them, looking for angles. *Just doing 'hood rat shit with our 'hood rat friends*, thought Ginger. *Enjoying the weather, enjoying the sounds of artillery whistling over our heads.*

On the SOPHIE, Riever saw a Russian drone come up. "Hey," he called over the radio, "there's a drone up there." They ducked for cover. Two minutes later, it was overhead.

Ginger and Tex moved up to a spot on the edge of town that was part of a farm, with an old fence that ran parallel to a perfect line of sight towards their target. "Dude," said Ginger. "I guarantee you that if I can push up there, I can get a Jav shot off."

"You think?" asked Tex.

"Yeah," said Ginger. He went and got Riever. The Ranger set up the SOPHIE, double-checking the thermal signature. It was solid.

The three men moved back to Prym's basement. "Alright, Prym, this is the deal," said Ginger, pitching his plan for hitting the target building with the Javelin. "I can take the building out, or we can wait until morning and see if we can find a better target." Once they hit with the Javelin, they would have to egress: the Russians would be able to figure out exactly where they were. They'd been hitting them all day with 82 mm mortars, trying to take out their vehicles.

Prym was adamant: "We're already burned. We need to hit our objective and leave."

"Alright, dude, whatever," said Ginger. He and Riever wanted to stay the full twenty-four hours, waiting to see what they could observe overnight. At the very least, Riever suggested that they stay until dark and egress under better cover. But Prym and Marti wanted to leave then. Ginger was irritated. They were semi-safe: they weren't concerned about enemy rolling on them; they were just concerned about artillery. *And if that's what you're worried about, you're always going to be worried.*

They set everything up, then waited an hour. The three Americans did one more recce, looking for a crossing spot down on the river.

When they returned, Loup said something in French; the sniper wanted to set his gun up and see what he could see. Marti translated. The Georgian had brought a chem light. He wanted to pop the chem light at night and throw it into an empty building to see if they could get the Russians to give away their position by shooting at it.

One of the most horrifying individuals I've ever had the pleasure to meet, Ginger thought. "Fuck, yes, Loup! That's that fuckin' shit I'm talking about! That's a great idea, dude!" It wouldn't even seem like a trap; both sides had awful nighttime discipline. Walking around with white lights on wasn't uncommon. "I one hundred percent think that they would fall for that."

I wish he would say more shit like that, Riever thought, watching.

Marti and Prym were against it. Prym was in charge of the operation, and he ordered Ginger to take out the building with the Javelin.

"Alright, dude, listen. We've fuckin' said our piece. If this is what you want to do, this is what we'll do," said Ginger.

He picked up the Javelin. Riever carried a spare missile in case there was an issue, staged about 150 meters back, with overhead cover. Ginger and Tex moved forward to the firing position.

Ginger looked at the position again. The chain-link fence he wanted to brace the Jav on sat between two trees in a pasture. *Like a fuckin' goalpost. Awesome.* The house was centered right in between the trees. *Money.*

He lifted the Javelin up, bracing the front of the rocket on the top of the fence, which came to eye level. He leaned forward and spread his legs wide, trying to get as stable as possible. He built the box and locked onto the target as a gentle breeze waved the lush green bushes next to him. *Eeeeeeeerrrrr*, whined the Javelin. Then silence. Ginger stayed perfectly still. A bird chirped. "Fire, fire, fire," he said steadily. "Firing missile," confirmed Tex.

Boom! The missile burst out, yellow flame shooting six feet behind Ginger, propelling the soft launch forward. On the other side of the fence, the missile lit its own ignition, and flame flew out of the back of the rocket. Ginger pulled the Javelin down to the ground, packing it up. "Let's go, let's go!" said Tex, moving towards the gunner.

They took off, running towards Riever and the trucks. Riever was already running to the Land Cruiser with the spare missile.

Marti sat behind the wheel of the Black Mazda, with Prym beside him, while Loup drove the old Land Cruiser. They heard the Javelin fire. Prym shouted behind to Loup to get ready.

Tex came over the radio. "Target hit." ETA was five minutes.

"Yes, yes!" said Prym as Marti pulled out from their tree cover, in English. "Stop, stop, stop!" he said to Marti. "Fuck. C'mon, c'mon, c'mon guys. C'mon, c'mon, c'mon." The tank could spin up at any moment; there might well be a drone with eyes on them.

Marti gripped the wheels, hands at ten and two. The three men came running into view. "Okay," sighed the Hungarian. "Come, come, come, come!" Riever ran past his window, with the missile over both shoulders, dumping it into the Land Cruiser and jumping in with Loup. He looked over and realized that the Georgian had the entire mission map set out on his personal phone, just in case. Marti drove up to Ginger and Tex, running to him on Prym's side. "Come, come, come, come!" shouted Marti.

"Stand by, stand by," said Ginger as they loaded up. Everyone piled in.

"Drive, drive, drive!" said Prym, holding up his phone for directions as Marti took off. "Left, left," he said in French. "Too far right!" They bumped over the dirt road, banging everywhere.

"Nice job!" declared Marti. "Now, we should survive!" The truck was everywhere; Marti's foot was nearly to the floor. His gloved hands ripped back and forth on the wheel as he tried to keep them straight, while Prym directed left and right in French. Loup, flying behind, nearly flipped the Land Cruiser. They were out in the open again, in perfect view of the Russians. The holes in the hardball road were full of mortar fins.

"Come on, Black Mazda!" shouted Marti, in English. "Go!" called Tex from the back.

Ternivka was smashed after they left, standard Russian retaliation for the Javelin hit. Back at base, everyone was surprised to see them back so early. Likewise they were surprised to see Dan's team back—another planned twenty-four-hour op that had been cut dramatically short. Ginger watched Dan's videos of the mines and trip wires. *A shit show.*

They debriefed each other and met the area commander. They planned to get back to business as usual, but Dan was called away to advise on a different op, further east, by himself. It was good work for him, but it let the wind out of the sails of everyone in B-town. *Man, I miss Dan*, thought Riever: the SEAL's often silent presence loomed in his absence.

20

A TALE OF WOE

Now the Ukrainians approached with a new request: a forty-eight-hour, nonstop eyes-on for Blahodativka, from two different locations. Dan, Riever, and Ginger got together with Symon, the local commander, and an SBU-Alpha man in the vicinity. "Can you do it?" the Ukrainians asked.

"Yes," the Americans confirmed. "We'll develop everything we need to." They could get their drone teams out as well.

Riever would take a sniper team to a treeline northeast of Ternivka, overlooking Andrivka. Ginger would take his team back to Ternivka, from where they'd launched the Javelin. Prym led a small sniper team to overwatch Ginger's men in Ternivka.

Riever took George and Mykola, plus three new additions. There was a young American infantryman named Aaron and Ben, the former Marine sniper. They also had a sharp, experienced Estonian who had served with NATO forces in Afghanistan, a perfect gentleman named Ragnar who also happened to be a tough anti-tank specialist. The start of the war had fallen on Estonian Independence Day. "It was easy to go to Ukraine because the fact was that if the Russians win there, then Estonia and the other eastern nations are next," Ragnar said. "The less tanks they have, the less tanks are going to drive into Estonia."

Their role was to sit in a treeline north of Andrivka and east of Ternivka, overlooking the Ukrainian-held town and McDonald's. They would provide suppressive fire and recon assistance, operating close to several Ukrainian Stinger teams that also used the treeline as cover. Ben had a sniper rifle in addition to Riever's British .338, and Ragnar brought the Javelin CLU, with Aaron as his assistant gunner carrying the missiles. Mykola served as both drone operator and translator so they could speak to the Ukrainian Army units around them.

They parked their vehicles at the end of treeline, far to the north of the river and Andrivka. Ahead of them was a long, two-kilometer infil on foot. *This fucking treeline*, thought Riever as they walked into the narrow set of scrubby bushes and tiny trees that served as their cover, *it's a deathtrap*. George added up the Stinger teams in this line and all those belonging to the fifteen or so trucks that were parked further back, behind theirs. *The Russians could shell this whole thing and kill, like, five hundred people.*

George, Aaron, and Ragnar set up their rear position. The existing holes there were fairly deep; even George's head and shoulders only poked above the top as he tucked in to set up his space. The sky went grey, and the wind started to whip. They pulled old wooden ammo crates to the edges of their holes and used them to help hold down their tarps. George worked carefully, pulling his dark green tarps taut. He dug at the dirt around his hole with his hard-knuckle gloves, placing large clumps to anchor the tarps and cover half of his position. He ducked down into the narrow, grave-like space, where he had stored his backpack to keep it dry. To his left, Aaron and Ragnar did the same.

Riever took Mykola and Ben forward to recce for a sniper's hide. The team carried two sniper rifles, Ben with a massive M107A1 Barrett .50 cal complete with the huge long suppressor. He had taken the gun apart to carry it, and its components dwarfed his small wiry frame. In the lead, Riever was shouldering his big British .338 rifle with one hand and he held a small shovel in the other.

Near their planned position was a Ukrainian Stinger team in their own foxholes. They were two forty-something salty hillbilly types, probably farmers or farm laborers before the war. They were lean and tanned and kitted out in flip-flops and fatigues. The men said something in Ukrainian. Mykola was still a way behind him, so Riever just shook his head. "Americans," he said.

"Americans?" one of the Stinger men said, brightening. He turned to his companion. "Americans! Fuck yes!" They talked for a minute and Mykola arrived to translate. In contrast to their casual appearance, their hole was a very professional construction about eight feet deep with layers of dirt-filled ammo crates forming a protective overhead cover. It housed the two men, their Stinger missiles, and the small comforts of a hole in the ground. *We're going on a forty-eight-hour op*, Riever thought, *but these guys* live *here*.

Ben and Riever crawled up to the edge of the woodline and discussed the various options for a shooting position. They eventually decided to lie there with the rifle parallel to the woodline, aimed at the Russian position at McDonald's. The place had no cover but was only a few feet from a foxhole that they could improve and deepen. It would have to do.

The Ukrainian Stinger team came over and offered them some coffee. They drank from the small cups as they chatted. Ben and Riever had more or less decided on the position when a peculiar sound made them all perk up. It was a fast mover, some kind of MiG doing a bombing run somewhere. The sky was too overcast to see it, but the Stinger has an infrared seeker, and the Ukrainian team grabbed one out of their hole and lined up the shot. They got a lock, but the shot was likely low percentage. Riever, acting cautiously, decided to pull back after that.

The Ukrainians readied the Stinger missile in front of them, one of them popping out to confirm before jogging back to his mate and saying something in Ukrainian. *Boomsnap!* Pale, almost silver-blue flame shot out of the back of the rocket: it was off. *Boom!* went the soft launch.

"Let's get the fuck out of here," said Riever. The shot was hardly out of the tube when he was shouldering the rifle. They were now a prime target for counter-battery. In seconds they had dropped off the coffee cups at the hole and were headed back up the long woodline.

The noise from nearby explosions was constant. The Russians seemed to be firing the full range of their repertoire. Back at the rear position, George peered over the top of his hole, looking towards Andrivka.

"Cruise missiles," he said at one point, noticing a difference in the sound. A squeezing, afterburner sound came from even closer to them. "That sounds like anti-air going off," the Canadian said.

TO DIE WITH SUCH MEN

"Yeah," agreed the men in the next hole. Overhead, the sky still rumbled: another incoming round?

"I'll bet you it's a jet," said George. "That's why we hear it still in the sky. And they're shooting some big-ass standoff munitions at us."

"I definitely don't like these trucks driving by us," said Aaron, watching the road that ran parallel to them. "In my mind's eye I'm imagining a truck driving by and just getting smoked by a Kornet," a wire-guided missile of the same type that had nearly taken out Greg and Dan's truck a few days before.

"Don't look behind you," said George. "There's a fuckin' truck right there." More booms rolled through the air. "I don't think a Kornet could hit them here," he continued. "Because that treeline's blocking it. But once they get past that treeline right there, that's when they're gonna be …" He trailed off, listening. "Yeah, there's a fuckin' jet up there somewhere."

The only time the artillery stopped was when the jets were just overhead.

Riever, Mykola, and Ben trudged back in.

"Dude, we heard some anti-air going off," George said.

"Yeah," Riever replied, "we were right next to it!"

They finished setting up camp and waited for dark. Then they began the long, heavy walk again, in order to dig deep holes and covered positions at the spot they had recced near the Stinger position.

They found their forward position and started digging. Riever wanted it all done right: "We're gonna fucking dig in. We're not gonna get killed by artillery." The Ranger had gone around and sharpened each shovel before they left, to make the digging easier. They dug near an old well, to give even greater protection, then added overhead cover as well to protect themselves from being spotted by drones. The positions dug, they retreated back to their safer rear positions to sleep.

Riever picked a spot right under the tree next to George's hole. The Canadian looked at his hole, considered the incoming rain, and chose a spot a few feet from Riever. He was too big to sleep in a hole anyway. When he woke up, Riever was surprised to find that he had slept quite well.

250

At the same time, Ginger's team had been tasked with clearing a small, wooded area and another, secondary neighborhood in Ternivka that was partly detached from the town, about three or four hundred meters outside it. They were also going to find suitable basements to stage troops for an assault across the river. Ginger took a bunch of new guys they had picked up in Kyiv: a sniper, a former Marine with some medical training called Zach, a drone pilot, and a machine-gunner, plus Noah, who could double as a Jav gunner.

Their first day was quiet. They'd gone in at night, driving along the bad approach in the dark. Once Ginger hit the hardball tarmac, his foot pinned to the floor and did not let up: they were taking no chances on the Russians sighting them with thermals. As they peeled off to drive over the fields into Ternivka, the vehicle bounced and flew over the bumps and holes. *I don't give a fuck about Russian artillery*, thought Noah, hanging on as Ginger drove, dodging shell holes. *I just don't want to die if we roll this truck!*

They made it. *Pretty kosher*, thought Ginger. He put everyone in a basement and toured through the trenches. He put his drone man and a communications man in one position, about 350 meters from Ginger's position, close to the river bank, to observe and listen. It was a standard drill, called SLLS in the U.S. Army: stop, look, listen, smell. "Boring as fuck," as Ginger put it, but the information was crucial: Were there animals around? Lots of people? Did noise carry? Can you see cars, or hear voices? and so on.

Ginger radioed for a drone in the air. There were no issues surveying the river. The small drone came down. In a few hours, they would send up the bigger one, over the Russian town. It was still quiet, a pretty standard first day. Ginger and Noah checked out one trench and found an enormous hedgehog the size of a volleyball. The animal had fallen in but was unhurt. Ginger climbed down to help him out.

"Wait, wait, do hedgehogs bite?" he asked.

"Nah, they're cool, just pick it up," said Noah. "Just put your gloves on, it's going to be a little pokey." Ginger lifted the hedgehog out of the trench and the animal trundled away down the path and into the bushes. They spent the day doing map reconnaissance, found good buildings for staging troops, and marked them on the maps. At night they regrouped in the basements and trenches near the river.

At dawn Riever's team moved forward again, bringing the whole team but for Aaron, who stayed with the truck to serve as a medevac in case of emergency. They passed a neatly laid-out pup tent that would have made a Boy Scout proud, in standard civilian colors but well concealed in the foliage. Ahead of them was a Ukrainian soldier, seated on a camp chair. Riever paused. "Wanna let them know what we're doing?" he asked George, who served as translator to Mykola, their only Ukrainian speaker, who spoke only a little English. The Legionnaires conferred. "Just continue," said George.

The brush thinned out, revealing a gap in front of them. George and Mykola paused while Riever moved through the gap. When he was across, George approached the opening, then sprinted the twenty meters or so across the gap. They looked up. There was a Russian Orlan drone right above them.

Riever kept a log, beginning at 4:45 in the morning, when they heard the Orlan. A little after 7:00, the Russian mortars started. Then came fire either from a light personnel carrier or a large grenade launcher. By 7:30 they could hear the helicopters doing gun and rocket runs on the town.

From then on, there was almost constant fire: mortars, grenades, light tanks, and small arms fire, plus artillery, all aimed at Andrivka. At 11 a.m. they put up their own drone, and Mykola was able to locate the Russian positions at McDonald's, getting eyes on two Russian soldiers hanging out laundry on a scruffy pine tree near their holes. The position was strong and the drone could see the entrance to a deeply dug underground position.

Twenty minutes later, a heavy chopper attack came in. Mykola still had the drone up, so they stayed in their holes and watched the choppers with the drone. They came in with their flare launchers at full speed, the choppers launching rockets as the flares peeled off in long strings at right angles to the flight path. Riever heard the Stinger team yelling into the radio, obviously asking for someone to bring them another Stinger. *Shouldn't have wasted the last one on that jet*, Riever thought. *These choppers are sitting ducks once their flares run out.* The choppers were too far to hit with the Barrett, and were a moving target to boot, but Riever always wished afterwards he had gone out to shoot at them, just to say that he had.

He later joked about it with George. "Holy fuck, man, I know we wouldn't have hit it, but what if we did? We'd be the only team in history to put down an alligator with a fucking rifle."

"If we did that, I would stop by the presidential mansion and demand a medal from Zelensky and then just go home," George laughed. "You are never going to top that."

Ginger never slept on ops. He had stayed up overnight in Ternivka, sitting on the SOPHIE, watching the Russians and cranked up on energy drinks.

Everyone else was woken by something much louder than artillery; to Ginger it sounded like five-hundred-pound bombs. Everything shook. *Wow, that was nasty.* He got everyone up, and ordered two men to a new position to send up a drone. They didn't catch much, though they saw some entrenched positions across the river but no Russians. It was too early for the Russians to be up. *These dudes,* sighed Ginger. *They got to take their morning shit, smoke a cigarette, and drink a cup of coffee before they start soldiering.* His own men were up and moving.

Ginger and Noah went out, flying drones and watching through the SOPHIE. He left his team with instructions. The two men went out up the road, going north through the town. The artillery changed that day—they could hear the treelines getting smashed; Andrivka was getting smashed too. Rounds were flying over them, aiming for what must have been a larger target to the north. One round just missed Prym's team. "And thanks for God we are still alive," said Marti quietly after it hit. "So, hoo-ray."

Ginger and Noah kicked in the door to a house and found a dog: mangy and big, a German Shepherd-style mutt. He ran up and rolled over, friendly and happy. Ginger ignored him, and they moved on. The dog followed as they cleared a woodline, checking for mines. Every time they stopped, the dog would find a tree to hide under. *Mad smart,* thought Ginger as he worked. *A very smart dog.* It was a bad position, so they pulled out. The dog followed.

They fed him and gave him water. He was nice and friendly and seemed chill, despite the circumstances. As Ginger and Noah patrolled back, they found the drone operators, broke them down, and collected together in their main basement.

It was a tiny, crowded space. The men in kit barely fit. They needed to go over the drone footage with everyone, and Ginger wanted to send the dog out to make room. He grabbed the dog and started nudging him up the stairs. Then Ginger moved to lock him out, and the dog turned and growled.

Motherfucker, thought Ginger. *Don't do this to me.*

"Just close the door!" called one of the men from below.

"I'm fucking trying!" Ginger said. He pushed the dog back. It bit him on the arm. "You fucking motherfucker!" he exclaimed, trying to push the dog out. This time the dog bit him on the hand. "Alright, motherfucker, this is your last goddamn warning." The dog stepped back. Ginger grabbed the door, but he had to put his foot out to close it. The dog bit his ankle, through his pants and over the bone. "You son of a bitch!" Ginger kicked the dog off his ankle and shot him.

Pandemonium broke loose. The dog raced down the stairs, biting Ginger again, then fell down the rest of the stairs. There was blood everywhere. Something stank. Zach saw the dog huddling in a corner. He shot it in the head to spare it more misery. "What the *fuck?*" he screamed, furious.

"Get the fuck outside! Go in the goddamn trench!" Ginger snapped. He went downstairs. He could hear everyone talking shit as he picked up the big dog and carried him up the stairs. He took the animal outside, put him in a mortar pit, said a little doggy prayer, and buried him.

He limped into the trench. "What just happened?" demanded the men there.

"Dude!" snapped Ginger. "The dog bit me. Four fuckin' times, dude."

"Show me," demanded Zach, still angry. Ginger showed him the skin broken over his ankle bone. "Whatever. You need to get tested for rabies now. It's very serious." He started cleaning Ginger's wound.

"What are you talking about? It's just a fuckin' dog bite."

"Exactly! Rabid dogs, you don't want to fuck with it. We need to get you out of here."

"You're joking," Ginger insisted, still upset over how upset everyone else had been.

"We need to get you medical attention. If that dog had rabies or any sort of bacterial infection, you're going to be in trouble." Zach explained how bad rabies was and just how gruesome a death from it could be. *I did not know that rabies was fatal*, Ginger thought in surprise. They patched Ginger up and gave him some vodka. He kept insisting that it wasn't a big deal. Everyone else was adamant.

Ginger called Prym on the radio. "Zach says I need to evac."

"What happened?" asked Prym. Ginger explained.

"*Pizdets, blyat!* Yes, we need to get you out of there right now!"

"Damn, so this is real!" exclaimed Ginger.

"Yes, mate! It is very bad to get bitten by a dog here!" replied Prym.

"Well fuck, if someone had told me that, I would have shot the dog before it even started following me, dude! That's Afghan rules, dude! Can you at least call Greg and ask what he thinks?" Ginger called back.

They stood in the trench, waiting for Prym to get back to them. Ginger was slightly salty from the vodka, staring off into nothing. *Whomp, whomp, whomp.* "What the fuck is that?" he exclaimed.

Noah was standing on top of the trench. "Yo, Ginger!" he shouted. "Ka-52, twelve o'clock!"

"You're fucking with me," Ginger said.

"Ka-52, and there's more than one of them!"

"How many?"

"Uh, four!"

I'm going to shit my pants, Ginger thought. "No." He started wobbling towards Noah. Everyone was standing in line, looking out over the field, straight at four of the infamous Black Sharks flying over the horizon. All the helicopters dumped every one of their rocket pods straight into Andrivka. Each chopper carried twenty-four per pod, two pods apiece. *That's a large number which I can't comprehend right there*, thought Ginger. *Fuck ton of rockets.* They flew away. *That was crazy.*

Ten seconds later, two jets flew over and bombed the treeline.

Oh my God, this is it. They're going to take Andrivka right now.

"We need to set the Jav up! This is going down!" exclaimed Ginger.

Greg called Ginger on the radio. "We need to get you the fuck out of there."

"Dude, there's gonna be a scrap."

"Exactly. You need to get the fuck out of there."

Goddammit, thought Ginger.

Riever watched the mortars and artillery that followed the combined chopper and attack jet run that Ginger had just seen. At 1 p.m., the team saw Ukrainian casevac vehicles flying up their road. A Ukrainian had stumbled towards them, without his weapon and kit but with holes all over his body. Ben and Ragnar moved off the gun to give him first aid. Twelve minutes later, the casevac left with the wounded man, and Ben and Ragnar returned to the sniping position. The artillery continued, with Grad by 3 p.m., then more rockets and, finally, heavy artillery. The casevac team returned to evacuate a few more men.

Riever, taking his turn on the big Barrett watching the Russian position, was counting the explosions. His log recorded all the different types of fire and, when possible, the time of flight. Occasionally, and particularly with mortars, you could hear the shot before the explosion, which might tell them how far away the guns were located. He got to two hundred explosions and stopped. He checked his phone: twenty minutes had passed. The Russians had lobbed two hundred large-caliber artillery rounds on a town of about thirty houses. *There is no way this is business as normal*, thought Riever. As he crawled out of the sniper position, trading places with the next man, he said to Ben, "That seemed like pre-assault fires. There may be an attack soon."

The Russians had been prepping; now came the full-on assault on Andrivka.

In Ternivka, Ginger's team broke down their position. Greg picked up Ginger at the halfway point; the rest of his team went back to the Lux House. Prym's team and Riever's team stayed put. Greg took Ginger to the hospital. They had no idea what was going on. *Dude,*

Andrivka's gone, Ginger kept thinking. *Riever's going to get overrun. This is fucked.*

"Hey, dude, listen, shit's going down and I need to be out there," Ginger tried to explain to the doctor.

"Yeah, we'll worry about that when the time comes," he was told.

"The time has already come! What's the word?"

"Well, you got bit by a rabid dog," said the doctor. He was an older man. He looked Ginger straight in the eye, then said, "Did you bring the head?"

"The fucking head?" exclaimed Ginger. "What the fuck do you need the head for?"

"We need to test it for different diseases," said the doctor.

"No! I don't have the fucking head."

Ginger looked at Greg, who was translating. "Dude, tell me this old man's fucking with me."

"He's deadass," said the tall medic.

"Oh, my God," exclaimed Ginger. "Y'all are gonna make me drive back into a fucking war zone and cut the head off a dog?"

Without the head, the doctor threatened an invasive procedure that involved forty—"four zero," Ginger noted for clarity—shots through the stomach wall over the course of forty days, for which he would have to stay in the hospital for the duration.

"Dude, I'd rather die," declared Ginger.

"I promise you," said the doctor, "you do not want to die this way. You would rather get the treatment than die of rabies, I promise," said the doctor.

"He's right," confirmed Greg.

"Fine, I guess I'll get the treatment," sighed Ginger. "But I'm not doing forty stomach wall injections."

"Then you need to get the head of the dog."

Fuck me.

As the Russian assault on Andrivka began, Riever's team moved into action. Mykola jumped from his hole and moved to the edge of the woodline to put the drone out, and flew it straight for the treeline across the river from where the Russians were attacking. Riever jogged from the holes up the treeline to the sniper position. They moved a short distance to where they could see the assault. Ragnar took out the Javelin, but there was no shot for the missile.

Watching on his gun, Riever saw the Ukrainian marines fighting with style. They had just crossed the river into the town and had taken numerous casualties moving through the tiny river crossing that Dan and Greg had used to get to Andrivka. Not two minutes later, explosions started hitting the crossing, four at a time: the same pre-sighted mortars that had pinned down Greg and Dan while they tried to evacuate their casualty.

Those fucking marines, man, Riever thought, watching. *You could not pay me to go across that. You could ask me and I would do it, but you could not pay me. Holy fuck.*

The marines were on the receiving end of a fires plan that would rival the Western Front in World War I: hundreds of rounds of mortar and artillery, augmented with gun runs from attack choppers, sniping, and constant drone coverage. Now with the Russians closing in, they emerged from their basements and shot the Russian advance flat. It may have been only a probing attack to find their positions for the development of another fire plan, but Ukrainian determination was on full display.

Ben had found a small tree with a branch that formed a V on its left side: a decent brace for his sniper rifle. Riever had taken the sling off his own rifle and tied the gun to the tree for a more stable position. The range was about 2,000 to 2,500 meters, and at that range Riever had no idea where to aim. He had dope, or data, out to about 900 meters, but anything beyond that was just a guess. His scope, however, was more powerful than Ben's, allowing him to spot the impacts of Ben's rounds and give him adjustments. Additionally the Barrett .50 had only one magazine. Shortages meant that Barrett magazines were hard to find, and they only had the one in the gun. Riever and Ben settled into a rhythm, pairing their gear for best effect. Ben leaned into his gun, left knee down and right knee bent. He was soaked in sweat under his plate carrier as the strong breeze blew. He zeroed in on his position, crossing his left arm to his right, and squeezing his bicep with his free hand for stability. "And firing," he confirmed. "Send it," came Riever's response. *Snap*. The big round ejected hard out of the gun. *Snap*. They looked for the hit, adjusting higher. *Snap*. Ragnar, sitting next to Mykola on the drone, gave confirmation: Ben was on target.

The range was extreme, but the big .50-caliber Raufoss bullets smashing through the brush would have a suppressive effect, and they might get lucky and hit an incautious Russian as he moved back from the failed assault. Riever and George had been on the receiving end of some heavy-caliber sniper rounds earlier in the day and knew its suppressive effects, a quick whipping smash as the round plowed through the heavy brush close to the team's holes. Ben fired rapidly for a sniper, squeezing off a round every five seconds or so. The range was so great that most of the impacts were invisible, but occasionally one would explode and Riever would give him feedback on the strike.

Riever took long drags from his e-cig with one eye on the scope as Ben fired round after round traversing up and down the treeline, calling out the count of Ben's rounds for the sniper. Every nine rounds Ben would hand Riever the empty magazine. Riever would reload quickly, stuffing in the massive rounds as Ben carefully squeezed off the last shot in the chamber. Riever would hand him back the full magazine, and the drill would start over again.

After a few minutes of firing, Riever ran back to Mykola's position. Mykola had the drone up and was observing the Russians in foxholes. Riever asked some questions, then ran back and walked Ben's rounds in on the area of the foxholes that Mykola had spotted. Round after round crashed into the woodline with the occasional tiny bright explosions of the Mk 211 Raufoss rounds. Mykola had comms with a mortar crew and started helping them drop their rounds, walking the explosions closer and closer to the Russian positions. It was surreal. Riever watched the rounds creep closer to the huddled figures in the foxholes.

"Take Ragnar and the Jav and the rifle, and start heading back," Riever told Ben, "and we will follow as soon as Mykola is done calling fires." They knew they needed to leave the area; they had fired about fifty rounds from an open spot on the edge of the woodline. If their fire had been remotely successful, the Russians would know that someone with a big rifle was firing on them, and anyone with a decent set of optics would be able to spot them. They needed to move before the inevitable artillery response.

"Goddammit," Riever said as they went, "I dropped my fucking e-cigarette."

Ben burst out laughing. "That's an accountable item, huh?"

"Yeah, we're going back for it," Riever kidded as he started his run to Mykola. He watched the Ukrainian finish his fire mission as the drone's battery died, effortlessly gliding the dead drone right back to his position. *Wow*, thought the Ranger, surprised and impressed, *Mykola is a shit-hot drone pilot*.

Mykola, Riever, and George started to exfil back up the tiny treeline to join the rest of their team. *The Russians are going apeshit with artillery*, Riever thought. Since the assault the explosions were everywhere; every treeline was taking fire, and they heard jets again in the distance. The Ranger had stopped counting, deciding that he really did not care as long as they made it out. The enemy response seemed almost petulant. *The Russians are just pissed off that their little attack failed*, he thought.

The men kept moving down the treeline. They would hear the whistle and instantly get down. With all their gear and the lack of protection, they would not dive for cover but simply crumble to the ground face-down. The round would explode, and they would spring up and keep moving.

Finally they reached a couple of shallow foxholes about halfway to the truck. They were old and very makeshift, the type that the U.S. Army calls "Ranger graves," just good enough to lie flat in and remain below ground level. They gratefully lay down in them as another round crashed into the field on their left.

All day, Riever and George had discussed their own plans at length. George said that he would stay for one more month; Riever planned to leave in mid-August. They were exhausted. They had agreed: when we get back, this is it. We're done. We're going back to Kyiv. *Goddammit*, thought Riever. *Just when we decided to leave, now we're going to get killed. How can they have this much artillery to throw at five guys in a treeline?*

The fire did not adjust, it just smacked down at regular intervals. They started discussing what was happening, and it occurred to them that the Russians were not trying to hit the woodline but were more likely trying to hit any reinforcement or medevac that would have to travel the trail next to the woodline. Riever pulled out his phone and took a video of a few explosions. The whistle and boom were textbook. Eventually the tempo of fire slowed, and the team picked up and made for Aaron and the truck.

"Okay," said Riever, "does anyone want to stay here and do this again tomorrow, or do we want to head home?" The team laughed. No one wanted to stay. It was a cover-your-ass kind of question, making sure there would be no dissent once they got back to the team house. They climbed in the Land Cruiser with Mykola at the wheel. He peeled out of the hiding spot and tore up the trail through the fields full of rocket tail sections stuck in the ground, and jounced onto the pavement next to a pile of empty ammo crates. They passed an ancient BMP-1 armored vehicle and its crew by the side of the road. They waved and smiled. *Good to be alive*, Riever thought once more.

Months later, George read an analysis by a British think tank of Russian assault plans for a village about one hundred kilometers away. The documents had fallen into the hands of Ukrainian intelligence. The fire plan came from the early twentieth century: a pre-set plan based on intelligence gathered days beforehand, with no communications and no space for adjustment or coordination between units. Just bomb, move forward, and assume it would overwhelm the defenders. It didn't work on either village.

Greg drove Ginger back to the Lux House from the doctor, and they dropped everything off. Ginger walked up to Noah.

"Hey, dude," he said. "I need you to do one last favor for me."

"Anything, bro."

"I need you to go back with me to Ternivka and cut the fucking head off a dog."

"You're fucking with me," Noah exclaimed.

"Not in the least bit," said Ginger.

They grabbed rifles and battle belts, and nothing else. In the truck they ripped down the road. The doctor had given him a hard limit: forty-eight hours to get the treatment, or else. At least ten hours had passed already. They still had no idea what was happening in Andrivka or with Riever's team.

As they ripped down the road, there was artillery everywhere. The Ukrainians were firing MLRS rockets, the Russians were shooting mortars, fires were all over. *Madness*, thought Ginger.

They got to their spot, jumped out of the still-running vehicle, and ran for the dog's makeshift grave. Ginger pulled the dog's body out and started trying to chop the head off with a shovel. He was sick to his stomach. He loved dogs more than anything else on the planet; he would rather have a dog than a child.

"Goddammit!" he shouted as he whacked. "Just! Cut! Off! I don't want to do this!"

Noah was cracking up. It wasn't working at all. "Dude, do you want a pocket knife?"

"Not really," said Ginger. "But I need it." He started sawing and chopping. Blood and tissue were flying all over Noah. Ginger heard the other man spit something out. *So nasty.* "I'm sorry, I'm sorry!" he kept repeating.

When he finally got the head cut off, he felt overwhelmed. The shovel was lying on the ground; Noah's knife was still in his hand. Ginger threw the knife down, picked up the shovel, and started running. A few steps later, he stopped. *What the fuck did I just do?* He turned around. Noah was on the ground, grabbing his knife. "Dude, I'm so sorry!"

"Dude, no, just run, let's get out of here!"

They threw the dog's head in the bed of the truck and started ripping down the road. They pulled up at a Ukrainian checkpoint. They had no password, and no Ukrainian between them. The young soldier on guard stopped them, speaking loose English. Ginger made him understand that he needed to call his commander for the password. He pulled the truck over. The guard turned and looked in the bed of the truck and saw the head of the dog. He looked at Ginger and Noah. He called the other soldiers at the checkpoint over. They stared at the Americans.

"Hey," said the soldier. "You can go."

The Americans started laughing. Ginger drove through. "They probably think we're some Satan-worshipping motherfuckers. We just drove to an active firefight with no kit, cut the head of a dog off, and threw it in the back of a truck and came back."

In the Lux House, they put the dog's head in a trash bag and stuffed it in the freezer.

When Ginger returned with the dog's head, Riever, George, and their team were back: alive and not overrun. Riever was exhausted.

Ginger thought he had the thousand-yard stare. The Ranger and his team had heard some back-and-forth about Ginger on the radio but hadn't been able to get a clear sense of what was going on.

"Man, I got bit by a fuckin' dog!" Ginger said. *A tale of woe*, Riever thought, hearing the story. *He's upset.* He knew that Ginger loved dogs. For his part, the Jav gunner finally learned that Andrivka was under siege and that the Russians had gotten smashed in their attempt to retake the town.

Ginger had only one option: a military hospital in Kyiv. He had to leave that night. Riever and George were offered a ride back to Kyiv. If they wanted to leave soon, this was it. Mykola would serve as driver and translator.

It felt like a spur-of-the-moment decision, even though each man knew he had to leave. George had promised Riever one more month when the American "bought him off," as the Canadian liked to say, back in Kyiv. And now Riever was nearly run dry: their pay was behind again, and living in Kyiv for a month when they had expected only days had drained everyone. The only thing in their fridge was a whole mackerel, scales and head and all. They were paid as Ukrainian privates—with combat pay, but even then it was nothing extravagant, especially once the exchange rate was factored in. They were all putting their money in the hat for food, for water, for renting rooms in local houses, for diesel for the generator, and gas and repairs for the trucks. The Legion did not have the logistics train of the U.S. military; they paid for much of their own gear and upkeep.

Riever and George packed quickly; everyone knew that they had been on borrowed time. The Ranger gave away all of the useful personal gear he could afford to leave: knives, a flashlight he had won in a shooting competition, a flashlight he had inherited from Dmitri, the IR laser from Oleksii, the Boonie hat with the mosquito net that had saved him on the peninsula, and other gear like the flip-down ear pro, which he left for Tex.

Finally, he took off his boots. He had bought them just before he left for Ukraine. Brand-new boots are not ideal for a combat deployment, but his old pair wouldn't have lasted. Just before he left, his girlfriend had driven him to an REI store in another state in order to get the best-fitting pair. They were Altras, and they had been perfect. Dan had coveted those boots: taupe with a strip of black just above the soles, and a dusty red stripe up the heel to the pull-tab. They were lightweight, one of the SEAL's obsessions. He asked Riever where he had gotten them, and had been hunting for a pair in Kyiv. They were dusted with Kherson dirt, but they weren't worn down, because the Ranger only wore them on missions. They had Riever's blood type written on them, and Oleksii's blood stained into them. Riever left them for Dan, knowing that they shared the same shoe size, and knowing too how much the SEAL liked them. Dan was still in Zaporizhzhia.

They shook hands with everyone; Riever was happy to get another hug from Marti. Just before they left, Symon approached. "I wish you weren't leaving," he said simply to the Ranger, and shook his hand.

They drove to Mykolaiv first, hoping to get the dog's head tested for Ginger. There the staff declared that they didn't have the capacity to test the thing after all. Defeated, they stopped at their favorite sidewalk shawarma place to grab one before the long drive to Kyiv.

There was a small municipal garbage can in front of the restaurant. Ginger, in a black mood, finished his food on the hood of the Land Cruiser, took the plastic-wrapped dog's head, and shoved it in the trash with the wax paper of his shawarma. Everyone laughed. *Too ridiculous to be real*, thought Riever.

They made it to Kyiv at the forty-hour mark of Ginger's forty-eight-hour limit. The doctors gave him the initial treatment—a shot in the arm, not the stomach.

"Do you have the body of the dog?" the doctor asked.

"I cut the fuckin' head off," Ginger explained, "and I brought it to Mykolaiv, but they said they couldn't test it."

"You cut the head off a dog?" the horrified doctor exclaimed. Mykola translated, laughing. The nurse looked at Ginger as if he was a monster. *Too bad*, sighed Ginger. *She's really cute.*

"This is what I was told to do!" protested Ginger. "I was instructed by a doctor to cut the head off a dog!"

"That's really old school," said the doctor. "You don't need to do that anymore."

"Well, fuck if I know! I'm not a fuckin' doctor! My medic and the fuckin' doctor told me to cut the head off a damn dog, so I cut the head off a damn dog."

"That's pretty messed up," Mykola translated for the doctor.

"Fuck you, dude!" exclaimed Ginger. "I'll never be able to sleep the same because of this!" At some point Mykola said that it had been a chihuahua. *I think he's fucking with me*, Ginger thought, eyeing the doctor. Sarcasm rarely translated.

"Y'all are talkin' some shit!" snapped Ginger. "Let me bite you and see if you wanna get some shots, motherfucker."

He was confined to Kyiv for a week, scheduled for a shot the next day, and another three days after that.

Mykola accompanied George and Riever to Legion headquarters, to turn in their guns and their green books. While they waited for the paperwork to be processed, the former French Foreign Legionnaires taught Riever the other Legion's term for REMF (rear echelon motherfucker), *branleur*. They were cracking up as they waited.

Finally, they went to turn in their pistols and rifles. George handed his guns in. The clerks took everything apart, checked it all, and recorded the serial number against their records. Then it was Riever's turn. He handed over the Makarov first, with its old leather Soviet holster, watching as the clerk checked everything. Then it was time to part with his Bren 2. He'd gotten it new out of the box, and had put thousands of rounds through it. He had hand-painted it in camouflage style, which was now wearing off. Riever took it off his sling, flipped the stock open, then gave it a kiss on the upper right, above the magazine. The clerks laughed, but he was deadly earnest.

21

A SPICY VILLAGE RAID

As Riever and George headed out and Ginger was confined to Kyiv for his shots, Symon began planning another mission: a raid on Blahodativka, the town across the river from Ternivka, from which Ginger had hit the machine-gun nest with the Javelin and where he had been bitten by the dog. The river in between was shallow in parts. Symon wanted to walk—literally walk—an entire battalion across it. Dan returned, saw the plans, and tried to make adjustments. "Hey, man," said Dan, "a lot of things can go wrong with that. Let me go down tonight and check it out myself."

But even SEALs don't swim alone: Dan needed a partner, and Riever was gone. "Well, who can swim?" Dan asked.

Tex piped up. "Doesn't Noah do free-diving?"

Fuck, thought Noah. He was an excellent swimmer, an experienced free diver and spear fisher. But he had no military experience in it at all: he was airborne-trained, not water-trained. *This is a crazy idea!* But he was game. "Yeah," he said. "I can swim real good. Let's go."

After dark, the SEAL took Noah, and the two Americans got into the river by themselves. Noah was happy with his minimal splashing and noise level, but he was astonished by Dan: the SEAL was completely silent. *Like the dude is made of oil or something*, thought the paratrooper. *The water is just parting around him. And he's so fucking fast.* The SEAL made everything look easy.

They walked about halfway to the village. The water level was fine, but the bottom was so sticky and muddy that at one point Dan nearly got sucked under; it was almost like quicksand. There was admittedly good cover. They put up a drone with thermal sights, and it never even saw Dan with his head sticking out of the water, despite knowing where he was. The river was a good way in for something like a commando raid. But what Symon wanted was not possible without a lot of guys drowning and making a lot of noise in the process.

Dan pitched a commando raid. Symon took about twenty percent of the SEAL's plan, then added his own. The new version was for Dan, Greg, and a member of the Ukrainian SEALs to swim in under dark and de-mine their approach to Blahodativka from the river. What remained of Alpha, plus Black and Charlie teams, would come down the river on boats. They would then establish a position on the beachhead, "fuck shit up," as Greg put it, and take over the first ten houses. At that point Ukrainian Army soldiers would back-fill while the Legion teams moved forward, and armor would come in to back them up as well. From there, they were supposed to take over the town. They were told there would be HIMARS rocket launchers, artillery, the works. The upside was that they would have a lot of help from the conventional side of the Ukrainian Army. The bad news was that they would have to do it on the army's timeline: close to daylight.

In the dark, in the early hours of the morning, Dan, Greg, and a Ukrainian special forces man slipped into the river. Dan felt as if he was crawling on top of the water. It was muddy, sticky, worse than before. There was a foot of water, and then six feet of mud; it was like swimming in dirty custard.[1] Dan bumped out to deeper water, where there was the same amount of mud but with a deeper water column in which he could float more than crawl.

I feel like a ninja, Greg thought, moving down the river in the dark with his NODs alongside Dan. *Holy shit*. It was going fine until he nearly drowned himself on a downed tree, hidden in the mud, which caught in his belt and dragged him under the water. *Not very ninja*.

Their original planned exit point from the river wouldn't work. They had spied it with drone footage, and the bank had appeared to be covered in tall grass. Now, in the early glimmer of the morning, it proved to be very thick shrub. They saw a small boat chained to a tree. There they found a tiny path up a steep embankment covered in vegetation. The trail led to the road, and beyond that was the village.

Dan had demanded that the teams behind him bring the boats in using paddles. "Do not start the motors," he had warned. He had suggested that some men travel in the water, swimming the boats along. "We only have two boats," Dan had insisted. "We can get twice the amount of dudes into the first wave if we have some hanging off the boat, and they'll provide the propulsion." The Ukrainian officers had refused, being worried about the swimming ability of their men. Paddles were the compromise.

A big, booming *brrrrrrr* sounded through the morning air, easily audible as the dawn started to break: motors. Dan could hear Prym shouting into his radio for what felt like all the way down the river. *Another Prym initiative*, thought Greg. *We're fucked*. He and Dan just looked at each other. *I'm going to get shot by a Russian with an AK from the bank*, thought the medic. *We're dead*.

Their boats had arrived, but everything had started late: the driver who had been tasked with taking the teams to the launch point had gotten lost. The Ukrainians had delivered rubber boats, but they didn't have air. An infuriated Marti, on the prep team, pumped while a few Russian shells hit near the town.

At the landing zone, there was no time left. Any sensible Russian would be on them in minutes. Greg threw his grappling hook up the bank in a hurried de-mining exercise.

Prym's boat was first, with Charlie Team and some Ukrainian special forces. There was only enough space for one boat at the new entry point. Prym unloaded and moved his men up the path, and then stopped, blocking it. They took Prym's boat out, but there was nowhere to unload everyone else.

Nearly thirty minutes had passed since Dan and Greg had reached the landing zone. To the SEAL, standing in chest-deep water, it felt like an eternity. His radio was flooded out, and he couldn't talk to Prym. *Why are we waiting? What is going on?* Dan was fuming and shivering.

Prym finally moved in, just as it got brighter in the open. He took his team and some of the Ukrainians and pushed forward but left Mykola with a PKM blocking the road and preventing the first part of Alpha from coming up. From his spot in the water, Dan could hear Prym banging around in the village, breaking glass and knocking over wood. Then, suddenly, Mykola opened up with his PKM.

Everything changed. The sun was up, and they'd just let off a machine gun. *Boom! They know we're here*, thought Dan. Noise no longer mattered. He crashed and pounded through the brush, trying to create a firing base for Aaron and Noah on the left flank. The rest of Alpha and Black Team, now flush with new men, landed just as the shooting started. If they pushed up, they could create a proper L-shaped ambush, with Dan's team coming up behind Black.

Dan peered at the houses. He couldn't open up, because he didn't know where Prym and his men were. Black Team advanced and flowed towards where Prym had moved in. Dan moved towards Black Team's trail. As he went forward, several Ukrainians were moving back with their first casualty, a Ukrainian. Dan looked down. The man's upper leg was snapped in half. Dan and Aaron cut through a chain-link fence to help the others bring the man through. Dan advanced and saw a new guy on Prym's team, another Ukrainian former French Foreign Legionnaire, being carried back with grenade frag wounds. Charlie had made contact, and things had degenerated into a grenade-tossing match.

Dan came around a corner and saw Prym and his team trying to assault a house. Charlie Team had gotten their bells solidly rung by the concussion from several grenades. One of the new men on Black Team said, "They're kinda running around like chickens with their heads cut off ... We've got to get this thing under control."

"See if you can call him back," Dan said, meaning Prym, "see if you can get him and his team out of that house, away from the house. I'm going to make sure my team knows where we're at." The SEAL was worried about what he called a Polish ambush: friendlies arrayed in a circle around a target, accidentally exposing each other to their own fire. They established a proper L ambush with a line of comms—not radios, but a visual communication link.

Frags flew back and forth; everyone shot into the enemy house. Dan called for Ragnar, who had already moved up; he carried the RPG. The Estonian also spoke Russian. Dan wanted him to do a callout to ask the enemy to surrender, an old-school counterterrorism tactic that the team had discussed beforehand. But the anti-tank specialist couldn't be heard over all the noise.

270

Dan ordered Ragnar to hit the house with the RPG. The Estonian hooked around the house and lined up on the target. Warning shouts of "RPG!" went down the physical line of comms to the other friendlies.

"Firing!" Ragnar called out; Dan's confirmation rang back. The RPG sailed through a window, into a wall on the first floor of the house: *shoooooom-bang* it went as it crashed into the house. A massive cloud of beige dust mushroomed back out. *A perfect shot*, Dan thought. The firing petered out.

Ragnar found Prym, who spoke good Russian, and sent him back to Dan. "These guys might just surrender," the SEAL said. "Grenades are flying into their courtyard, rockets are coming through their window. We might just be able to get them to come out." He figured there were probably only one or two guys left alive in the house. A former British SAS man with Black Team had an incendiary thermite grenade and threatened to use it as extra encouragement.

Prym did a callout in Russian, but there was no answer. The Ukrainian started to walk away. Then Dan heard a yell from the house and called Prym back. The enemy were surrendering.

Dan went to check on Tex and Greg, down by the river. By the time he came back, eight men had been brought out of the house.

Back at the boats, Greg was working on their first casualties. One of them was Zach. After Mykola opened up, the former Marine had moved up to shoot his 40 mm six-shot grenade launcher, the "40 mike-mike." One of his rounds failed to fire, and he turned to get more. As he was moving, a bullet ricocheted and hit him in the leg. "Fuck!" he exclaimed. Struggling with the velcro, he put on a tourniquet, then scooted down the hill towards Greg and the boats.

Greg reduced the tourniquet and put a pressure bandage on. He helped Zach down the hill and got him in the boat. The tall medic was also busy treating their other wounded, who had been carried back to him. A new man on Prym's team had four pieces of shrapnel in him. The Ukrainian man whom Dan had seen with his leg snapped in half had broken his femur. *No idea how he did that*, thought Greg. *But somehow he did.* He must have landed badly in heavy kit climbing one of the walls or fences in the overgrown compounds. It was the worst injury they had had so far. Greg sent the two more badly wounded men out first, then Zach was loaded into another boat and taken back to Ternivka.

Back in Ternivka there was no formal casualty clearing post, and the casevac that took out two other men missed Zach. He was forced to move from micro-terrain to micro-terrain with his numb leg; the bullet had hit his femoral nerve. He had to avoid artillery corrected by the drone hovering above for an hour and a half before he was finally taken out. Eventually he was so exhausted from moving while injured that he chose a spot under some small trees, stayed put, and waited for the casevac to return. He would eventually have to go back to the U.S. for surgery after several poor medical experiences in-country, but months later his leg still felt as if one had hit the funny bone as the nerve healed.

Now Greg moved in with Dan to take care of the wounded prisoners. One man was what he called "really fucked up"—he had taken the worst of the RPG blast, which had shredded his stomach and pelvis. The others had some fragmentation, but nothing worrying. They turned out to be DNR, not "proper Russians," as Greg put it, but "the village idiots."

Dan was torn. He wanted Greg to question the prisoners, but the younger man was in medic mode, trying to help. The SEAL watched Greg work on a guy with a mangled elbow—uncomfortable but not life-threatening. "I'll put this guy's arm in a sling," Dan said. "Talk to him about the village, and where the Russians are, and what we're going to run into, and I'll take care of his medical stuff."

Greg started talking in Ukrainian and Russian, but the man either didn't know anything or at least said he didn't. *We're not in a position to get solid intel unless they volunteer it*, thought Dan. They'd have to proceed on their own.

Greg bandaged the rest of the prisoners up, and they started to carry the badly wounded prisoner out. The wound to the man's pelvis was ugly. The internal bleeding was massive. Greg bandaged him, but it was obvious that he would not survive. The tall medic gave him fentanyl. It wasn't enough to kill him, but it was on the high end of the limit—palliative care for a dying man. "Still a person, right?" said Greg later of someone he considered a traitor, perhaps even worse than the Russians themselves.

They went trophy hunting, hauling out a bunch of AK-47s, a Dragunov, and a PKM (Greg still called it a Pokémon), several rockets, an RPG-7, and a new RPG-30, the new dual-tube rocket. Noah pulled security while other men inspected the captured items; his rifle looked out over a bunch of beehives in the back of the yard of the house they had been engaging. At the beginning of the fight a machine-gunner had pulled security with a small flock of geese nonchalantly fluffing their feathers a few feet away.

Dan looked at Charlie Team. They'd been badly smashed by the grenades. Prym was bewildered from the concussion. One of the new men on Black Team said to Dan, "Hey, man, I don't think he's really in this."

Charlie and the Ukrainian special forces man who had also been "kinda fucked up" by the grenades, as Dan put it, were tucked into a basement in their newly secured compound to guard the prisoners. The dead man's body was left outside the basement door. Prym had a radio line to the commander and HQ.

By now the Russians knew that they were there. That their own men were in the house didn't matter: they started hammering the location with what Dan called "pretty much everything in their arsenal." At one point Dan thought he heard a fast mover come in, dropping bombs on them.

In the meantime, the backfilling plan to support the Legion teams as they assaulted fell through. The first group of Ukrainians came in, but their rubber boats got smashed by the artillery. A de-mining crew made it ashore, but the boats were badly hit and the drivers fragged. The de-mining crew started working to help clear the way for the armor, but the Russians sent drones up and began hammering the crew, forcing them to take cover in a basement. The Ukrainian Army tried to get a BMP to them, but it got blown up by a landmine.

Dan checked his bearings. They controlled several houses at the north end of the village. The plan had been to move forward and get backfilled, but now they were pinned down and simply being smashed. If they went forward and either hit more casualties or took more prisoners, they would be overloaded. Their own wounded had been evacuated on their only working boat. The remaining boats were down. There was no way in or out, and they were stuck.

The orders came to push forward to a fork in the road, where it split into a small Y. "Okay, we'll do that," Dan agreed. "And then you'll get us what you promised, right?"

Alpha and Black moved forward, leapfrogging each other building by building towards the fork, keeping a good line of comms, while the artillery fell around them. In the nearby fields, the cows munched on grass, oblivious to the shells. Alpha and Black cleared up to the intersection. "Okay, we're here. Send us all the stuff!"

It couldn't come. There was no way to get anything down the river, as it was now broad daylight. They were going to be on their own. *We should've done this at night*, Dan thought in frustration. *We could've got a whole battalion in here, and the Russians wouldn't have seen us.*

They holed up in basements and got shelled for the rest of the day. Dan's radio was flooded out, so he had to run between buildings, checking on Charlie, Alpha, and Black. Several times, each team had to bail out of a good building because the Russians walked the mortars in too close and started to take the houses apart. A tank hammered them from McDonald's.

The fire wasn't perfectly constant. Dan would look for a lull, then make his run. As soon as he arrived at the next spot, the building would get hammered. *They can see me*, he thought. *There's an observer on McDonald's or there's a drone up.*

In the house Alpha had occupied, Greg was wet, cold, and exhausted. The swimming, the shelling, the fighting, and all the medical work had taken their toll. The day had been long as well; that morning he had driven the prep team in and had berated himself for accidentally beeping the horn as they arrived in Ternivka. Aaron had had to persuade him to shelter from an assault helicopter that morning after the medic declared that he didn't deserve a space in the basement after his mistake.

Greg climbed upstairs, took off his boots and socks, lay down on the bed and fell asleep. Tex and Aaron came up to check on him.

Tex decided to join Greg. Every ten to fifteen seconds a tank or artillery piece hit the buildings around them. *What do you do?* thought Greg. *At some point, you just get used to it.*

Then something hit their building. They jolted awake, covered in plaster, eyeing the blown-out windows. "Okay, time to go down," they agreed. The basement was usually safer though not always. Across the way, Black Team got an unlucky drone grenade dropped next to their basement. Marti was standing in the door and got fragged in the shoulder.

As dusk approached, they began to make their plans for an egress. The Ukrainians wanted them to hold, but there was no point in doing so: there weren't enough of them to hold the buildings, and the Ukrainian Army couldn't get more support to them anyway. Dan ran out to check on Prym. Outside, the artillery finally hit a cow. They could hear her screaming.

The village was completely transformed: burning, flattened, and apocalyptic, it was also extremely disorientating. Paths that had once existed were gone, along with the buildings that could be used as landmarks. Behind someone's house, a small shed that had once stored household and gardening items kept popping off: it was now a burning ammo dump.

Running behind the SEAL, Aaron noticed a grey material that looked like corrugated metal. Now it was making odd popping sounds everywhere. "What's that?" he asked. "Oh," said Ragnar next to him, "that's asbestos cooking off."

Dan had been demanding boats. One came and took the prisoners, the wounded Marti, and Black Team out, leaving Alpha and Charlie in the village. As the boats pulled out, everyone heard a cluster bomb hit right where the boat had been. They lost comms with Black Team; everyone assumed that the boat was hit and all were dead.

More than an hour later, the tough and combative British George, from Black Team, came over the radio: they had made it. He was sending the boats back to them, threatening to shoot the drivers on the water if they didn't go. The drivers started back down the river.

"They're coming to get you," Dan heard on the radio. Hours later, they hadn't arrived.

Okay, Dan decided. *Maybe they're high-centered or something; me and Greg will go up the river and see if we can spot 'em. If not, we'll come back and everyone's going to have to swim out.* The drivers had turned around once they realized that Black Team had left the beach.

Dan and the tall medic slipped back into the water and found the boats from earlier in the day, the ones that had been hit by artillery fire. The motors were no good, but they were still partly floating. The two men dragged one of the boats down the river.

The men left in the basement put on their kit in preparation for leaving; the impending sunrise might not give them time to wait for Dan and Greg. Noah said to Prym, "We're going to go out. You need to leave an hour after us, at most. We're gonna find out what happened to the boats, but if the boats don't come within an hour, then you need to do what we did and swim out."

Aaron went out and found the two swimmers bringing the half-sunken boat back, then rushed to collect everyone else. "Boat's here, let's go," he said.

Alpha emerged, expecting a Ukrainian boat to carry them out. But there was only Dan and Greg in the water, and the boat was partly sunk. "Throw your gear on, let's go," they said. The Javelin, the machine guns, all the heavy gear and anything that couldn't get wet went into the boat. Dan and Greg moved out to scout up the river. They finished loading, and the men from Alpha held onto the sides of the boat and started to swim it out while Greg and Dan scouted ahead of them.

The river was deep in parts and full of mud and chemicals from shell refuse; the water bubbled. The men would later realize that their skin had turned red. One man ended up with an infection from the water in an open cut on his knee. The nasty water was one of the reasons Greg had been so exhausted earlier. Ragnar's SCAR dipped in for mere seconds. When he went to clean the rifle the next day, there was rust everywhere. As they swam, artillery rounds landed parallel to them, and an illume round went up straight ahead, while everyone ducked as deep as they could, kicking quietly.

Dan had intended that everyone should come out at once. The SEAL, up ahead, didn't realize that Prym was not swimming out. It was only as they reached the far shore, up the river, that he realized that just Alpha had come out.

"Hey, man," said Noah, "someone's gotta go back for Prym. I don't know if he's gonna come out."

Aaron offered to go back and get them; Greg insisted that he would go too. Dan put his foot down. His men were exhausted from the day and the swim with heavy, waterlogged gear.

"No one's swimming back," Dan said. They didn't know if Charlie was actually willing to swim out or if they meant to stay. "At this point we're E&E-ing [escaping and evading]. He's going to have to come out. We don't have an asset to go and get him." The only way out was to walk several kilometers, through the area where Marti and Loup had driven like bats out of hell a week before, though it was safer now in the dark.

As they walked, they could see the town behind them being demolished by cluster munitions. Everyone was exhausted. Ragnar put his hands on his knees, leaning over, and saw ten or fifteen liters of water spill over his shoulder, out of the backpack that he had borrowed to carry RPG rounds. Finally, they made it to a spot safe enough for vehicles to come and get them, in a treeline on the hills outside the town. There they found Black Team and the wounded Marti. After hours of waiting, a Ukrainian unit came with Humvees and took them out. *Just a terrible extract*, thought Dan. *A full-on E&E.*

They trudged back into the Lux House and put down their gear. Marti walked into the room he was sharing to find Symon napping on his bed. The pirate looked up in surprise when Marti walked in. "Marti, what are you doing here?" asked the Ukrainian. "I heard you'd died."

They had not taken the town, but they had done something potentially more valuable. As the Russians opened up on them, they revealed where their positions were. *For me, it was a day of sitting getting the shit shelled out of me*, thought Dan. But the Ukrainian counter-battery had had an actual field day. They killed armor, mortar positions, artillery, the works. The Ukrainians sent up the drones, put up the 777 howitzers, and got the HIMARS set up.

Greg saw the video of the Ukrainian artillery hitting a column of Russian armor that was coming to their fight; it was smoking and burning. HIMARS hit a school that the Russians had been using as a headquarters position and killed several of the enemy there just as a platoon of men from the McDonald's position moved in to reinforce it. If one added in their group of prisoners, it was not a bad day. The Ukrainians took a video of the bombed-out village months later. The Russians had never bothered to retrieve the body of the DNR man: it was still lying outside the basement door where the teams had left it.

I thought it was a huge fuckin' shit show, thought Dan when he was told, *but apparently it was great. It was a success, it was just wonderful. I thought we botched a raid, got stranded, got none of the backup we were promised, had to escape and E&E out of a village and back to friendly territory, but apparently it was a huge success.*

22

ECHO

Dan's advising role, the one that had taken him away from the Kherson front before Riever and George left, involved water. It also involved something very, very big: the Zaporizhzhia Nuclear Power Plant at Enerhodar. They called the mission "Echo." The Ukrainians wanted to cross the Dnieper, assault the town, and take back the plant from the Russians. The SEAL then returned for what he called the "Blaho raid." But now it was going down: the Ukrainians were about to try to take back the plant. Black Team decided to go, and Greg jumped over to go with them. Dan, despite his misgivings about the effectiveness of the plan, went with him and officially joined Black Team.

The head of the International Legion insisted that his men go in the second wave. The Legion was first into Irpin, first into Severodonetsk; they can't be the front line of everything, went the argument.

A squared-away group of Ukrainian divers, whom Dan liked, went in and checked the beach for mines: it was fine. There were stories of the Russians playing volleyball on the beach, intelligence that was later contested. It looked hard—very hard. But the Ukrainians were willing to give it a shot.

The aim was to get across the water and lay siege to the plant. Dan's plan was to get from the beach into the city as quickly as possible, in order to find cover from the artillery. He urged the leadership to hit the place at night, as close to the city as they could, and beeline straight into the urban area. The Ukrainians without NODs would dig in and secure the corridor to resupply. It still wasn't a good idea, he thought. But they were sending all his buddies, so he decided to go.

The first wave, solely Ukrainian, had already left when Greg and Dan got to their staging point on the shore. Dan heard that one unit hit the beach and got artyed, but that another got shot off before they arrived. Both pulled back. The second wave never started the crossing.

Now the gig was up. "It went from a sneaky insertion to a full-on D-Day invasion," as Dan put it. There were tanks, artillery, constant overwatch, good intelligence, drones, trenches, thermals, IR floodlights; all the best equipment that the Russians had was guarding the town of Enerhodar. The remnants of Alpha Team, with Ginger having rejoined after his rabies treatment in Kyiv, came up to join them. So did Charlie.

The new target was a town just up the river, a bit further north of the power plant, called Ivanivka. The mission was to go and raid the town. There was intelligence that there was an armory, ammo cache, and possibly an electronic warfare (EW) system in a compound outside this little town across the river. There was a U-shaped spit of land that reached into the river, a rat's mouth on whose sides the teams would come ashore and assault. They were pre-approved for a HIMARS strike on any hard target they chose. The compound was one hundred meters off the beach. They would hit the building, then bounce. The goal was to get the logistics of the plan down and try to figure out how to do the waterborne mission properly.

They loaded in the buses and headed to their staging point across the river, about four miles across open water from their target. It was expected to take thirty minutes.

They were delayed. Ginger waited at the staging area with Alpha Team, lying with Greg and Tex under Greg's poncho, spooning to stay warm, while Prym played with a drone with a white light on the beach. *We are in visible range of Russians. Probably audible range of Russians*, thought Ginger.

Loading into the boats was a mess. They were unarmored rubber Zodiacs, suitable for quiet insertions but completely unsuitable for attack. *When you hear that there is a big cache of ammo, what does that typically mean? That there's probably a large group of people there, and that's logistically why they need that ammo there. They want to open up hot as shit with a HIMARS strike then roll a bunch of guys up like it's D-Day, but on rubber rafts*, thought Ginger.

Mother Nature didn't play along: a huge storm settled over the water. The wind picked up wickedly, and the water got very choppy. As people climbed in, some of the boats had water all over them; some men were sitting in water to their waists. After hours of waiting, the men started to get cold. Given enough time, cold injuries can set in under fifty-five degrees if you're soaked. Hands started turning blue.

"We stood for hours while they unfucked themselves," as Dan later put it. Two of the metal sharks with them were unable to dock at the beach, so some teams got ferried from small boats to larger ones.

The weather was a mess. *This is no-go weather*, thought Ginger. It was like a hurricane out there, and it was very difficult to navigate the little Zodiacs. The pilots were very brave but inexperienced. Many of them were members of the Ukrainian Territorial Defense Forces (TDF) with little previous exposure to boats at all, especially in four-foot swells. People were getting lost. *Super dangerous*, thought Ginger. *Dude, you're gonna get people killed, lost, captured before we even get to the mission area.*

Just before they left, Ginger was put in a "terminator" position: he was supposed to tank the mission if it looked untenable. "These dudes aren't going to listen to me," he protested. "Yes, they will," said the mission commander. "They've all been told to listen to you." The Westerners had already agreed: if anyone heard Ginger give the order, they would turn around.

Now they had a timeline problem: they started late, and loading had taken longer than expected because of the weather and the ferrying issue. It was 3:30 in the morning. There was just barely enough time to hit the target under the cover of darkness.

Everyone buckled down. As they were on their way, pedal to the metal, two minutes from their own shore, they saw an enormous flash of light, as a huge stream that looked like a giant sparkler flew through the air. *The fuckin' nuclear plant just went up*, thought Ginger; *we're all gonna die. A bright-ass flash of light. Holy fuck, they got us.*

In fact it was an S-300 missile taking out a Bayraktar drone that had been overhead, but no one knew that. The drivers on the boats reacted to contact and immediately began to return to base, which was what they had been briefed to do. The mission commander was shouting over the radio a word that he swore meant both "advance" and "go back" in Russian. Whatever he said, the drivers heard "abort," and the Westerners in the boats couldn't communicate. *A whole communications snafu*, thought Dan. The inexperienced drivers didn't have night vision or GPS. They actually had their phones out to navigate across the four miles of swollen river.

As they arrived back at the beach, there was only an hour left before sunrise. Greg and Tex jumped in Ginger's ear: "Man, you've got to put an end to this." Ginger agreed: they were done. He got on the radio and called it. The mission commander insisted that they go. Ginger put his foot down: "We can try again later."

They ruined two Stingers, which had fallen in the water, plus other personal gear. People had cold weather injuries. Ginger was woken two hours after he fell into bed, and dragged to headquarters for the debrief. He listened while everyone in front of him said what he called "respectful and well-worded things." Finally, it was his turn.

"Listen, everything I've got to say has already been said," Ginger declared, looking at the senior commander in charge of the entire overall assault, "but listen, brother, I understand that you have a job to do and you're in a little bit of a different situation than the rest of us. But when it comes to maritime operations, weather is a fucking no-go criterion."

Everyone behind him jumped in, in agreement. *Finally*.

"I don't think so, man," said the commander, shaking his head.

"You're smoking the glass cock, man! There's no way that you don't think that weather is a thing when it comes to operations like that," sputtered the American.

"We just need more experienced boat pilots. Why weren't you guys helping the boat pilots?" the Ukrainian demanded.

"I'm not a fuckin' boat pilot either! I don't know how to drive a boat in a damn storm!" replied Ginger.

For two weeks, they tried to plan a better way to do it. But they kept losing resources: units pulled out; the big guns got sent further south to help with the offensive in Kherson. They also lost Greg, who was called away for specialized training for medics in Poland. Their chances of success, already low, started to get lower.

They intensified their training, with big rehearsals on a beach further into their own territory. One day the Russians struck the beach with a missile minutes after Ginger and his team had left, hitting some Ukrainians who were still there. Another unit took serious casualties when they were missiled while out on a firing range nearby. Rumors started: there was an informant in the village. Red flares had been seen during their movements. Others suspected a mole within the unit that was hit at the range. Orlan UAVs were sweeping over their headquarters. Some guys started to get nervous. They were on twenty-four-hour standby for another raid on the power plant.

Ginger was given a mission to take a small team, go into the town at night dressed as civilians, and look for the flare-popping informant, while a Ukrainian unit, with Westerners manning the guns, got into boats and did a diversionary faux raid. *That is madness*, Ginger thought. *This is, first off, way too cool, but there's no way*.

Everyone received new civilian clothes and got dressed; Tex was mad because he couldn't come. "Sorry, buddy, you don't blend," Ginger said; a large Black Texan wasn't a common sight in eastern Ukraine. "Nothing I can do here, dude."

They took night vision and pistols, with rifles in the back of the trucks in case it went down; they didn't know if they were looking for a local civilian or a genuine Russian FSB agent (or agents) in a safehouse.

They waited all night, watching as the diversion team went out. It looked like broad daylight under NODs. All the Westerners had noted it: Ukraine was incredibly bright. *The brightest place I've ever been*, thought Ginger. *I don't know if it's a lack of cloud cover or some Soviet propaganda shit, I don't know man, but walking around under NODs is a cheat code out here.*

They never saw the informant, but what they saw, and heard, was worse. They heard the diversion team start their engines from four kilometers away. They heard them on approach the entire time. Ginger used his laser range finder and realized that the team could see them with bare eyes at over half a kilometer away. They saw the plant light up like a Christmas tree when the team was seven kilometers out, all the way across and up the river: no flare. There were helicopters, drones, IR floodlights, everything. The Russians didn't need an informant. They could see everything already.

The diversion team fired towards the beach and found Grad MLRS, not even bothering to arc, shooting directly at them. *Dude, they're fucking dead*, thought Ginger. *There's no way.* They tried to raise the team on the radio; nothing. *This is retarded. We came out here to catch some asshole and all it did was get thirty dudes on a boat killed. Motherfucker.* A FAGOT, the anti-tank rocket, followed them out over the water.

They could see the boats start to come back. Ginger counted them in: thirty men. The Russians had missed. *Oh, thank God.* They hopped in their trucks and exfiled out. *There's no way they don't know we're here.* They never saw any informant.

But the commanders decided to do it. Ginger got his team ready. It was awkward and uneasy; they had told themselves they wouldn't do this because they knew it wouldn't work. Ginger had a physical pain, specific pressure, in the back of his head. They knew that even if they made it across, they wouldn't make it back, and it would be for no good reason: everyone understood it would fail.

Dude, if we go over there, I've just signed all these guys' death warrants because I didn't have the balls to walk into Vadym's office and say "You're a fucking idiot and we're not going over there", Ginger thought. But none of them were willing to say no. Ginger had a standard joke that he used in Ukraine: "Man, I'm too old for this shit." It always got a laugh because he had only turned twenty-five that March, not long after he arrived in-country. But now he actually felt like it.

The plan was for them to cross the river and hold out for seven days while the Ukrainian Army planned a follow-on mission. There was no way they would last that long. Everyone packed for the endgame: very little food and gear. They took ammo, speedballed magazines, the works. Ginger had six rockets in his daypack. *I'm going down. This is it.*

Dan's team was set for the initial wave. One of the bigger boats that was meant to rendezvous with them got swamped on the way, flooded, and sank. Near shore, they waited for hours, but had no idea that one of their larger escorts was in the process of sinking.

Eventually the rest of the larger boats arrived. Another Ukrainian unit got close to the beach and started taking fire. Dan could see tracer rounds going from the water towards the beach. Then flares started going up, lighting them up. The SEAL looked ahead and saw several gunboats coming right for him. *We're dead*, he thought. *Those are Russian boats and they just lit up flares to see us and they're going to come and just lay into us with machine guns.* But they were Ukrainians, pulling back.

They tried to call in artillery support to take out a tank on the beach. Russian artillery started landing in the water near them. *Really cool at night*, Dan thought, watching the rounds explode just below the surface, producing a glow under the water and an illuminated fountain in the air. *I've never seen that before.* It was starting to get closer, and as they pulled back, lines of Grad starting hitting the water right where they had been.

Ginger's team was assigned to the second wave. They were sent to a TDF outpost in a basement close to the river crossing. Their job was to leapfrog the guys who landed first. Ginger took a look around and realized that there were way too many people there. It would be a good target once the artillery started. They pulled out, found a smaller place, and tucked in.

They heard the boats go over, and the small arms open up. Then they heard the tanks, BTRs, and cluster munitions. Their own artillery was going nonstop right behind them. HIMARS was working, but they were hitting targets too far away to see: twenty-two targets, all successfully. *The sky looks insane*, Ginger thought. The barrages back and forth were constant.

They never got the call to go. "I just sat there and got pounded," Ginger said afterwards, "like a jailhouse pretty boy for six hours."

A big waste of time and assets, Dan thought when it was over. There were big guns tied up in the area that could have been better used for something else. *Heck, if you had all of the resources of Joint Special Operations Command, it still would have been a very difficult op to do.* They didn't have the specialized gear, like water wings, or the proper boats. It was just too big, and there wasn't enough experience operating on the water.

It was the end of Alpha Team. Everyone scattered. Dan had already moved over to Black Team permanently. Greg was in Poland for medical training. Ginger and Tex went on two weeks of leave back in the United States; they would figure out the status of the team when they got back. They planned to reconnect with each other, plus a few newer additions to the team like Noah and Ragnar, when they returned. As they checked out, they passed through Legion headquarters in Kyiv, where they found their medals, plus Riever's, in someone's desk drawer. They were the Order for Courage, a white Greek cross with the Ukrainian trident in the middle, resting on a golden laurel bed and two crossed swords, and hanging from a blue ribbon. The paperwork had been signed by President Zelensky himself.

On landing at JFK, Ginger was immediately singled out for interrogation by Customs and Immigration, who accused him of traveling abroad to train white supremacists. "You were there for ten months, what other reason could you have been there for?" the agents demanded.

"To fucking kill Russians?" snapped Ginger. "Why are you sending weapons and advocate that people help if when they come back you slap a fuckin' terrorist sticker on 'em and give 'em a hard time?"

The agents took his passport and cell phone, and detained him for hours. "I thought I was gonna get a thumb in the butt," the Jav gunner said later. He missed his connecting flight home to Ohio. *Fuckin' JFK*, thought Ginger. *Never again. A nightmare.* Agents there had pulled him off his plane on his initial flight to Poland nearly a year before.

Everyone they knew who had flown through JFK had been harassed in similar fashion, though with nearly a year having passed since the start of the war, and billions of U.S. dollars and equipment having been sent in support of the side he had risked his life for, Ginger had not expected this. Other parts of the country were very different. When Riever landed in Chicago, the border agent asked where he'd been. The Ranger gave him an honest, if limited, answer: Poland and Ukraine. "Visiting family," the agent had said firmly, pushing the passport back across the desk and opening the gate. "Welcome home."

That December George rejoined Tex and Ginger: he was going back for good. He shipped his truck by freighter ship to Belgium and flew to the East Coast, where George spent a week with Riever and his girlfriend before Christmas, prior to flying to France. He and Tex picked up the truck at the port and drove it across Europe. In Ukraine they had it hand-painted in a green camo pattern, just like the truck that Greg had rolled back in Mykolaiv. The three planned to join a Ukrainian SSO team, but it fell through, leaving them cooling their heels in Kyiv while they searched for a new team.

23

BAKHMUT

Dan had stayed with Black Team, moving out to the Bakhmut area soon after the power plant raids finally fell apart in the fall. Loup and Marti joined Black as well. The team had changed since Severodonetsk and Kramatorsk, though Artem still had the Portuguese Pedro, from Severo, plus Jock, the Scot, and the British Rory with him. Even during what Dan called "the Blaho raid" Black had added several new men. Two were not just brothers, but twins, from New Zealand. One was a sniper named Ramsey; the other, Will, was NZ SAS. There was a British machine-gunner named Owen as well. Greg joined Black Team a bit later, after he returned from his medical training in Poland to find that Alpha's successor had fallen apart and that Tex and Ginger were on leave. Out east Black Team reconnected with the Mexicans, whom they'd met in Severodonetsk, as well as a new group called Grey Team, led by Ginger's old buddy Rob, the posh British officer they'd fought with in Irpin, Zaporizhzhia, and early on in Mykolaiv. Doug had moved from Black over to Rob, whose Grey Team was operating as a pure quick-reaction force.

Their first day in Bakhmut was slow and miserably cold: told that a Russian assault was expected, they went to reinforce the line but saw nothing. Loup, frustrated, went upstairs as the sun went down. With a thermal scope on his bolt-action .50 cal bullpup, he had five confirmed kills on Russians that night.

Damn, thought Dan, *this is sniper playground. This is what we need to be doing, not planning assaults and doing all that stuff*. The Ukrainians still wanted an assault, so they went out the next day to recce a quarry, bringing all three of their snipers. Ramsey, their Kiwi sniper, got one kill. The third night they sent out both Loup and Ramsey, and both men got one kill each. Three nights, eight dead Russians: the math made sense to Dan. He pushed for more sniper ops, and for money to buy a thermal sight for his third sniper. With active night sniping they could deny Russians the use of cover for entrenching, and keep them awake, scared, and immobile. They could deny the Russians movement and the use of entire areas. But the Ukrainian commanders saw it differently: they wanted assaults, ground to be taken, something easy for Western supporters and the press to understand.

I don't want to get my guys schwacked on some crazy assault when we're getting eight Russians in three nights with very minimal risk to ourselves, thought Dan. *Why change what we're doing?* But the commanders wanted an assault. Dan went out to recce through the rubble between apartment buildings one night with Will, Ramsey's twin and the Kiwi SAS man. The two crept forward in tandem, Will on thermal and Dan on his night vision. As they bounded forward, Dan confirmed that they could get the team through, and put together an assault.

Grey Team got called away, to support the Mexicans further north. Black went on with their assault, now at half strength for the operation without Grey. Before they left they heard the news: the other teams had gotten hammered. Several Belorussians and Georgians were dead. Grey Team had been hit by a tank.

Owen drove four trips, one of them at night, to get the wounded out. One Canadian was killed, as well as a Brit named Si, one of the original Alpha Team members from Irpin. One former British SAS man suffered severe head trauma and ended up in a coma. Doug had been standing in between the two men who were killed; his right hand was badly damaged from holding it over one of the other men. He twice signed paperwork in two different hospitals for the hand to be amputated, but he held the surgeons off, saved the hand, and was back fighting again within a few months. Rob had a chunk taken out of his leg and was evacuated to Poland. His leg was later amputated.

Black went out that night, Dan and Will going first to get eyes on the Russians to prep beforehand. The illume was high. As the pair bounded up through the rubble, tank rounds came in. The two men hit the ground. "Was that for us?" asked Dan quietly. The second round hit even closer. "Yeah," said Will, "that's us." They picked themselves up and ran for cover; a third shot followed them. *A top-end thermal tank would have got us*, Dan thought. *The round didn't seem as big as at other times when tanks have shot at me.* Perhaps it was a smaller tank, or a BMP with a bigger gun, but it didn't matter. Dan aborted the mission. They couldn't bring the team through that.

Higher command intervened. There were too many dead and injured Westerners in the news. Black and the rest of Grey were sent back to Kyiv for leave through Christmas. Grey Team was completely reconstituted under new leadership, but it kept the same name.

Just before the Kyiv break, Greg was out with Loup when the sniper killed fifteen Russians in twelve hours. *He is one scary man*, thought the tall medic. Dan wanted to run simultaneous sniper ops in different positions, though it brought him into conflict with the Ukrainian commanders. Meanwhile, Loup chose to move over to the Georgian Legion, whose tough, charismatic commander would let him kill as many Russians as he liked.

"Russians don't care about them," the Ukrainian commanders would say of the snipers' kills. "They're prisoners, they're conscripts, they're mobilized guys. Russia has more of them, they'll keep throwing them out."

"But eventually they'll run out!" Dan would say. "If you lost five dudes the night before, you're going to be pretty affected probably most of the next day. And you're not going to move around at night." One of the men Loup shot in the quarry had a night sight up to his eye, scanning, on watch. "Now the next dude who's told 'Watch out tonight' isn't going to do a very good job, which means we can sneak up on those positions at night 'cause everyone's going to have their heads down knowing that there's snipers with thermals out there picking dudes off," the SEAL would explain. But it was lost in translation. As Dan put it, there was a local mentality of "If you're not taking casualties, you're not doing work."

There was pressure, too, from others who wanted bigger roles for soldiers other than the snipers. "Yeah, it's not great for the rest of us, none of us are getting to pull the trigger," said Dan, "but at this point I couldn't care less if I'm pulling the trigger. I want to win."

This was Bakhmut, the city that had come to stand in for Ukraine itself. The Ukrainians thought they could bleed the Russians, and bleeding them they were. The beleaguered city kept the war in the headlines and kept pressure on Western governments to send more support. The war was nearing its one-year anniversary. Western tanks would be arriving soon, a fact that had pressured the Russians into committing to an early offensive that they didn't have the manpower, or the armor, to win. *Never interrupt your enemy while he's making a mistake*, the saying goes. The Ukrainians needed to bleed the Russians, hold the little city, and gather momentum for an offensive that could regain territory before the West lost interest. As Bakhmut went, so went Ukraine. They would assault.

Black Team rolled back out to Bakhmut on January 10. They had one more new addition: Ragnar had gone home to Estonia on leave after Alpha broke up. He returned just after Christmas. Since Alpha was no more, he joined up with Black, officially becoming a member of the team on January 3. It was an easy choice. *I have so much to learn from Dan and Greg*, thought the Estonian, who was always trying to challenge himself. They trained together for a week, allowing Greg to spend Orthodox Christmas with his family before he headed back east.

The small city was cold and apocalyptic, with the sound of guns and artillery booming almost constantly, a Stalingrad-like feel with oddly modern twists, like the little quadcopter drones Ragnar spotted overhead dangling grenades under their bellies.

They started to settle in after the long drive, organizing their gear and looking for work. A mission came up quickly. Black Team was asked to hold a house on the eastern side of the city. The Russians had gotten into the houses on the edges, and command wanted Black Team to assault there soon.

A six-man team went out: Artem, Ragnar, Greg, Owen, Jock, and Rory. Dan and the others were still en route from Kyiv. On the overnight, the firing was intense; there was shooting just one hundred meters from them, in the direction that they were planning to assault. When the small team returned to their safehouse, the rest of the team had arrived. They stole a few hours of sleep, briefed, and headed out again on a raid.

The plan was simple. They would form a large, L-shaped ambush. Another team of foreigners serving as a quick reaction force (QRF), along with some Ukrainians, were holding a house at the corner of a residential block. Moving south from their position were six houses in a row. Houses 1 through 3 were expected to be empty, but houses 4 through 6 were suspected enemy positions. A fire support team would set up in the house they had just held, to the west of the target houses, with rockets and machine guns, while an assault team moved south and cleared the Russians out.

Intelligence indicated three to four Russians per occupied house: it seemed solid. Dan had talked to the commanders at rear headquarters and in Bakhmut. The SEAL was pleased with the intel and the plan, which gave the rest of the team confidence. *We all know the risks*, thought Ragnar, *but the size of the risk has to be controllable.* Like everyone else, the Estonian knew that Dan wouldn't take a mission that was too risky.

In the early hours of the morning, armored vehicles dropped them off at the QRF team's house, which also held a small Ukrainian unit. Artem had initially planned to go with the assault team and leave the highly capable Ragnar in charge of fire support, but Ragnar had pointed out that he couldn't shoot the Gus and command the GUR (Ukrainian military intelligence) men and Owen at the same time. They would need someone to command the whole thing and be able to be in radio communication with both the assault teams and headquarters.

Artem led Ragnar, Owen, and six Ukrainian special forces men from the GUR around a long block, about a kilometer's walk, to the fire support location. Ragnar noted how incredibly dark it was. If during the Echo mission the big skies of Ukraine had been the enemy, tonight it was difficult to see even under NODs. Bakhmut was loud and full of fighting, but at least for now the big Russian artillery was to the north of them, assaulting the town of Soledar.

Meanwhile, Dan conferred with the QRF team leader. He briefed them on the plan; Rory added that the team would be the QRF and casevac if Black got into trouble. The other team agreed.

In the fire support house, the small team set up. Ragnar manned the Carl Gustaf, the hard-hitting Swedish rocket, armed with both high-explosive and anti-tank HEAT rounds. Owen had his 5.56 SAW, and one of the GUR men had a PKM machine gun. They had radio links with the assault team, the QRF team, and headquarters.

Rory led the assault team as point man, followed by Marti, Dan, Will, Ramsey, Jock, Pedro, and Greg. They cleared houses 1, 2, and 3 easily: they were empty, but it was awkward going. As in Blahodativka, they were in a residential area. Each house had a fenced yard, with multiple little outbuildings. They moved carefully in the thick dark, maneuvering their way through broken fences that could snag men and gear.

Between houses 3 and 4 were the fences belonging to each yard, and a small road that ran between them. Together Dan and Rory crept forward to scout house 4. Returning, Dan got on the radio to Artem: they were ready. With an IR laser, he confirmed identification of the first target house and the team's own location. The fire support opened up. Ragnar heard Dan on the radio again: "The fires are good, keep it up."

Once contact opened, Russian RPGs started flying towards the fire support team, though Ragnar thought they looked small in comparison with the massive rounds of the Gus that he was whipping into the position. The assault team took contact and put their own Matador and LAW rockets into house 4.

The assault team broke the fence and moved carefully across the road, taking cover behind some outbuildings in house 4's back garden. Dan lasered house 5, indicating that the fire support should shift to the next building so that they could assault house 4. The fire support team confirmed and shifted their aim south. The assault team moved through a rubble-strewn opening, probably a hole in a concrete wall like the one through which Alpha had pulled Oleksii in Severodonetsk. Now they were closer to house 4. Greg popped a grenade through the window.

A massive explosion shook the assault team. Afterwards Ramsey thought it must have been an RPG fired from an elevated position in the house, because it was so accurate. Ramsey saw his twin brother Will, who had been standing right in front of him, go down. In the fire support house, Ragnar heard Marti's pained voice on the radio: "I'm hit! I'm hit!" Beside him, Dan was down hard.

Ramsey, nearly blind in one eye from debris and bleeding from shrapnel in his leg, leapt forward with Greg to pull the three wounded men out of the line of fire as the enemy started to shoot airburst munitions at them. The rest of the team tried to fire to suppress the enemy, and called for help.

Will had bad injuries to his chest and abdomen; one leg was ripped open. Ramsey put on tourniquets as best he could, then went back to link up with the QRF. When Ramsey returned, he briefly helped Greg, who was working alone to save Marti and Dan under heavy fire.

Expecting help from the QRF he had led in, Ramsey stripped off his kit and his brother's. He put Will on his shoulder and ran with him back to the QRF team house.

A second explosion went off: a massive blast with a sharp, bright flash; they thought later that it might have been an 82 mm mortar jerry-rigged with a booster to an RPG launcher. Everyone went down. In the fire support house, the rest of the team was firing to suppress. On the radio Artem kept calling for casevac vehicles and for the QRF to help his men.

When Jock came to, he thought he had been hit in the hip by a sledgehammer. At first, he couldn't hear anything. Instinctively he rolled to cover and shouted for a medic, but there was no response. Finally, he could hear Rory's voice. Was he okay? Could he walk?

Rory ordered Pedro to get a radio from Dan's or Marti's kit. In the fire support house, Ragnar heard Rory's voice on the radio and knew that Dan and Marti must both be badly wounded. The point man took command, requesting rapid fire from the fire support team and laying down heavy fire on his own. Jock realized that he had been hit badly in the leg by shrapnel. He put a tourniquet on himself and struggled forward to help Dan and Marti. None of them could see Greg anymore. Rory reported to the fire support team: the medic was missing.

When Marti got hit, he realized that he couldn't feel his legs. He assumed they were blown off, then looked at the sky and closed his eyes, expecting to die. After a few minutes, he realized that he wasn't dead yet, and started talking. When Jock found him, Marti kept repeating, "I can't feel my legs, I can't feel my legs." The Scot patted him, reassuring the big Legionnaire that both legs were intact. But Jock wasn't sure what was wrong—he could feel cold, but he wasn't sure if it was blood or if his hands were just cold. Beside Marti, Dan begged Jock to take his sling and weapon off. "It's choking me, it's choking me. Jock, take my weapon off, I can't breathe," Dan said again and again, trying to raise his right arm.

"There isn't a weapon on you, mate, just relax," Jock said, trying to calm the SEAL, and reached forward to remove Dan's helmet in case the strap was the culprit. As he removed the helmet, he found pools of blood coming from the top of Dan's head. Rory, desperately requesting help on the radio and not seeing the QRF anywhere, handed Jock a first field dressing. The Scot tried to wrap Dan's head, but there was blood everywhere. He worried that he wasn't doing a good enough job, struggling at the same time to remove Dan's body armor in case it was causing the breathing problem. Meanwhile Pedro was trying to help Marti while Rory fired alone. "We're going to get you both out of here," Jock said to Marti and Dan.

Now Rory could see the small QRF element, and they began to try to move the wounded towards better cover. Then Rory finally saw Greg, slumped over a little fence. "Greg! Greg!" Jock shouted, in an attempt to get a reaction. The Scot got to the tall medic, feeling for a pulse, but he couldn't find anything. He leaned his cheek alongside Greg's mouth to feel for a breath; still nothing. He tried again for a heartbeat: nothing. Greg was cold, and Jock knew that he was gone. In the fire support house, still firing at the Russians, Ragnar heard Rory's voice on the radio: "The MIA is KIA."

The fire was starting to come from three sides. The Russians had trench lines to the east of the houses. They were fighting at least a squad, if not a whole platoon, and the enemy was maneuvering on them.

"Brother, we need help. We can't get out. Somebody come and help us. We're going to die here," Rory called on the radio. Ten minutes had passed since the first explosion went off.

Artem left most of the GUR team on the support position, then took Owen, Ragnar, and three GUR men with him. The gunners laid the Gustaf and the heavy weapons on the floor. They were 150 meters from the firefight as the crow flies, but they had no knowledge of the terrain or the enemy flanking movements. They chose the proven route, running the kilometer back to the QRF's corner house flat out in the dark.

On the ground Rory ordered a machine-gunner from the QRF to set up his gun, and indicated where he wanted suppressive fire. Jock got someone to help him pull Marti and Dan about twenty meters into better cover. But the fire was increasing, and now it was clear they were being surrounded. Briefly, they pulled back behind a garden shed.

The QRF men started to panic. "We're all going to die!" they cried. "We need to get out!"

Jock started to move back to pull Dan and Marti towards further cover behind the shed. "Don't you leave us! We have wounded men and we're not leaving them!" the Scot shouted, seeing them panic. "If you leave now, I'll kill you," he threatened. "I'll kill you all," he shouted, turning to push through the rubble opening, with the tourniquet still on his leg, in order to pull his men to safety.

Pedro and Rory put down covering fire as Jock moved to pull Marti out. The QRF machine-gunner threw his PKM on the ground and ran; the others followed him, except for one man, an American veteran called Nick, who stayed. As Jock struggled to pull Marti through, he was shot in the arm. He tried to pull Dan, but the SEAL was stuck on something. Putting a tourniquet on his arm, he went back with Rory and Nick for Dan, and together they dragged the SEAL behind cover. Rory was shot through the leg. The radio filled with Scotch invective: where was the rest of the QRF?

It took Artem, Ragnar, Owen, and the three GUR men five to seven minutes to race the distance to the QRF corner house on foot. When they burst in, they found them all sitting in a room: the QRF was back, quiet and embarrassed. Fifteen men were in the house, but no one was helping Black Team.

Ramsey was there, checking Will's tourniquets as the casevac vehicle arrived. The driver wanted to look for more wounded before he went to the hospital. Outside, Ragnar explained in Russian that there were more casevacs coming and that Will needed to go to the hospital immediately. As two men were speaking, the vehicle started moving. Ramsey had jumped into the driver's seat and was turning the vehicle around, ready to drive his brother to help on his own. The driver jumped back into his vehicle, threw Ramsey into the back with Will, and drove them straight to the hospital.

Artem commanded the QRF outside. "Let's go," he said. They assembled in the yard, but the QRF just stood quietly, telling Artem to calm down.

"Ragnar, take five guys and go," Artem said.

"Who's been there?" the Estonian demanded. Two men raised their hands.

"Come, you can show me where," Ragnar said.

"I don't remember," said the men quietly.

Artem erupted, yelling in anger.

"Artem, you ready?" Ragnar asked. "Owen, you ready? Let's go."

The Estonian turned and ran into the dark, still struggling to see even with NODs. They could hear a single rifle firing back at the surrounding Russians. It was Rory, who had brought eighteen magazines. He was firing so much and so fast that he had been forced to grab one of the wounded men's weapons. His own had overheated, and now he was running low on ammo. The rest of the team ran to the sound of their gun. Behind Ragnar were Owen, Artem, and three GUR men.

In front Ragnar was focused on finding his own men. As they arrived, Artem fired at the second floor of a house to their right side: Russians that Ragnar hadn't had time to see.

"Is it okay to come?" Ragnar yelled to Rory as he approached.

"Yeah, it's okay, come here," the point man responded.

Ragnar saw Dan and Marti on the ground, unconscious. He noticed a very neat wound dressing on Dan's head, the one that Jock had worried over. Nick, the one QRF man who had stayed, was trying to stabilize the SEAL. Pedro was shooting and trying to help Marti. Rory directed Ragnar's fire as Artem took blast injuries and shrapnel to both shins, but he and two GUR men picked up Marti and started to run with him.

As they started to help Rory, the point man broke down. "Greg is fucking dead," he cried. But they didn't have enough men to help the hobbling, double-tourniqueted Jock, whose leg was numb, let alone carry the 6′ 5″ medic. Ragnar, Pedro, and the remaining GUR man picked up Dan, while Owen and Rory laid down suppressive fire to cover the evacuation.

One of the hardest things I've done, Ragnar thought later, *and the ugliest casevac I've seen*. They had no stretchers; each wounded man was carried bodily. Dan was unresponsive. The path was difficult, especially in the dark. The broken fences were a nightmare: kit caught, bodies caught, clothing caught, everything caught. Watching the wounded Jock hobble alone was terrible. The Scot got stuck badly on a fence and Ragnar tried to pull him but only managed to put his finger right in the bullet hole in Jock's arm. The Scot yelled in pain. "Sorry, man!" said the Estonian.

They tripped and fell over and over. Ragnar fell once more, his face landing close to Dan's. Then he heard a voice, very quietly. "Pick me up," the SEAL said. "Pick me up on your shoulders so I can walk." It seemed impossible, but Pedro heard it too.

On his own the Estonian carefully pulled Dan up and put him to his shoulder. Pedro took Dan's other shoulder, and the SEAL began to push with his legs. *I don't know what this guy's made of, but that's something like out of a movie*, thought Ragnar. Dan had blast injuries all over his body. He also had a bullet in his brain.

Near the QRF's corner house the QRF men and the other Ukrainian team ran out to help. Ragnar and Pedro handed Dan over, and the Estonian turned to provide additional suppressive fire. Dan, Marti, and Jock were loaded onto casevacs. Pedro climbed in to help stabilize Dan on the way.

Artem, Ragnar, Owen, and Rory returned to the QRF's corner house. They had gotten the wounded out, but they had had to leave Greg's body. Now it was time to get him.

They refilled their magazines from an ammo box and asked for the QRF's help again. "But we're out of ammo," came the excuse. *They haven't fired one shot but they're out of ammo*, thought Ragnar. Rory had fired all eighteen of his magazines trying to suppress the Russians.

"It's just a body," someone said, as the remainder of Black Team stared. *Someone could've gotten shot*, the Estonian realized, *but everyone kept their cool*.

Artem was furious; he moved to throw the QRF out of the house. Then Ramsey walked back in: still mostly blind in one eye, limping and still bleeding from a shrapnel wound to the leg.

"Ramsey, what are you doing here?" everyone asked in confusion. "Didn't you take your brother to the hospital?"

"Will is okay," Ramsey explained. The doctor said that he could be stabilized. "I came back to see how my other brothers were doing." He had refused treatment, hitchhiked back to Bakhmut, fired up ATAK on his phone, and run the last kilometer back to the house on his own. They tried to send Ramsey out with the QRF to get medical help. "No, I'm not going anywhere," the Kiwi said, "until all my brothers are safe."

"I know we need to get Greg's body out," Ragnar said to Artem, "but we can't go in with four guys."

It was now five in the morning. Artem called to HQ for help and got Vadym on the line. They went back to headquarters to get organized. Within three hours, a BTR with a 30 mm auto cannon and a Humvee with a Mark 19 grenade launcher, specially approved by the senior area commander at Vadym's request, had been loaned to a Ukrainian unit who would help. They persuaded Ramsey to stay at headquarters. He agreed not to go on the ground mission but still refused to go to the hospital. He wasn't going anywhere, he said again, until all his brothers were safe.

A drone confirmed the location of Greg's body. Ragnar led the ground force while the BTR drove parallel to them on the road, smashing the Russian buildings. Ragnar and Owen made it to Greg first: he was stuck under debris from a collapsed part of house 4. A beam had fallen and it prevented them from moving him. Rory arrived in the Humvee with Artem and a few Ukrainians. Despite being shot through the leg, Rory was still mobile. The point man broke the beam, and they were able to move Greg from under the debris. They loaded Greg on the vehicle and took him out.

The wounded were evacuated to Kramatorsk, where Jock stayed; he nearly lost a big toe but otherwise was healing well. He would spend time on crutches, with some nasty contusions to his head, plus the bullet wound in his arm and the shrapnel wound to his leg. The bullet hole in Rory's leg turned out to be a medically simple through-and-through; Artem's shins healed as well. The very badly wounded Marti, Will, and Dan were sent on to the big hospital in Dnipro.

Will's guts sat on a table next to the rest of his body while the doctors operated. He pulled through. Marti had a shrapnel wound to the lungs; the doctors drained eight hundred milliliters of fluid from them. Another piece of shrapnel had penetrated parallel to his spine, just barely to the left of it. It was the reason he had initially been unable to feel his legs. The doctors operated, creating a nasty-looking scar several inches long. "Will be okay 100% just minor scratches," Marti posted on his Instagram, with a laughing face emoji. He ended up temporarily on crutches from a nasty cyst of blood that pressed on a nerve, making it impossible for him to control his right leg, though he retained feeling in it. Through significant pain he pushed himself to heal. By May he was still in pain but running again, tough as nails and determined to pass the tests to join the Ukrainian special forces.

Dan had a bullet in his brain and extensive blast injuries. In Dnipro the doctors stabilized him, using adrenaline to keep him alive. They tried everything they could. There was even a Johns Hopkins-trained surgeon on hand to examine him. Black Team arrived on January 16, the day after the mission went bad. There was talk of sending Dan to Poland, but there was no way to move him safely.

When Ginger arrived the next day, the hospital was a madhouse. The city had recently taken a missile strike and there were severely wounded people everywhere. Then the doctors brought the news: Dan's not going to make it. You can say goodbye now.

Two by two, they were allowed into his room to say their final words to Dan. Ginger sent a voice message to everyone who couldn't be there, his voice cracking as he explained what was happening. *One of the craziest days*, thought Ragnar. The SEAL hung on for another day, but there was nothing anyone could do. Dan died in the early hours of January 18, Ukraine time.

EPILOGUE

'Still? That was finished long ago.'

'When everyone is dead the Great Game is finished. Not before. Listen to me till the end.'

— Rudyard Kipling, *Kim* (1901)

They buried Greg outside Kyiv; the blast that killed him had somehow allowed his funeral to be open casket. The Ukrainians held a funeral for Dan in Lviv. His body was repatriated to the United States, to be buried near his family on the West Coast. At the end of her tearful eulogy, Dan's mother paused in her own grief to ask the assembled mourners to remember Greg also, the man who had died trying to save her son.

After Riever returned home he went back to his old job working as a defense contractor, deploying around the world. Dmitri went to get his degree. Michael had already preceded both men back to the civilian world, for his part returning to his job at a major tech company. He flew home on a Friday and was back at his desk the following Monday morning. On the way he had found a home for Matador near Lviv, after escorting the kitten to the vet and paying for his shots. The new family regularly sent him update photos, which the former Marine used to pass on to Greg. Ragnar returned home to Estonia with a precious prize: the Happy Meal toy from Greg's final trip to McDonald's before they went to Bakhmut. It was Superman's Superdog, wearing a cape.

Ginger, Tex, and George stayed. "Just turn that hourglass over, you know what I mean? When's that shit gonna run out? That's the game we're playing out here, it seems," Ginger said before signing back on to a new Legion team to do medevacs out in Bakhmut with

303

Tex, George, and Oleksii's former aide, the young man named Borys, in January 2023 after Greg and Dan had been killed.

Under damp, grey skies they drove out to the Bakhmut operational area in their vehicles, George in his newly camo-painted truck traveling behind Ginger and Tex in a little blue crossover; his map app gave directions in English with the signs showing in Cyrillic. Both vehicles had the standard white Ukrainian identifier crosses taped to their windows. George kept a Ukrainian trident keychain hanging from his rearview mirror, a Ukrainian flag sticker on the driver's-side lower windshield, an energy drink in the cupholder, and his rifle ready, propped between the floor and the passenger seat beside him. The neat and tidy highways that looked like anywhere else in Europe yielded to the carnage of collapsed bridges, flattened and burned-out houses, cars, and armor, and spiked, artilleried treelines that could have come straight out of the Western Front. The temperature dropped; a light dusting of snow covered the unpaved surfaces as a miserable cold rain began to drift down on them.

They had been issued with new rifles: no more Brens. These were AR-15 variants made by Sig Sauer. They sighted in at a craggy range in the operational area, a former quarry with a small lake at one side, listening for the telltale *pings* of the steel targets. George stood, aiming out of the roof hatch of an MRAP light tactical vehicle, while, below, Tex gently teased Borys about his new rifle's shooting ("Did you fix the flux capacitor?" "I don't know what that means"). Ginger, in his "live large" hoodie, grumbled as he zeroed in. "These aren't 2 MOA rifles. Not even close," declared the Jav gunner. "Not even a little bit."

"This is like that one spot when we were in Kramo last time," Tex said one day, eyeing the open terrain as they bounced in an MRAP across the partially frozen mud towards the bombed-out apartment building that served as barracks near Bakhmut. Ginger was driving, with his kit over his "live large" hoodie and a pair of knee-high gaiters pulled up over his boots to protect him from the cold mud, a modern version of old-style puttees. They had a tiny, empty room, its window blocked with gardening pavers, while a small generator provided electricity for their Starlink and cell-phone chargers.

It was a neighborhood, or it had been, full of mid-rise apartment buildings, with what had once been neat, grassy courtyards with intersecting paths between them. There was a playground in one, the fixtures painted a cheery red and yellow. Windows were broken; the buildings all had holes in them. There was rubble everywhere, and trash, seemingly endless amounts of trash, as well as mud. They had seen it before, but somehow the dust of Severodonetsk looked less depressing than this dark, muddy garbage pile. Loose, abandoned dogs nipped in and out of the paths. Ginger, rocking a LAW under each arm in addition to his rifle, ignored them, even the tiny one that looked like a mottled-brown Shih Tzu mix, which trotted near his feet.

An absolutely massive artillery round sang out overhead and struck nearby while they waited for instructions. Regrouping, one of the Ukrainians translated the new directions. "Don't run because … this is friendly area. It's normal!"

George chuckled. "It's normal, *blyat*," he muttered to himself as he rose from kneeling cover.

Vadym had called them out for an emergency mission. They posted up in a high-rise as medevac support to other teams, including the snipers tucked high above them. Their position was lower than the snipers but still upstairs, a change from the usual underground shelters generally used to avoid artillery. George and Tex sat at the end of a stairwell, facing into a big, empty room painted a searingly bright shade of blue. A United Nations refugee agency banner, turned lengthwise, was pinned to cover the hole in one window. Outside, artillery boomed and sporadic gunfire ripped through the air.

George opened an MRE as he debated with Tex the source of all the noise. "Just a tank, probably," the Canadian said, his mouth full of imitation cheese tortellini. They discussed the merits of their position (fire coming from multiple sides) and the MRE (too much sauce) as the *booms* got more intense.

"Well, we've got two stairwells, so if one gets collapsed …" Tex said. "Yeah," said George, "we can go out the other one."

They ended up exiting through a lower-level balcony of what had once been someone's apartment, climbing down a rickety wooden ladder with parts of one side missing. A tank scored a direct hit on their building, cooking off the generator room and burning all the diesel and plastic inside, and rapidly creating an impenetrable cloud of black smoke. Soon everything else was burning, and nearby ammunition started cooking off. Their sister unit emerged with blackened faces, some of them looking like dynamited figures from an old Bugs Bunny cartoon.

Everyone piled into an old M113 personnel carrier. "We're not goin' far, we can be a little uncomfortable," Ginger said from his seat near the rear door. Their Ukrainian sister unit jammed in as George handed energy drinks around. "We're not out of the woods yet, guys!" George chuckled as everyone climbed in and traded fist bumps, with the artillery booming outside.

The driver struggled to close the doors and get the beast in gear. The Ukrainians started yelling directions at the driver, who was tucked up in his forward compartment.

"Oh, my God," laughed Ginger, "what an endeavor!" The motor rumbled and whirred and whined. "He's gonna blow this fuckin' thing up." More shouting ensued. Artillery boomed; the volume increased. Finally, the doors closed. *"Davai, davai!"* the men shouted.

George laughed. "What the fuck, man? How did I get here?" The old tracked vehicle rattled down the roads, finally stopping at their bombed-out safehouse.

"Now," muttered George, "does he know how to ..." as they all wondered whether the doors would open. More whirring and whining sounds followed. *"Suka!"* Then there was daylight. They clambered out, counting and double-checking their gear. They would get a short break, then a small team would go back out to find new positions for the next sniper rotation.

They started a four-day rotation, with the medevac teams operating in pairs, while the Legion teams they were supporting swapped out on staggered forty-eight-hour missions, in an eerie reflection of Greg's early days as a medic in Moschun. George put his emerging Ukrainian language skills to use, his second foreign language for a second foreign army. He also nearly ate an artillery shell one day, watching it explode in front of his face as he ducked. The debris rained down on top of the bombed-out building they called "the supermarket," its open floor with the incongruous, museum-style tracked lighting now home to damaged light-skinned trucks. There were holes, debris, and above all trash everywhere at the small base.

They would drive to the injured men in their MaxxPro MRAP, George bitching in frustration about the difficulty of opening the passenger door. Tex took the lead in the medical work. The men they rescued ranged in age from young to Santa Claus; one old man had a thick, white mustache that nineteenth-century British generals would have envied, and a bullet lodged just to the side of the front of his neck. Somehow, it had missed everything important. Once it got so hot that they did their final pick-up of the day in the M113 instead of the MaxxPro, with George serving as the .50 cal gunner.

"On one hand, I'm disappointed I didn't get to shoot anyone," George said to Tex when they got back; "on the other hand, I was happy for five whole minutes!" On his return he tucked away the round he had cleared from the chamber as a souvenir.

Ginger called Bakhmut the "death trap," and everyone nearly got smoked again by a tank that barely missed them in the M113 with five separate shots. They settled in for the long haul just as the new Ukrainian offensives near the city opened up in May. Tex shifted over to an NGO, doing fundraising and support work. George got the medic's role on Prym's team for one last-ditch mission as the city finally fell, moving forward to a house on the edges of a city with rockets flying overhead, rifle fire very close, and a beautiful set of lilacs brushing his left shoulder. Some of the last men out, they were forced to evac themselves on foot all the way out to Ivanivske, followed by an adorable and determined old Lab mix they named "Bakhmut." In the little village they were finally loaded into vehicles under red lights, the dog happily panting in their laps. When they brought the dog home, Ginger just shook his head and laughed. The infantryman had marked his second birthday in Ukraine that March, in Bakhmut, a little more than a week after Dan would have turned thirty-six. Riever now called the Jav gunner the oldest twenty-six-year-old in the world.

* * *

I was officially brought into this story in July 2022. I had just turned in the manuscript for my World War II book, *A Quiet Company of*

Dangerous Men, to my editor, expecting to have a breather. Then Riever called and persuaded me to write a book about this team. I was strangely well qualified: a professional historian, I had been educated on the history of Ukraine in college by the now-famous Tim Snyder; I spoke enough French to understand the French Foreign Legionnaires' conversations, even in combat; my specialty was military history; I had just written another "band of brothers" kind of book for a big publisher. There had been discussion about one of the guys maybe doing it, and I fervently hope that everyone who walks out of there does write a memoir. All stories are individual, and the more the better. But Dan was adamant: "Let's have the professional do it." He was always so practical. I was a historian: someone who, if worst came to worst, was trained to tell the stories of people who could no longer answer her questions directly. But I was also a woman, an American woman, the one person involved who was virtually guaranteed to survive in order to tell about it.

The truth is that I had been involved since the beginning. Riever and I have been together for years. It was my house that Dmitri's kneepads were delivered to, my name and number on the "in case of death please notify" message on the lock screen of Riever's phone. I drove to the next state over to help pick out the boots that Riever eventually left for Dan, and I received the "road trip to the end of the world" message, which I feared might be the last. I knew not to ask questions. My job was to be as supportive as possible, and pray that he would survive. He told me very little until after the big fight in Severo, when I caught a glimpse of Samuel's footage, which had been picked up by Sky News. After that, I was clued in. A month later, we started this book. I spent hours with each of them, recording their stories, watching their videos, getting as close as possible to their experiences, reliving with them the proudest and the worst moments of their lives. Sometimes they told me things they hadn't even told each other.

They became my friends. I never got to meet Oleksii and Jordan; I came in after they were killed. But I prayed that the rest of them would survive.

I always knew that I was on borrowed time with Dan, and he did too. The day after Christmas he asked me to edit a historical novel that he'd written, about a group of Varangian Guard, an elite Byzantine unit of the Middle Ages. He'd long had an interest in the Varangians; at one point he had suggested using their name for Alpha Team. The slogan of the warriors in the book eventually became the tagline for Black Team: *Long Live the Brotherhood*.

"I kinda want to self-publish it before I get killed," Dan texted. I edited it over the holiday week, we passed it back and forth, and he self-published it on Amazon before they went back out to Bakhmut. It was excellent (entitled *The Forged*, it was written under the pen name Eugene Ryder). I begged him for a sequel, an unspoken "please come back." He said he was working on one, planning to add his teammates in Ukraine as characters.

Dan was careful to make sure that I had everything updated before he went out to new operational areas: he would label photos and videos for me, call and give details of his work. On one hand, losing him seemed impossible. Who could kill *Dan?* But his complicated home life, his tragic past, his inherent warrior nature: I knew that Dan was going to Valhalla, just like several of the characters in his book. It was what he wanted, and I respected that, though it took some getting used to. I'd been mourning Dan since the day I met him. He was never going to walk out of Ukraine.

He sent me the link to his novel when he published it. The last thing he texted was "Thanks for everything." He knew.

But I was not emotionally prepared to lose Greg. God loves medics. He loved this one too much.

I remember, vividly, getting the call: a Sunday morning. My Apple Watch started buzzing. I looked down. It was Riever. The clock said 7:41 a.m. I went to get my phone; I just missed the call. I called him back. That was before.

"Can you hear me?" he said, his voice different from usual— harder.

"Yes," I replied.

"We got the call," he said, slowly and carefully. "… is dead. Dan and Marti are in the hospital." The beginning was garbled. Or maybe his voice caught. It wasn't real; my brain wasn't adjusting fast enough. Maybe it was outright denial. I had always expected this. I wasn't ready.

"*Who* is dead?"

"Greg is dead."

"*No.*" Not Greg. *Not Greg.*

That was after.

A few days before he died, Greg texted me a photo of the team from Severo: Tex and Riever standing in the bed of the Black Mazda, then himself, Michael, Ginger, Dan, and Dmitri from left to right in front of the tailgate. He was flashing his standard V for victory sign, that goofy grin on his ridiculously handsome face as usual. "*Nastalgia,*" he said. He was on his way to the front. He'd been there for a month before the new year; now they were heading back out. "But you're all in one piece?" I asked. "Headlines look scary."

"Yeah we good, going to be in bakhmut area today," he wrote back. "Starting to work this week."

I sent two crossed-fingers emojis.

"Everything will be good:)," he wrote.

For the next few days we tried to connect to talk on the phone. It kept falling through. Finally, just before the order came to hold the house for the first part of what became his final mission, he wrote, "Heyo yeah I'll give you a call in 10 min cool?"

I replied "perfect, yes, of course." A few minutes later he texted back, "Fuck sorry it's not going to work:/ I'm very sorry. Would tomorrow be cool?"

"No worries!! Yes tomorrow is great," I wrote.

"Thank you! Sorry about that," he wrote. "No problem!" I replied.

It was the last I ever heard from him.

I reread those last conversations, that last week, all the time. I think he too knew that something would happen. He always asked about this project. "How is the book coming along?" he said in one of our last conversations. "I've written up both big Severo missions. About 32k words so far. Reads like *Black Hawk Down,*" I told him. "Haha looking forward to reading it:)" he replied.

He wanted to make sure that I had certain stories, that I'd talked to Dan. He wanted to tell me more, wanted just, I think, to talk, which we enjoyed. And he always tried to make me feel better. "Now going back for a long time I think," he'd said. "Everything will be good:)"

Everything will be good, Greg. Everything will be good. I won't get to see you tomorrow, Greg. But Ukraine will have a tomorrow because of men like you and Dan, Oleksii and Jordan. The main character in Dan's novel noted that a God who could turn water into wine would want company. He could not ask for any better than you four.

A NOTE ON SOURCES

When I first met Riever, he said, "You know everything about war but what it's like." I was younger then. I still believed in perfect objectivity and analysis and professional omniscience. I'm not a fighter, and no one's ever shot at me. But I've been along for this whole ride, exposed in one of the worst ways: emotionally naked and unable to fight back.

I am not a journalist, and I have no truck with giving equal weight to either side, not that that profession has ever managed to do such a thing anyway. Nor do I hold to the academic high horse of objectivity, where people who have rarely ventured out of a warm, comfortable library judge others as though humans were emotionless automatons, assuming that we in the present somehow have the moral high ground over those in the past, who did things the hard way.

Accuracy I believe in. This book is as accurate as humanly possible. I have compared timestamps; isolated audio; cross-checked quotes, stories, after-action reports, timelines, and photographic and video evidence; gone back and asked clarifying questions over and over; checked kit; compared suppressed versus unsuppressed fire; examined bullet reports and impacts. I am sure that there are errors; memories are imperfect and don't always align. Obviously, this story follows only a specific group of people, and it is not possible to tell a story from every single angle while keeping the page count reasonable. I have had to use my best judgment. But we will never get closer to accuracy than this until every single person involved wears a perfectly operating camera with the ability to capture high-fidelity surrounding audio at all times. I don't expect that day will come soon, if at all.

But objectivity is a myth, and as far as I'm concerned objectivity can go fuck itself. We've all read about the Russian playbook in the news: invading the neighbors, torturing prisoners military and civil-

ian, stealing children, committing murder, vandalism, and terrorism, and paving the way for genocide. Some people say this is the
Soviet model reborn, that Vladimir Putin just can't shake his KGB
habits. But this playbook is one that the latent historian in me rec-
ognizes as the pattern of centuries, not decades, one familiar to the
Finns, the Balts, the Poles, the Czechs, the Slovaks, the Hungarians,
the Moldovans, and of course the Ukrainians, not to mention the
many peoples of Central Asia. The Soviet Union just dressed up an
old emperor in new clothes and added nukes to what we used to call
the Great Game. Whatever you might say about the Russians, you
can't deny that they're consistent.

What the Russians taught me was different. It happened despite
those conscripts the Western journalists liked to report on, the ones
who complained about their awful treatment and then always said
something along the lines of "but I guess we have to do it anyway,"
that classic Russian mix of nihilism, denialism, and imperialism, not
unlike that of the babushkas who said, "If only Putin knew!", just as
their sixteenth-century predecessors had said of the czar. It was
something that years of the finest schools and careful experience
combing through evidence could never teach me: the last key to
history, the final bridge to understanding. I could finally comprehend the old men who never stopped using the term "Jap," and the
ones who would never buy German cars. The Russians killed my
friends. And they taught me how to hate.

For
Oleksii Chubashev
Jordan Gatley
Greg Tsekhmistrenko
Dan Swift

Your cause of sorrow
Must not be measured by his worth, for then
It hath no end.

William Shakespeare, *Macbeth*, Act V, Scene 8

ACKNOWLEDGMENTS

I must thank Ian Kemp, whose friendship I am daily more grateful for. He also volunteered to serve a fellow country; he won a Silver Star in Vietnam for his bravery on one of the worst days of his life. He was the first person I contacted on the worst day of mine. Though there is one ocean, one sea, and nearly half a century between us, it feels like nothing at all. He was the only person not on the team whom I could truly talk to. I don't know where I would be without him, but I do know that I would be lost.

It is one of my great regrets that I met Keith Wrightson as late in my student years as I did; it has been my great good fortune that he has continued to grace me with his wit, his wisdom, and his kindness. He listened as I lived, and wrote, this book. It was he who taught me how to write about real people, and he was instrumental in getting this book to the right publisher at the right time.

I am grateful as well to Stacy Schiff for her remarkable generosity and mentorship, and to Roger Freet, Terezia Cicel, Michael Kaler, Atifa Jiwa, Richard Bassett, Patrick Radden Keefe, and Xan Smiley for their encouragement as I pushed to finish this project. I am thankful, as ever, to Karen Heath and Tom Jehn for their patience and benevolence as I attempted not just to teach, but to do.

This book would obviously be nowhere without Hurst, and I am deeply grateful to Michael Dwyer and his entire team for their work, enthusiasm, and partnership, and to Niko Pfund and Oxford University Press for their work in distributing this book within the North American market.

And, finally, the boys themselves. I could not possibly express what I and the rest of us owe to all of them. I will simply borrow from Dan: thanks for everything.

NOTES

1. THE BATTLE FOR KYIV

1. Where appropriate, names have been replaced with pseudonyms for security purposes.
2. Peter Kemp, *No Colours or Crest*, London, 1958 (reprint 2020), p. 85.
3. *Suka*: Ukrainian swear word roughly equivalent to "bitch," and used similarly.

4. BEHIND ENEMY LINES

1. John Masters, *The Road Past Mandalay*, London, 1961, reprint 2002, p. 258.

5. WHEAT FROM CHAFF

1. *Pizdets*: Ukrainian swear word roughly equivalent in English to "shit." *Blyat*: General Slavic swear used as an English speaker would say "damn," "shit," "fuck" or anything else used to indicate strong frustration.

8. A LITTLE NIGHT RECCE

1. Antony Beevor, *Stalingrad: The Fateful Siege, 1942–1943*, New York, 1998, pp. 169–70, 435–8.

9. NO MAN'S LAND

1. *Kurwa*: Polish swear word, also used commonly in the French Foreign Legion, meaning "whore" or "bitch" but also sometimes used in the sense of "fuck!" in an exclamation.

10. URBAN JUNGLE

1. George MacDonald Fraser, *Quartered Safe Out Here*, London, 1993, p. 200. Said wit was talking about a PIAT, which was a World War II-era British-

made anti-tank rocket, not a tank round itself. The process, however, remains the same. For an excellent description of tank rounds, see Michael Skinner, *USAREUR*, Novato, CA, 1989, pp. 47–50.

2. If you know, you know: *Forgotten Weapons* is a YouTube channel popular among weaponry geeks of all stripes. It reviews examples of unusual, weird, and historical weapons used and manufactured all over the world.

11. "REGULAR DAN"

1. It is called *The Fall of a Man*, written under the pen name Ryder Thompson, and self-published on Amazon.

21. A SPICY VILLAGE RAID

1. For this visual I am indebted to George MacDonald Fraser's description in *Quartered Safe Out Here* of his own wading in the Sittang River during the British campaign in Burma in 1945.